SEATTLENESS

SEATTLENESS

A CULTURAL ATLAS

TERA HATFIELD, JENNY KEMPSON, AND NATALIE ROSS

Foreword by Tim Wallace

SASQUATCH BOOKS
SEATTLE

CONTENTS

87 | LINES

FOREWORD BY TIM WALLACE

What's your favorite thing to do when you visit a city for the very first time?

For me, it's getting lost for a few hours. As in, well and *truly* lost. I head to a known landmark, then put away my phone, guidebooks, and whatever else I have that might want to tell me what I *should* do in this new place. And I wander.

I do this because for me, getting lost in a new place for a little while is one of the most enjoyable ways to establish a personal connection to it.

We all likely remember the first time we ventured far from home, but we almost certainly remember that moment, that journey, and that place for different reasons. Each of us establishes these personal connections a little differently. Maybe some of us found the landscape especially beautiful, while others were taken with the strange road signs helping us navigate that landscape. Maybe you thought the people were unusually friendly—or not friendly enough. Maybe the trees were greener than you ever thought possible.

Whatever it was that first stuck out in your mind from that trip became the first pin in your mental map of that place, permanently fixing, in a highly personal way, your memory of what you saw or smelled or tasted or did in that space and time.

I savor being in a place for the first time and, through wandering, identifying that very first pin. Eventually, I know, there will be many more as I start to build out a brand-new mental map.

Sometimes when we've visited a place several times, or when we've settled in one spot, we forget to keep adding pins. The personal lens through which we view that area can become fixed. We get stuck in our routines. We start focusing more and more narrowly on what we know to be true about a place because we've seen it and slogged through it over and over again.

But I think the magic of geography and the magic of mapping are that, with a little nudge, we can see everything afresh—and, even better, that *everything is always fresh.*

Seattleness will nudge you in countless ways and challenge you to see the city and region through new, crisp, and yes, sometimes even warped lenses. Some of what is presented here may even find its way onto your own mental map of Seattle and its hinterlands. You will be introduced to a city of flannel, pinball wizards, extraordinary women, and rain, rain, rain (but not the world's *most* rain, just really frequent rain).

Through the maps, charts, diagrams, illustrations, and photography in this book, you will be treated to a perceptive visual tour of Seattle. This tour may confirm some things you think you know about the city (e.g., seriously good coffee), but it also will inevitably spin what you know in a way that surprises and excites you (e.g., the greatest concentration of seriously good coffee shops is around Pike Place, the neighborhood home of the first Starbucks). At the same time, this book is also a tour that will smack you in the face with information that is truly bonkers (did you know sightings of UFOs of all shapes and sizes have been reported across Washington state?!).

How we experience places and how we use maps (be they paper, digital, augmented, or virtual) are constantly changing. But it seems fair to say that the global usage of maps that are made by just a handful of companies worldwide does not bode well for people hoping for a means to explore a place's true nature and spirit. Map conventions designed for quick reading—and for an audience of billions—have oversimplified landscapes and made cities that are thousands of miles apart look identical.

Seattleness stands strong in the face of maps that present places as if they are devoid of geographical, political, or cultural diversity (but it also shows you when such diversity is lacking in a particular area).

It embraces the far-flung and wacky as much as the more comfortable and familiar. And it brings to the forefront the historically underrepresented and forcibly hidden aspects of what makes Seattle, well, *Seattle*. In so doing, it puts forth a clearer, more complete, and valuable picture of the city.

The creators of this volume all experienced Seattle, synthesized those experiences, and portrayed them in their own unique way. I recommend you enjoy their efforts the way I enjoy a new city. Put away your phone, extricate yourself from the internet, and wipe your mental map clean. Dive in, start to wander, and ultimately, get lost. By the time you put *Seattleness* down, these authors will have inspired you to see and think of the city afresh—and to rebuild your personal collection of mental maps of the region into a full-fledged mental atlas of Seattleness.

Tim Wallace is a geographer and graphics editor at the New York Times, *where he makes visual stories with information gathered from land, sky, and space. He has a PhD in geography from the University of Wisconsin-Madison, but he first got into mapping as an undergrad at Macalester College, where he also met Natalie Ross, one of the authors of this book.*

Seattle field notes: A 1910 Edward E. Curtis profile of a young Chinook (Wishram) woman, wearing abalone-shell disk earrings, anchors this informal portrait of place while the North Cascades range and Minoru Yamasaki's iconic arches stretch upward in the ever-present Northwest veil of cloud, mist, and distant calls of seabirds.

INTRODUCTION

Before Rand McNally, there was Mercator. In 1595 he brought us the first self-described atlas, titled: *Atlas or cosmographical meditations upon the creation of the universe, and the universe as created.* Subsequent atlases appear mundane in contrast, filled with pages of highways and terrain that are all too real and tangible. Mercator's "cosmographical meditations" are an intriguing foundation for a book of maps, and one that struck a chord with these authors. Seattle, our own little slice of heaven, is a mythical notion as much as it is a real city, storied with fact and fiction that all tie back to place. Meditating on both the geographical and the cosmographical seemed an appropriate way to navigate this project.

Through maps, diagrams, visualizations, and illustrations, we examined Seattle and the surrounding Puget Sound region in the spirit of Mercator. The resulting collection of impressionistic and ephemeral explorations were undertaken as portraiture, and by no means is this portrait complete or definitive. The moment it is published a map is outdated, and so our attempts to depict the real Seattle can only be a snapshot in time, a captured memory. To initiate our meditation, we retreated into a midcentury city bungalow with a view of Elliott Bay and discussed what makes Seattle special, what drew us to it, and what pushed us away. It was gray skies, frontier psychology, strong women, and strong coffee. Together we collaged a landscape of impressions that, when squinted at with lowered eyelashes, had the quality of "Seattleness."

From here, we dove deeper into the quirks and characters, letting Seattle's exclamation points draw us into more complex stories and associations. The construction cranes that loom so large in the current zeitgeist led to the discovery of subtler subterranean shifts in the urban strata. We discovered that CenturyLink Field isn't just for football games and that the skies over Seattle are 3,650 colors of blue-gray. These were the points and lines that began to make up a more recognizable likeness of the city we sought to discover.

Like Italo Calvino before us, we allowed ourselves to be lost in the real and imagined spaces of our city's past and future. We invoked the names and genre-bending works of W. G. Sebald, John McPhee, Lygia Clark, and Buckminster Fuller (to name a few) as a means of inspiration to explore beyond the spurious boundaries and fortifications set up between people and place, architecture and landscape, past and present, the individual and the collective. We sought to grapple with the dynamic entropy of place and memory, all in an effort to look beyond our everyday silos and experiences to see greater connections to one another and this city we precariously inhabit at the edge of the sea. We soaked up the stories of Paul de Barros and Paul Dorpat, essays by David Williams, Charles D'Ambrosio, and Lindy West. We got lost in the fictional fever dream of Shadowrun's near-future apocalypse and watched the tides rise to bury the Seattle we know today. The expertise and imagination of these Seattle storytellers would take a lifetime to explore, and could fill a thousand books.

Seattle's representations also take on a multiplicity of personalities, ranging from brooding and solitary to bursting with song. Like the expressions of a moody teen, these faces and traits layer over time and space to create an individual likeness, albeit a murky and mysterious one. We sought to capture that in our own portrait on the adjoining pages, made entirely of the stories and data we have collected on this journey. Our investigative sojourns led us into creative territories and down rabbit holes. We often found ourselves dangling from compelling and gnarled loose ends, where

both humble fictions and monumental myths were clearly entangled with human recollections and history. These points of interest, with fact separated from fiction, are represented in the first section of this book. Represented in the second half are many of the linear and nonlinear threads—illuminating connections between natural phenomena, historical events, current events, people, the past, the present, and the very soil in which we've put down roots. The portrait brings together these two sections. Data from points and lines take shape, like a half-developed Polaroid, to embrace the city's oscillations, its poetic flaws of both past and future.

We emerged from these meditations changed, as the city itself shifts. Armed with stories and blueprints, familiar scenes were transformed, as if with X-ray vision, to become radically altered and tenuous, on the brink of further mutation. The mythical and real converge and loop. The reader may find this portrait familiar, or possibly unrecognizable, to the Seattle they know. But we hope that it inspires you to see the city anew, as an ever-changing collection of imprints, marks, and traces.

POINTS

The points of a portrait, marks of interest in place, time, and history.

AGAINST THE GRID

Seattle is a city of steep slopes. Its towering, unstable bluffs were once camouflaged in rich conifer stands of Sitka spruce, Douglas fir, and western red cedar with an almost impervious understory. When early white settlers sought to impose ruler-straight order onto the rebellious topography, the glacier-carved hills quickly dis-abused them of the notion. The city street grids were warped from the start with remarkable and uncanny style, leaving inconvenient and mysti-fying dead ends, drop-offs, obtuse triangles, and five-way intersections, which remain to this day.

Seattle's hills were all formed by a three-thousand-foot sheet of glacial ice. Subglacial rivers carved curvilinear troughs and valleys as deep as thirteen hundred feet to birth Seattle's surrounding water bodies, like Puget Sound, Lake Washington, and Hood Canal. The daunting topography didn't stop early settlers from notoriously regrading over seventy-five million cubic yards to manufacture flat land and a more "manageable" 15 percent average street grade.

In May of 1853, the city planning and platting process started with an inauspicious argument between Seattle's three primary founders: David Swinson "Doc" Maynard, Arthur Denny, and Carson Boren. Maynard purportedly showed up "stimu-lated" (nineteenth-century-speak for inebriated) with a grid system that followed the cardinal direc-tions, blatantly ignoring the towering topography that surrounded his relatively flat parcel of land, which would come to be known as Pioneer Square.

Denny and Boren similarly fought for orientations that befit their parcels (32 degrees west of north, and 49 degrees west of north), generally running parallel to the Elliott Bay shoreline. The result is a three-way head-on grid collision in downtown, with Maynard's rigid grid extending out to the rest of the city, troubling topography be damned.

As Seattle grew in the early twentieth century, annexed towns like Ballard (1907) and Georgetown (1910) added their own curious grids to the mix. In 1903, the Seattle City Council hired the Olmsted Brothers to begin work on a system of major parks. The work continued until 1937, resulting in a series of lush green spaces along a twenty-mile-long linked park-and-boulevard system that defiantly ignored the grid, instead following the natural organic contours of the land and water bodies, making it easier and more enjoyable for citizens to explore their city.

The graphic at right takes all the land parcels (or units created by real-estate lot lines) and re-organizes them to resemble and follow the growth rings of a native western red cedar tree. Look between the two wood blocks to see the shape of the Lake Washington Ship Canal, Lake Union, and the Montlake Cut. You can also find recognizable parcels like Green Lake, Discovery Park, and Pike Place Market. The odd-ball shapes created by property boundaries vary from gigantic (one marine terminal parcel is over 115 acres) to tiny townhouse parcels less than 800 square feet.

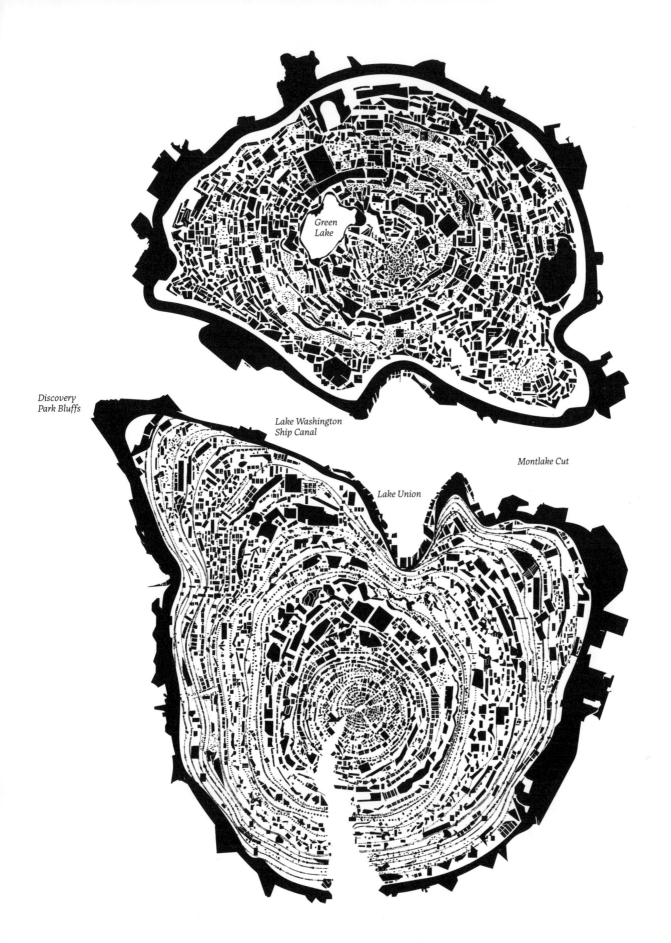

Green Lake

Discovery Park Bluffs

Lake Washington Ship Canal

Montlake Cut

Lake Union

3

GRAY ANATOMY

Seattle is defined by its big natural features and big weather—in 2015, the city tied for first with Buffalo, New York, as the dreariest city in the United States. Seattle's ashen forecasts are almost mythical, thanks to cult films like *Singles, Hype!,* and *Kurt Cobain: About a Son*; sweeping essays by Charles D'Ambrosio; and seminal graphic novels like Charles Burns's *Black Hole*. Old and new TV shows alike (*Frasier, Grey's Anatomy,* and *The Killing*) all cast the city as a stark gray and soggy backdrop. Benjamin Moore and Sherwin-Williams have even produced multiple paint colors based on the city's pale pallor (Seattle Gray, Seattle Mist, and just plain Seattle).

On average, Seattleites bear the emotional weight of living under 240 days of cloud cover—nine months of cool dampness that seeps into the bones, and a fog of compressed gray skies that often drive nonnatives right up the wall. Locals are up for the challenge, patiently waiting for the perfect summers that often lure unassuming visitors to think they've found a sunny and temperate paradise, until late October brings the inevitable fog of melancholy. Google "Seattle gray weather really" to find numerous online threads asking, "What's the deal—is Seattle really that gray?" Yes, it is.

Pacific Northwest natives tend to have, even if begrudgingly, an appreciation for the nuance in winter light and shadowy gloom, often finding beauty and difference from one gray day to the next. To illustrate these color nuances, turn the page to find a histogram featuring 3,650 color samples from the Seattle sky— that's ten color samples per day over the course of 2015, using 360-degree panoramic images from a camera on the tippy-top of the Space Needle. The color samples were further broken down into percentages of color—the longer the bar, the larger percentage of the sky was that color on that particular day. The cloudless blue skies during the summer and early fall months stand out in stark relief against the backdrop of gray hues that were present for the rest of the year.

100%

90%

80%

70%

60%

50%

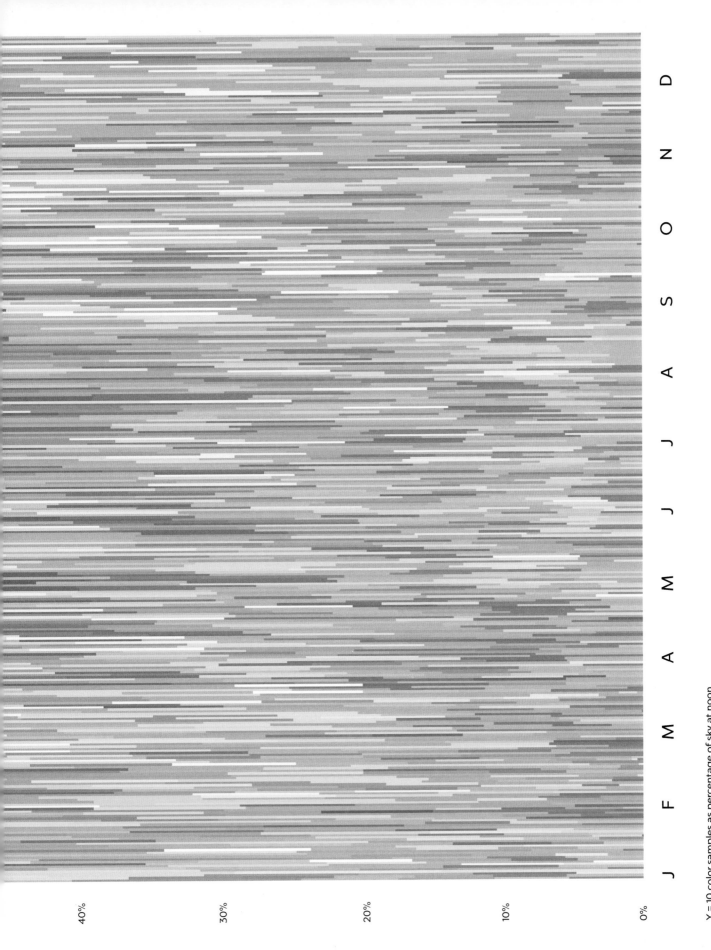

J F M A M J J A S O N D

40%

30%

20%

10%

0%

Y = 10 color samples as percentage of sky at noon
X = 365 days of the year

JET CITY

Pilots and aviation enthusiasts will recognize the lines, codes, and symbols in the map on pages 10–11 as icons from an aircraft navigation chart. When using a visual flight rules (VFR) sectional map, prominent observable checkpoints are highlighted (e.g., stadiums, the Space Needle, etc.), along with topographic notes and boundary zones, as guides for slow- to medium-speed aircraft. The dark lines and coded names (e.g., NORMY, FLAAK, etc.) refer to airway routes and radio navigation aids, and come from the instrument flight rules (IFR) low- and high-altitude en route charts. This pilot's-eye view, hybrid map of aeronautical information centers on a city at the forefront of aviation, a city that helped launch the United States into its illustrious Jet Age.

Seattle's first aerial endeavors occurred in balloons and dirigibles. A popular attraction at the Alaska-Yukon-Pacific Exposition in 1909 was going up in a tethered hot-air balloon fifteen hundred feet above the fairgrounds. Never before had Seattleites seen their growing city from such a heavenly vantage.

Five years later, and many advances in "flying machines" hence, aviator Silas Christofferson flew his Roman candle–emblazoned floatplane off Lake Union to encircle the newly opened Smith Tower in a nighttime display of derring-do. Aviation fever was ignited, and Lake Union became its hub. On its shores in 1916, lumber-wealthy shipbuilder William E. Boeing erected a three-plane hangar to build and fly his first airplane: the B&W seaplane.

With World War I, a new market emerged, and Boeing converted his Duwamish River shipbuilding warehouse, a.k.a. the Red Barn, into an aircraft factory. Displaying a knack for innovation (and securing lucrative government contracts), Boeing soon ventured into chartered passenger flights and airmail flights, including the first international airmail route, between Seattle and Victoria, British Columbia (which, in Prohibition-era Seattle, may have been a bootlegging operation!). By 1929, the Boeing Co. was both the largest manufacturer and operator of commercial airplanes in the United States, flying over ten thousand miles daily and delivering 30 percent of the country's entire mail load. A graphic elevation timeline explores the heights of Seattle aviation history in more depth on pages 12–13.

Aircraft design and manufacturing produced thousands of specialized skills and positions, and thus the rise of an entire aerospace industry centered around Puget Sound. The area is home to hundreds of companies related to aviation, engineering, and travel, many with their start as Boeing businesses. Seattle-Tacoma International Airport (Sea-Tac) is the ninth busiest in the United States and hub to hometown carrier Alaska Airlines. And Lake Union remains an active seaplane base, one of the busiest in North America. Kenmore Air, the largest operator on Lake Union, flies over forty-five thousand taxi and sightseeing operations annually from its base, just a short jaunt from where Boeing built his first hangar.

Left: December 1942, sections of the Boeing B-17F framework hang above female plant workers. The aircraft, nicknamed the Flying Fortress, was used prominently for strategic bombing raids in World War II.

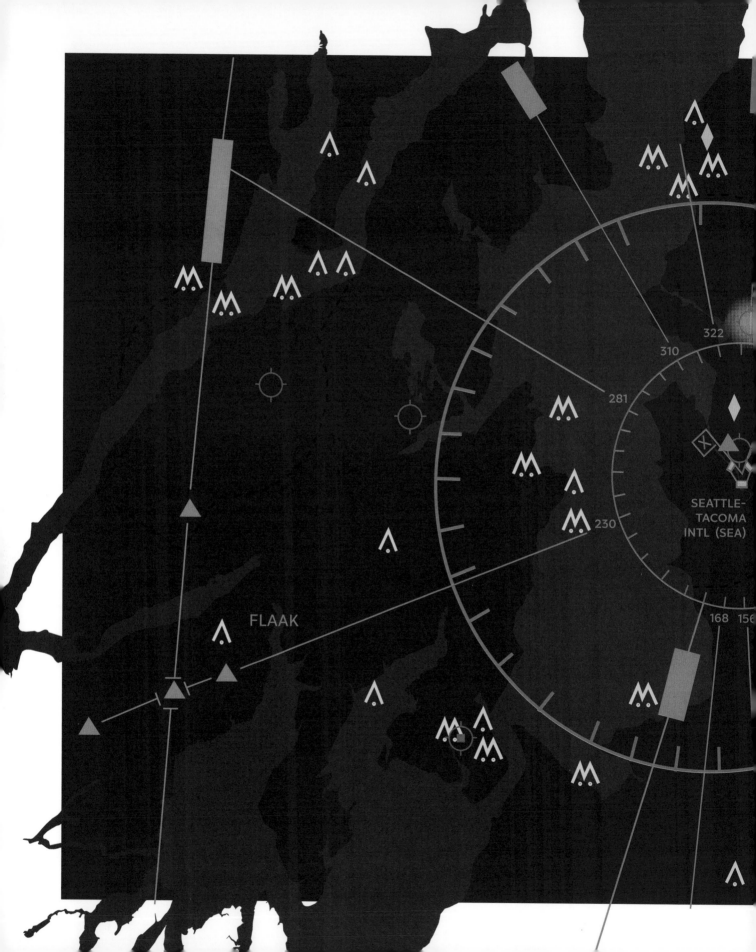

A PILOT'S VIEW OF SEATTLE

A constructed map replicating the most interesting symbols and lines from the FAA's published VFR (visual flight route) and IFR (instrument flight rules) "sectional" charts. Numbers surrounding the inner ring represent radial mileage for en route pathways.

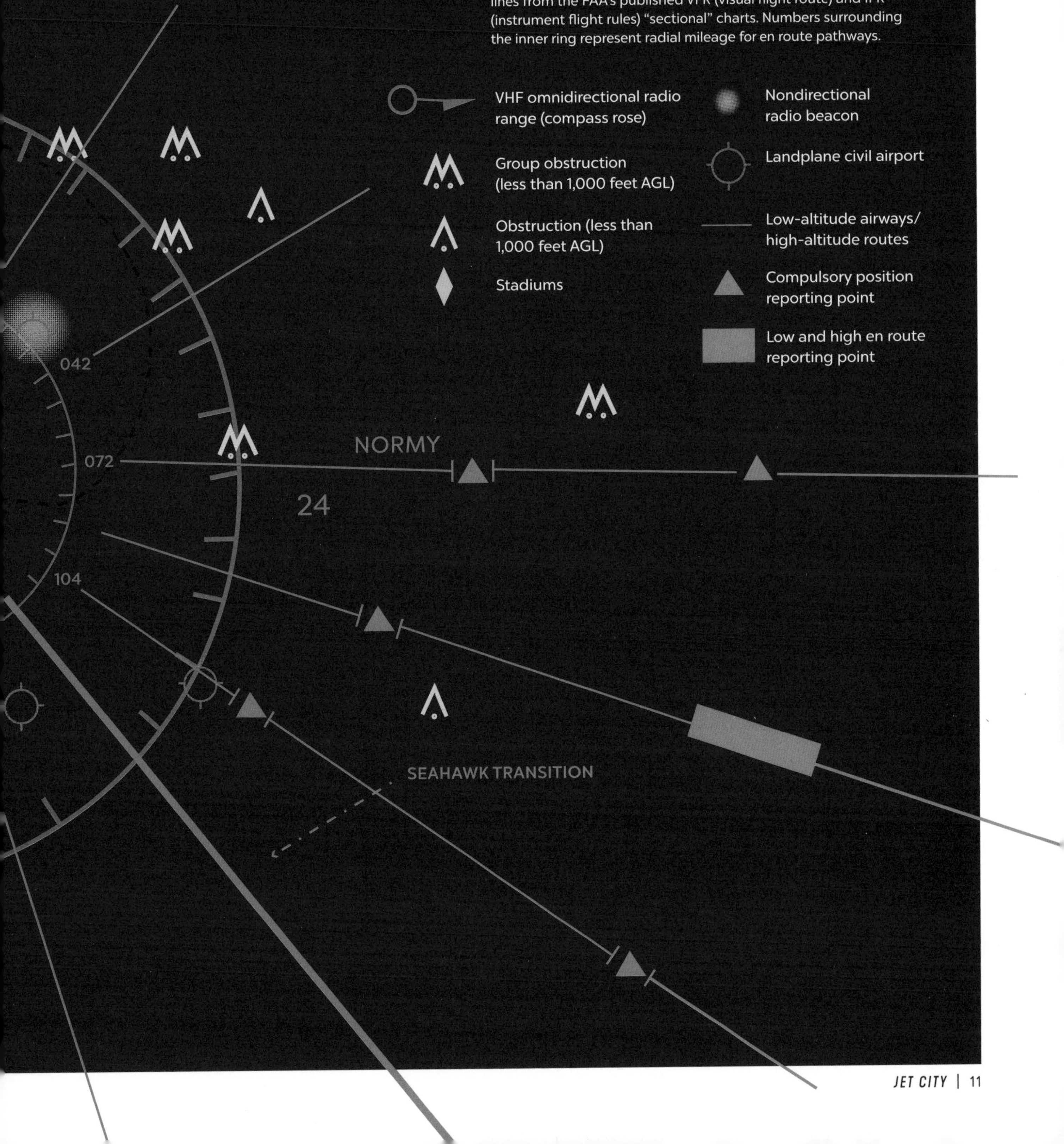

VHF omnidirectional radio range (compass rose)

Nondirectional radio beacon

Group obstruction (less than 1,000 feet AGL)

Landplane civil airport

Obstruction (less than 1,000 feet AGL)

Low-altitude airways/ high-altitude routes

Stadiums

Compulsory position reporting point

Low and high en route reporting point

042

072

NORMY

24

104

SEAHAWK TRANSITION

FLYING MACHINES:
AVIATION ELEVATION TIMELINE

1980 *VOL LIBRE*

Boeing engineer and UW grad Loren Carpenter used fractal geometry to generate algorithms that revolutionized computer graphics in every industry (including aviation design) with his seminal short film *Vol Libre*. Carpenter went on to create the first-ever fully computer-generated sequence, for the feature film *Star Trek II: The Wrath of Khan* (all computed on a VAX-11/780, a machine the size of a refrigerator) and eventually cofounded Pixar.

102,100'

1967 BOEING'S X-15 RESEARCH JET

The X-15 still holds the world record for the highest speed ever recorded by a manned, powered aircraft, flying Mach 6.72 at 102,100 feet.

19,600'

1938 BOEING'S MODEL 314 "CLIPPER" FLYING BOAT

The 314 Clipper, built for Pan American World Airways in 1938, was the first long-haul passenger plane to complete a transatlantic flight. Regular service included a six-day trip from San Francisco to Hong Kong.

14,411'

1951 MOUNT RAINIER

In April 1951 an AWOL US Air Force lieutenant landed a Piper Cub on the highest peak on Mount Rainier and then promptly got stuck. He was charged $350 for illegally landing in a national park without permission.

14,000'

1928 BOEING 80

The first regularly scheduled American airliner to transport passengers.

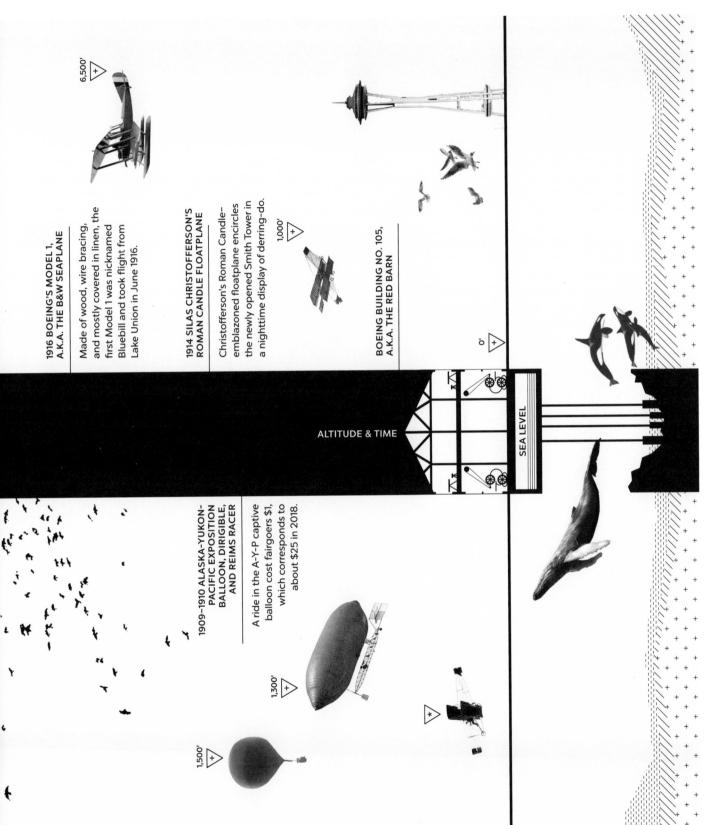

ALTITUDE & TIME

SEA LEVEL

1916 BOEING'S MODEL 1, A.K.A. THE B&W SEAPLANE

Made of wood, wire bracing, and mostly covered in linen, the first Model 1 was nicknamed Bluebill and took flight from Lake Union in June 1916.

1914 SILAS CHRISTOFFERSON'S ROMAN CANDLE FLOATPLANE

Christofferson's Roman Candle–emblazoned floatplane encircles the newly opened Smith Tower in a nighttime display of derring-do.

BOEING BUILDING NO. 105, A.K.A. THE RED BARN

1909–1910 ALASKA-YUKON-PACIFIC EXPOSITION BALLOON, DIRIGIBLE, AND REIMS RACER

A ride in the A-Y-P captive balloon cost fairgoers $1, which corresponds to about $25 in 2018.

6,500'

1,000'

0'

1,300'

1,500'

*Charles Hamilton crashed his Reims Racer (also known as a Curtiss No. 2) into a lake at the A-Y-P. Suffering only minor injuries, a few days later he was back in the air.

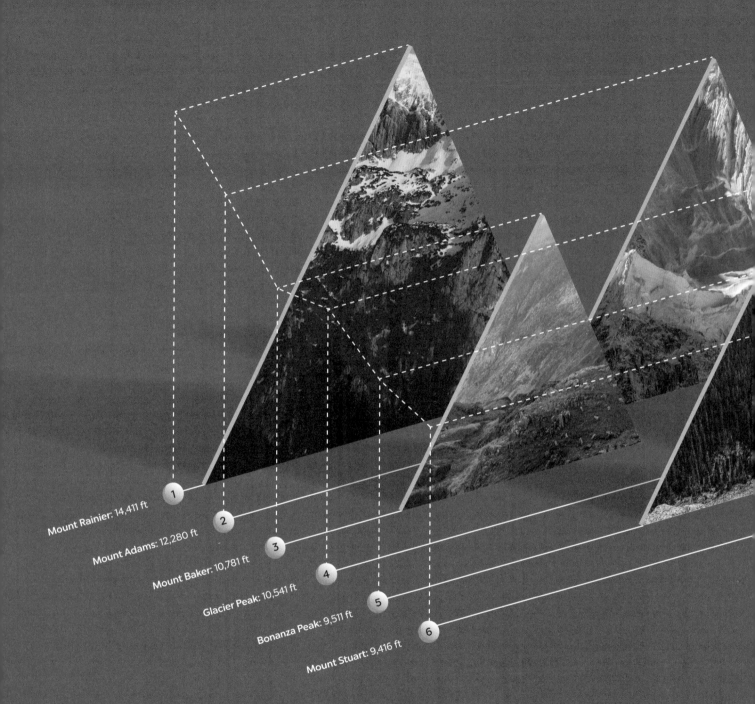

1 Mount Rainier: 14,411 ft

2 Mount Adams: 12,280 ft

3 Mount Baker: 10,781 ft

4 Glacier Peak: 10,541 ft

5 Bonanza Peak: 9,511 ft

6 Mount Stuart: 9,416 ft

MOUNTAIN
MORPHOLOGY

There are sixty-three named mountain ranges located in Washington State, including the Cascade Range, the Olympic Mountains, the Stuart Range, the Enchantment Peaks, and Horse Heaven Hills.

Happily, Seattleites don't have to travel far to enjoy some fresh alpine air. The iconic Mount Rainier is visible from the city. Towering at 14,411 feet, this volcano is the tallest peak in the state. Mount Rainier National Park, located just seventy-five miles from Seattle, is a quick weekend trip and is beloved by mountain climbers, hikers, and campers. This mammoth mount is also home to more glaciers than any other peak in the United States. The trails leading up to these glaciers wind through majestic forests and vivid subalpine flower meadows. South of Rainier sits the infamous Mount Saint Helens. While still impressive at 8,363 feet, this peak has sat slumped over like a petulant teenager since a massive eruption in May of 1980 that spewed 540 million tons of ash over the region. This blast currently holds the record as the largest volcanic eruption to ever occur in the United States. The giant crater left in the eruption's wake is now a popular attraction for hikers.

In addition to the Cascades, Washington is also home to the Olympics. Olympic National Park is just a ferry or highway ride away for Seattle residents. Once there, outdoor enthusiasts can explore not only the mountains but also over a million acres of fern-filled rain forests, spectacular seascapes, and tide pools teeming with colorful aquatic critters. At 7,979 feet, Mount Olympus, the range's tallest summit, may be shorter than many other Washington peaks, but it is definitely still mighty. A round-trip to the summit takes most climbers three or four days, trudging across glaciers and rocky terrain for over eighteen miles—but the stunning vistas are worth the struggle.

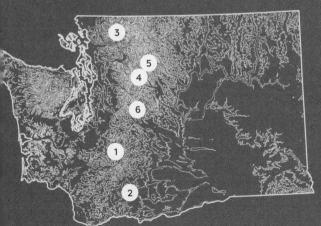

VOLCANOES

Mount Rainier/Tahoma, 14,411'
Mount Adams/Pahto, 12,280'
Mount Baker/Kulshan, 10,781'
Glacier Peak/Dakobed, 10,541'
Mount St. Helens/Loowit, 8,366'
Goat Rocks, 8,182'
Indian Heaven, 5,925'
Signal Peak, 5,100'
Silver Star Mountain, 4,364'
West Crater, 4,360'

9,000–11,999 ft

Little Tahoma, 11,138'
Bonanza Peak, 9,511'
Mount Stuart, 9,416'
Mount Fernow, 9,249'
Goode Mountain, 9,199'
Mount Shuksan, 9,131'
Buckner Mountain, 9,114'
Mount Logan, 9,088'
Mount Maude, 9,060'

8,000–8,999 ft

Mount Spickard, 8,980'
Black Peak, 8,970'
Mount Redoubt, 8,970'
North Gardner Mountain, 8,957'
Dome Peak, 8,924'
Boston Peak, 8,894'
Eldorado Peak, 8,868'
Dragontail Peak, 8,842'
Forbidden Peak, 8,816'
Oval Peak, 8,800'
Mesahchie Peak, 8,795'
Fortress Mountain, 8,760'
Mount Lago, 8,745'
Robinson Mountain, 8,726'
Star Peak, 8,690'
Remmel Mountain, 8,685'
Mount Custer, 8,630'
Clark Mountain, 8,602'
Cathedral Peak, 8,601'
Kimtah Peak, 8,600'
Mount Carru, 8,595'
Monument Peak, 8,592'
Raven Ridge, 8,590'
Cardinal Peak, 8,589'
Osceola Peak, 8,587'
Buck Mountain, 8,528'
Reynolds Peak, 8,512'
Cashmere Mountain, 8,501'
Big Craggy Peak, 8,470'
Lost Peak, 8,464'
Chiwawa Mountain, 8,459'

Tower Mountain, 8,444'
Dumbell Mountain, 8,421'
Azurite Peak, 8,420'
Pinnacle Mountain, 8,402'
Spectacle Buttes, 8,392'
Devore Peak, 8,380'
Martin Peak, 8,375'
Golden Horn, 8,366'
McClellan Peak, 8,364'
Snowfield Peak, 8,351'
Windy Peak, 8,333'
Mount Formidable, 8,325'
Flora Mountain, 8,323'
Luna Peak, 8,310'
Castle Peak, 8,306'
Andrew Peak, 8,301'
Apex Mountain, 8,297'
Booker Mountain, 8,284'
Mount Fury, 8,280'
Spider Mountain, 8,280'
Big Kangaroo, 8,280'
Sentinel Peak, 8,266'
Tiffany Mountain, 8,245'
Riddle Peak, 8,220'
Mount Arriva, 8,215'
Johannesburg Mountain, 8,199'
Gilbert Peak, 8,184'
Fool Hen Mountain, 8,168'
The Needles, 8,160'
Mount Terror, 8,150'
Ba Peak, 8,142'

Armstrong Mountain, 8,139'
Wolframite Mountain, 8,137'
Crater Mountain, 8,128'
Buckskin Mountain, 8,124'
McGregor Mountain, 8,122'
Agnes Mountain, 8,120'
Mount Hardy, 8,100'
Mount Rolo, 8,096'
North Star Mountain, 8,096'
Big Chiwaukum, 8,081'
Hozomeen South Peak, 8,071'
Hozomeen North Peak, 8,066'
Cutthroat Peak, 8,050'
Bauerman Ridge, 8,044'
Gilbert Mountain, 8,023'

7,000–7,999 ft

American Border Peak, 7,999'
Eightmile Mountain, 7,996'
Mount Olympus, 7,979'
Graybeard Peak, 7,965'
Mount Daniel (Northwest Peak), 7,959'
Horseshoe Mountain, 7,956'
Skeptical Butte, 7,949'
Mount Berge, 7,948'
Indecision Peak, 7,945'
Three Fools Peak, 7,940'

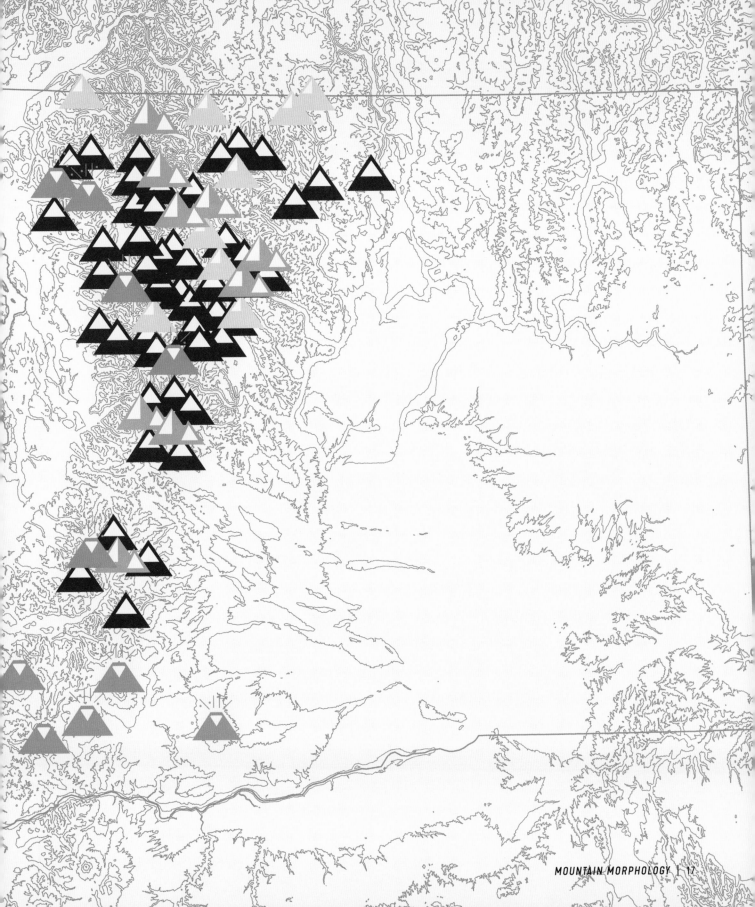

MOVERS +
SHAPERS

Massive industrial-scale terraforming was and still continues to be a Seattle specialty. The controversial State Route 99 tunnel, dug by the four-million-pound boring machine named Bertha, is just the latest in a series of undertakings to radically reshape the city's landscape.

Hills regraded, entire rivers shifted, miles of tideflats filled, and the United States' largest artificial island are the profound (and environmentally dubious) legacy of the last century. The heavy lifting, shifting, sluicing, and dumping of approximately seventy-five million cubic yards of rock and soil was primarily done by a few key pieces of machinery, which were marvels of their time. The steam shovel, the pile driver, the hydraulic pump and hose, and the self-righting barge were all elemental in the radical reshaping of Seattle's terrain.

Bertha was the largest tunnel-boring machine in the world when it was built in 2013 by Hitachi Zosen Sakai Works in Osaka, Japan. The drill, fondly named after Seattle's first female mayor, Bertha Landes, bored through more than seven thousand feet of subterranean Seattle and created a 57.5-foot-diameter tunnel to replace the Alaskan Way Viaduct along Seattle's downtown waterfront.

The steam shovel and the hydraulic pump hose excavated centuries-old strata from several bluffs in Seattle to manufacture flat land.

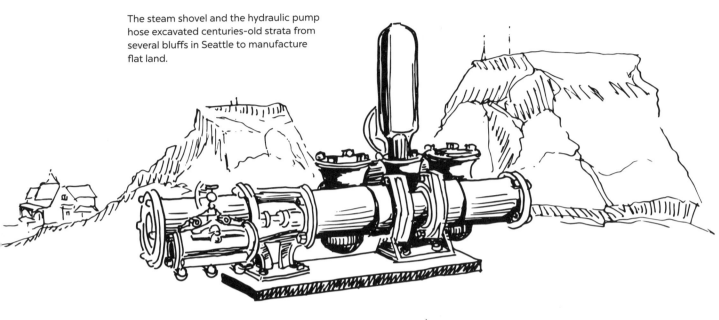

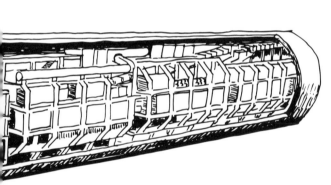

The pile driver made it possible to bridge gaps over tideflats, effectively connecting points between sea and land for rail services.

Gravity and conveyor belts delivered soil directly into Elliott Bay. Self-righting barges carried tons of soil into open waters before overturning and discharging their loads into the murky Puget Sound. Harbor Island was created in 1909 from the relics of the Jackson Street and Dearborn Street regrades, which razed parts of Beacon Hill.

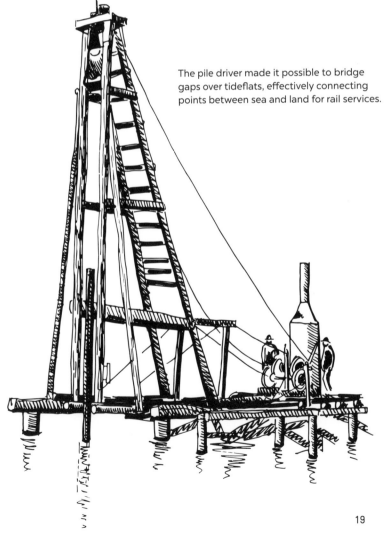

RAISING SEATTLE

There are strange birds roosting in Seattle. Towering over streets and sidewalks, their rigid wings sweep back and forth, slowly erecting nests of glass and steel and concrete. In January 2017, there were sixty-two of these creatures in Seattle, according to Rider Levett Bucknall's North American Crane Index, more than in any other US city. (San Francisco had around twenty-two.) Though they concentrate around downtown, nearly any view in the city is sure to contain at least one of these lumbering ersatz fowl.

Construction cranes signal a building boom commensurate with Seattle's status as the fastest-growing city in the United States. Like in previous boom times, the demand for housing and work spaces has led to radical changes in the landscape and, many would argue, the very identity of the city itself. Beloved (if also neglected) places have been demolished to make way for taller, denser structures with new tenants. The cranes produce uneasy feelings in many Seattleites who have spied them before.

Each boom seems to reflect something of the nature of its time. During its midcentury boom, Jet City built infrastructure—freeways, bridges, airport expansions—to better serve the commuting and leisure classes produced by Boeing. In the 1980s and '90s, Seattle aggressively overcompensated for its earlier bust by erecting seven of its ten tallest buildings, nearly all of them corporate financial centers.

The current boom has yet another flavor. The newest buildings are mostly mixed-use commercial and residential. They collocate realms that were distinct during previous booms, reflecting a desire for dense urban living and working. Another trend is the urban corporate "campus," multibuilding complexes within a tight radius, exemplified by Amazon in the South Lake Union neighborhood.

The following pages present the skyline as synecdoche for Seattle: an agglomeration of height and bulk and style where disparate structures born of disparate ages share present-day streets in a gallery of time.

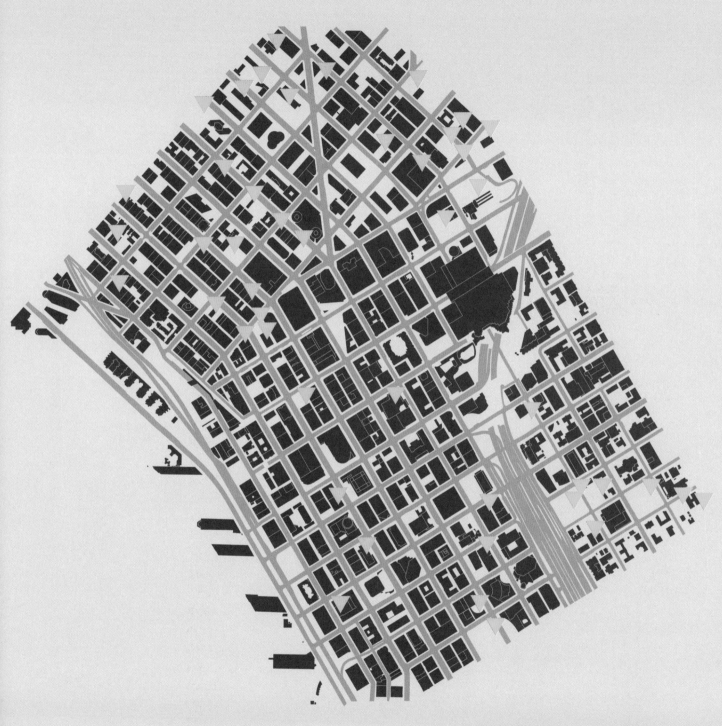

This map of downtown Seattle shows projects that have applied for building permits or are under construction as of 2017.

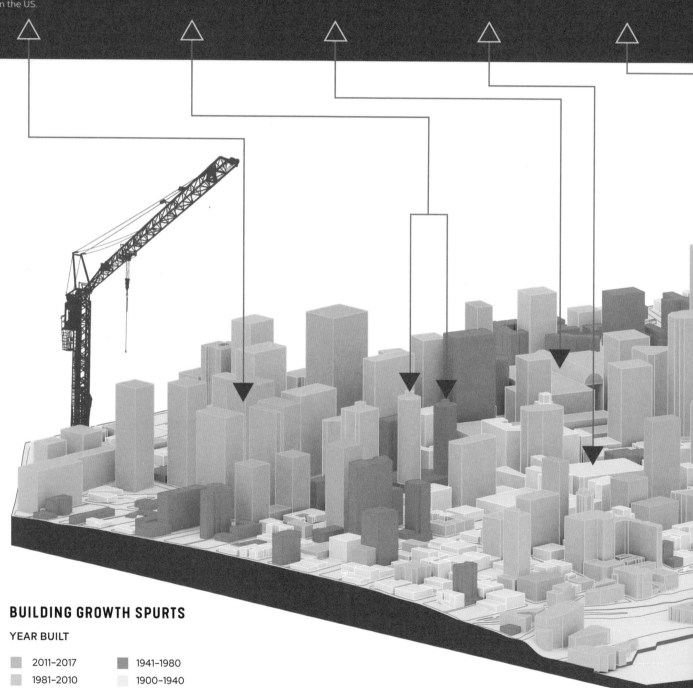

AMAZON HEADQUARTERS CAMPUS

2014 (Doppler) | 524' | 37 floors
As of August 2017, Amazon's complex of seven buildings, including three five-hundred-foot-plus skyscrapers and the famous glass Amazon Spheres, occupied 19.2 percent of all office space in Seattle, twenty times the next-largest employer's footprint, and the biggest percentage of any city in the US.

WESTIN SEATTLE TOWERS

1969 (south), 1982 (north)
449' | 47 floors
The high-rise hotel was built on the site of the Orpheum Theatre. Its towers are pictured on the cover of Modest Mouse's 1997 album *The Lonesome Crowded West*.

WASHINGTON STATE CONVENTION CENTER

1988, 2001, 2010 | 339' | 22 floors
The complex, spanning the I-5 freeway and notable for its glass atrium across Pike Street, has hosted Emerald City Comic Con, PAX (originally known as Penny Arcade Expo), and the Global Specialty Coffee Expo.

MACY'S BUILDING

1928 | 80' | 7 floors
Originally the Bon Marché department store, famous for its Frango mint chocolates, this landmarked building features bronze-colored panels, entitled *The Spirit of Northwest Industry*, created by artist Dudley Pratt.

TWO UNION SQUARE

1989 | 740' | 56 floors.
Topped by a ninety-foot flagpole that occasionally flies a twenty-by-thirty-foot American flag, this skyscraper is Seattle's third-tallest building.

BUILDING GROWTH SPURTS

YEAR BUILT

- 2011–2017
- 1981–2010
- 1941–1980
- 1900–1940

1411 FOURTH AVENUE
1928 | 162' | 15 floors
A magnificent modernist stone facade with remarkable art deco bestiaries earned this building a place in the National Register of Historic Places.

RAINIER TOWER
1977 | 514' | 41 floors
Sometimes called "the Wineglass Building," thirty of this skyscraper's floors balance atop an eleven-story concrete "vase."

1201 THIRD AVENUE
1988 | 772' | 55 floors
Nicknamed "the Spark Plug," Seattle's second-tallest building was the home of Washington Mutual Bank (WaMu).

F5 TOWER
2017 | 660' | 44 floors
This skyscraper is the tallest building constructed in Seattle since 1990 and the first tower in the city designed to LEED Gold standards. In addition to the technology company F5 Networks, it houses a 189-room luxury hotel.

COLUMBIA CENTER
1985 | 937' | 76 floors
Victor Steinbrueck, former dean of the UW's school of architecture called Seattle's tallest building "probably the most obscene erection of ego edifice on the Pacific Coast."

SMITH TOWER
1914 | 462' | 36 floors
Seattle's neoclassical gem, Smith Tower was Seattle's tallest building until the Space Needle bested it in 1962. The pyramid atop is a much-coveted private residence.

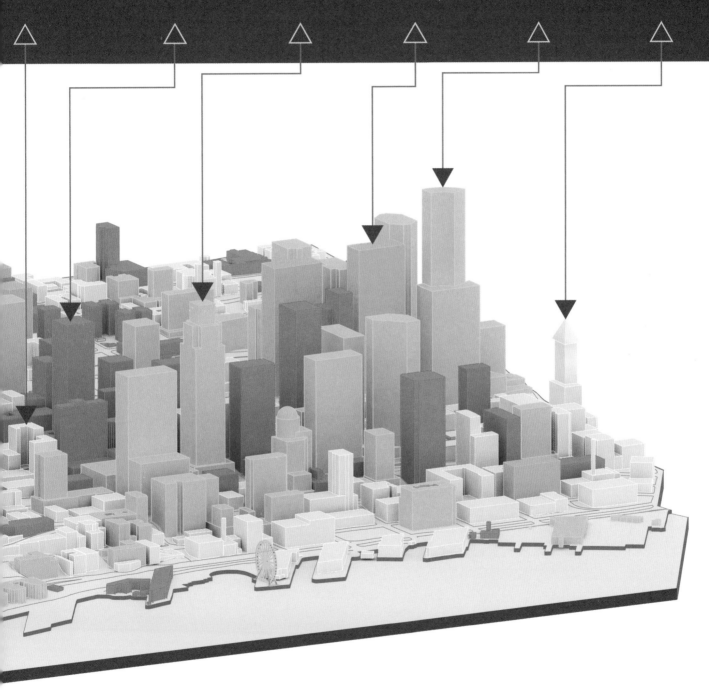

RAISING FOURTH AVENUE

1865–1940

 CENTRAL LIBRARY
A Carnegie library was opened downtown in 1906 after an arson at the original library site possibly involving the city librarian. (See more about this story on page 76.)

 SEATTLE GENERAL HOSPITAL
This hospital, the second in the city, opened in 1900 with financial ties to the nearby First United Methodist Church.

 COLMAN 8 COURT

 FIRST UNITED METHODIST CHURCH
Built in 1908 in the Beaux-Arts style, this church served as a place of worship into the twenty-first century. The E-shaped building, one of many buildings there, was the nurses' home for Seattle General.

 RAINIER CLUB
The Rainier Club was founded in 1888 by civic and industry leaders. The clubhouse was built in 1907 and has storied connections to a variety of Seattleites. During the first half of the century, it maintained an all-male, all-white rule.

BURNETT FAMILY HOME
This home, built in 1865 by Hiram Burnett, housed three generations of Burnetts and was built with wood cut at the Burnett's Port Ludlow Mill.

 COLMAN FAMILY HOME
Agnes and James Colman built their house in 1883. Their granddaughter Agnes lived there until her death in 1936 at the age of ninety-four. She would frequently come down to Fourth Avenue to hand out meal tickets to the unhoused and out of work. Reportedly among them were many drunks, who had to listen to Agnes expound on the virtues of temperance.

OAKLAND HOTEL
The Oakland Hotel was built in 1911.

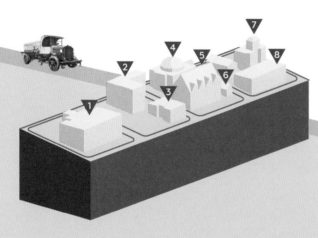

1941–1980

 CENTRAL LIBRARY
The Carnegie library was demolished, and in 1960 a new International Style library was constructed.

 SEATTLE GENERAL HOSPITAL
In 1944, artist Dudley Pratt unveiled relief panels above the hospital's main entrance, a notable attraction until the building was demolished in 1971. Four years later, Seattle General merged with Doctors Hospital and Swedish Hospital.

 UNION BANK OF CALIFORNIA BUILDING
At the time of its construction, in 1973, this forty-one-story structure was the second-tallest building in Seattle.

 FIRST UNITED METHODIST CHURCH
In 1951, the church added an education wing.

 RAINIER CLUB
The club admitted its first Japanese American member in 1966, and its first African American and female members in 1978.

 AL'S PARKING

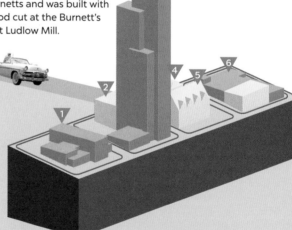

1981–2010

1 CENTRAL LIBRARY
A new glass-and-steel library, designed by OMA + LMN, opened in 2004.

2 FOURTH AND MADISON BUILDING
This forty-story skyscraper was completed in 2002. It has a rooftop garden on the seventh floor, which is a privately owned public open space.

3 COLUMBIA TOWER
This 937-foot skyscraper dramatically altered downtown Seattle. Designed by Chester L. Lindsey, it was the tallest building on the West Coast when it opened in 1985. Its massive presence caused ire among residents who did not agree with developer Martin Selig's desire to dominate the city's skyline. Selig wanted to break the one-thousand-foot mark, but his goal was denied by the FAA, citing airline restrictions. Today the building is ranked fourth-tallest on the West Coast, but it remains the tallest in Seattle.

2011–2017

1 FIRST UNITED METHODIST CHURCH
The church was listed in the National Register of Historic Places in 2011, but after pressure from developers, church leaders agreed to a deal to knock down the newer education wing to build the F5 Tower. The older part of the building that remains is now known as Daniels Recital Hall.

2 F5 TOWER
This forty-four-floor luxury hotel and office tower was the most expensive building under construction during the recent boom. Work began in 2008 but was paused due to the recession, not resuming until 2014.

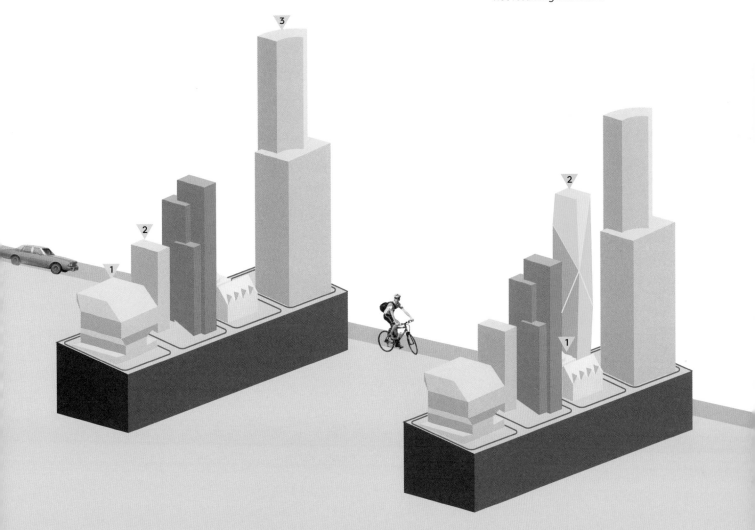

FLOATING FORTS

Above: Hidden Lake Lookout's gabled L-4 fire tower overlooks an array of storied giants, all with their own impressive histories. Many of them bear foreboding names like Torment, Forbidden, and Sharkfin, perhaps to keep the faint of heart from scaling their heady peaks.

The Cascades, a lumbering system of intimidating white peaks that extend from Canada to the northern border of California, tower and collapse around the delicate exposed neck of Seattle and the greater Puget Sound, holding the region loosely, but effectively, in a convincing headlock. From a Queen Anne Hill rooftop, take a look around and you'll find you're surrounded, a gang of over seventy-five gulp-inducing peaks looming large in the distance. The highest summits are home to exposed humble structures, sparse cabin variations bolted and cinched to bedrock, making it possible to bear the brunt of scouring winds and wet weather systems blown in from the Pacific Ocean while affording wildly graceful and immaculate views in all directions.

The fire lookouts of the Pacific Northwest and their supporting trail systems are the direct legacy of the 1910 Big Blowup (a disastrous series of fires in Washington and neighboring states that burned more than three million acres of land) and the epic efforts of the 1933 Civilian Conservation Corps (CCC). The 1910 event caught the newly established US Forest Service off guard, and it quickly sought to establish an aggressive fire suppression policy. Unfortunately, the policy fundamentally misunderstood the important role of fire and adaptation in forest ecologies, but in the end it produced a vast infrastructure of extraordinary and remote architecture.

Most of the Forest Service's Region 6, a.k.a. the Pacific Northwest Region, was built out by the late 1930s, during the Great Depression, by the CCC, resulting in over 685 timber structures overlooking Washington forests. Men and women then became fire spotters, particularly during World War II, earning between $150 and $230 a month (about $3,000 in today's dollars) to live a season of solitude on top of the world, eating canned food and communicating only with the help of a heliograph and Morse code. Lookouts were built with a singular architectural function, which viewed the landscape with what some might argue was a too-narrow perspective. However, despite the advent of aviation technology in the 1950s that quickly threatened the fire lookouts' obsolescence, their relevance to regional identity, environmentalism, and Western literature was cemented by the literary mythmakers of the Beat generation, who found profound intimacy, connection, and inspiration on those desolate peaks. They recorded their experiences in the form of powerful poetry and essays, along with chapters that would become central to novels like *The Dharma Bums* and *Desolation Angels*.

Twenty-two-year-old Beat poet Gary Snyder was the instigator, spending the summers of 1952 and 1953 in the North Cascades as a logger, trailhand, and fire lookout up on Crater and Sourdough Mountains. He inspired fellow friends and lonesome travelers to make their own pilgrimages up into the air. Poet Philip Whalen followed Snyder's lead in 1953 as a lookout on Sauk Mountain and again the next year on Sourdough. In the summer of 1956, Jack Kerouac followed suit after Snyder persuaded him at the famous Six Gallery reading in San Francisco the preceding fall. Kerouac spent sixty-three days in isolation atop Desolation Peak with enough food supplies to last the season along with a single book (Dwight Goddard's *A Buddhist Bible*) and a Golden West spiral notebook. He had no liquor or cigarettes to distract from the slow shift of geologic time and space.

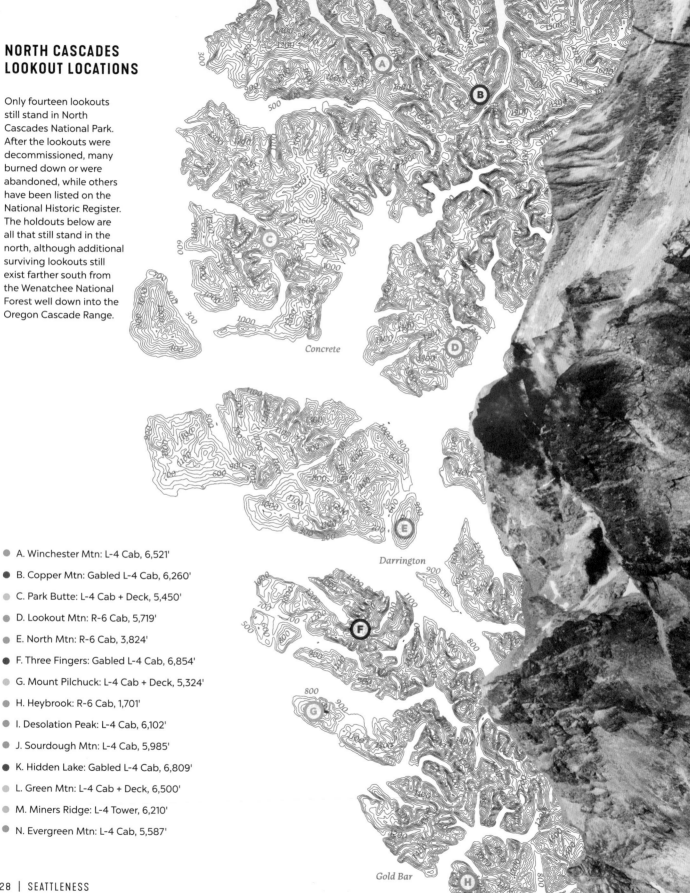

NORTH CASCADES LOOKOUT LOCATIONS

Only fourteen lookouts still stand in North Cascades National Park. After the lookouts were decommissioned, many burned down or were abandoned, while others have been listed on the National Historic Register. The holdouts below are all that still stand in the north, although additional surviving lookouts still exist farther south from the Wenatchee National Forest well down into the Oregon Cascade Range.

Concrete

Darrington

Gold Bar

- A. Winchester Mtn: L-4 Cab, 6,521'
- B. Copper Mtn: Gabled L-4 Cab, 6,260'
- C. Park Butte: L-4 Cab + Deck, 5,450'
- D. Lookout Mtn: R-6 Cab, 5,719'
- E. North Mtn: R-6 Cab, 3,824'
- F. Three Fingers: Gabled L-4 Cab, 6,854'
- G. Mount Pilchuck: L-4 Cab + Deck, 5,324'
- H. Heybrook: R-6 Cab, 1,701'
- I. Desolation Peak: L-4 Cab, 6,102'
- J. Sourdough Mtn: L-4 Cab, 5,985'
- K. Hidden Lake: Gabled L-4 Cab, 6,809'
- L. Green Mtn: L-4 Cab + Deck, 6,500'
- M. Miners Ridge: L-4 Tower, 6,210'
- N. Evergreen Mtn: L-4 Cab, 5,587'

Cedar Crossing

Mt. Rainier National Forest

Lake Wenatchee

LOOKOUT ARCHITECTURE

L-4 CAB

By far the most common live-in lookout for Region 6 from early 1930 to 1952, the L-4 cab has a standard hip roof, where all sides slope down from a single peak, like a pyramid. This particular shelter model is found on Sourdough, one of the first lookout points established by the Forest Service, and Desolation Peak. Both lookouts are still in operation for recreational use and, year after year, continue to house travelers, authors, and poets.

L-4 CAB + DECK

This model is a slight variation on the L-4 cab design, with the addition of (surprise!) a wraparound deck. Earlier lookouts constructed without a uniform design were often crafted of sundry materials found on-site. The L series has its origins in the Pacific Northwest, which is why this particular architectural typology and its variations dominate the region.

GABLED L-4 CAB

An earlier generation in the L-4 series, this style of lookout was constructed primarily from 1929 to 1932 and is distinguished by a two-sided wood shingle roof atop the standard L-4 14-foot-square wood frame. The L-4 structures were often referred to as "Aladdin cabs," named after the mill in Vancouver, Washington, where they were manufactured as modular kits.

L-4 TOWER

This lookout launches the traditional timber design high into the air, reaching at its tallest a cringe-inducing one hundred feet to withstand deep snowpack. The 1933 to 1953 designs have four-sided hip roofs and bolted ceiling joists to hold the shutters open (as seen above). The last of these relics stands twenty feet tall atop the bald summit of Miners Ridge, overlooking the alpenglow of Image Lake and Glacier Peak beyond. Active for sixty-five years, the tower is well maintained. It has been listed on the National Historic Lookout Register since 1994.

R-6 CAB

Also originating in the Pacific Northwest, the early 1950s R-6 cab design is considered relatively modern. It has a 15-foot-square plywood frame construction and a flat tar-paper roof, which extends a few feet beyond the cabin to offer shade to its residents. Examples of the R-6 design float among the evergreens atop Heybrook Ridge, Lookout Mountain, and North Mountain like the most epic of tree houses. Don't be intimidated by the challenging staircases; the views at the top are well worth it.

D-6 CUPOLA

First prototyped atop Mount Hood in 1915, the D-6 cupola features a square 12-foot-square frame complete with wall-to-wall windows and a second-story observatory. It was the first standard design of the Forest Service and thus a stalwart structure in Region 6. Many of the peaks in the North Cascades started with D-6 cupolas before moving on to more economical designs. One of the few examples still in existence sits atop North Twentymile Peak about ninety miles east of Ross Lake in the North Cascades.

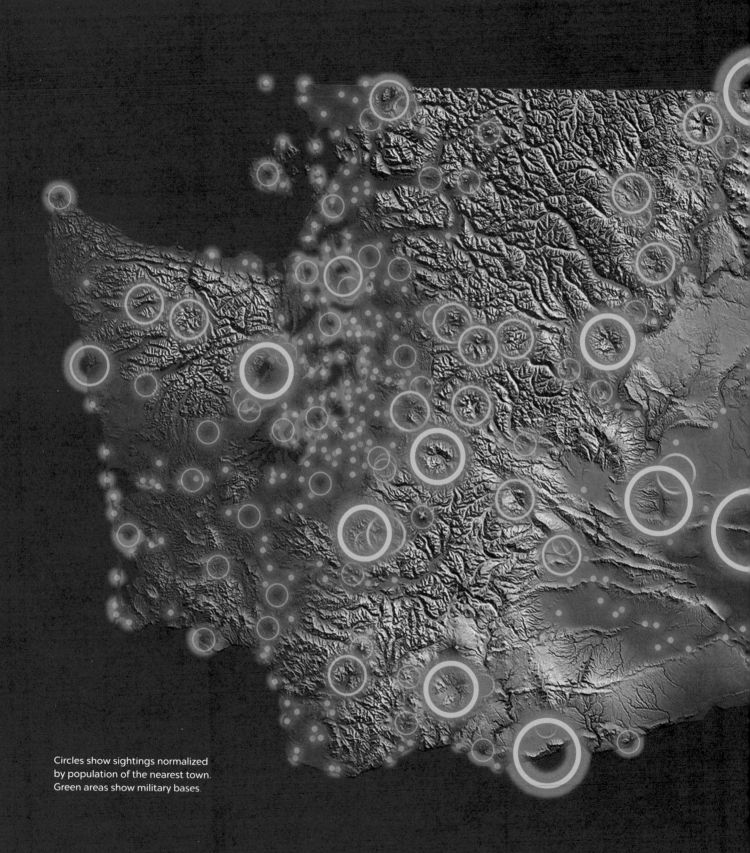

Circles show sightings normalized
by population of the nearest town.
Green areas show military bases.

SAUCERS IN THE SKY

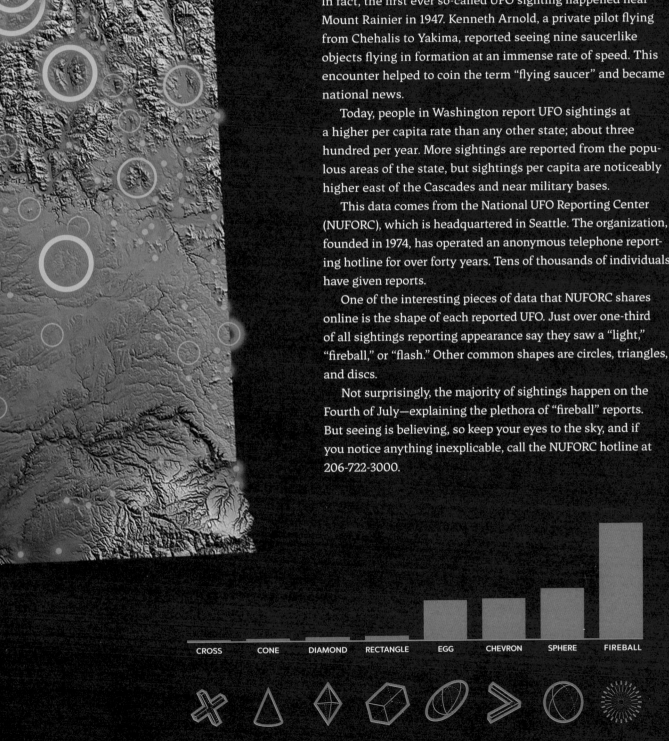

Washington State has a long history of close encounters. In fact, the first ever so-called UFO sighting happened near Mount Rainier in 1947. Kenneth Arnold, a private pilot flying from Chehalis to Yakima, reported seeing nine saucerlike objects flying in formation at an immense rate of speed. This encounter helped to coin the term "flying saucer" and became national news.

Today, people in Washington report UFO sightings at a higher per capita rate than any other state; about three hundred per year. More sightings are reported from the populous areas of the state, but sightings per capita are noticeably higher east of the Cascades and near military bases.

This data comes from the National UFO Reporting Center (NUFORC), which is headquartered in Seattle. The organization, founded in 1974, has operated an anonymous telephone reporting hotline for over forty years. Tens of thousands of individuals have given reports.

One of the interesting pieces of data that NUFORC shares online is the shape of each reported UFO. Just over one-third of all sightings reporting appearance say they saw a "light," "fireball," or "flash." Other common shapes are circles, triangles, and discs.

Not surprisingly, the majority of sightings happen on the Fourth of July—explaining the plethora of "fireball" reports. But seeing is believing, so keep your eyes to the sky, and if you notice anything inexplicable, call the NUFORC hotline at 206-722-3000.

CROSS   CONE   DIAMOND   RECTANGLE   EGG   CHEVRON   SPHERE   FIREBALL

AW, SHUCKS!

Whether you prefer the sweet petites or love the brave and bold, when it comes to oysters, Seattle is the place to shuck.

Oysters serve a vital ecological function, filtering an enormous amount of plankton and algae, leaving the surrounding water clearer and cleaner. Native cultures have harvested the tasty bivalves for centuries in Puget Sound. Raw oysters surged in popularity in the 1850s when white settlers began to exploit the local resource and send shiploads down to San Francisco. The state of Washington is the only state in the United States that grows all five major edible oyster species. Within each of these five species, there are multitudes of flavor profiles and texture varieties for oyster lovers to explore. Each oyster is a direct reflection of the environment in which it was grown. True connoisseurs will enjoy savoring the subtle distinctions each inlet and cove provides.

Of the five types of oysters grown in the Seattle area, the Pacific is by far the most pervasive. Approximately 98 percent of oysters grown in Washington are Pacifics. This oyster variety is not a native of the area; it was brought to Washington in 1919 by two Japanese oyster farmers. All oysters have some degree of salinity, and this is impacted by their growing environment. Pacifics tend to be on the sweeter side, and some even have a fruity finish.

Eastern oysters, which are also grown around Seattle, have smoother shells than their counterparts. They don't grow as easily on the Pacific coast, but they seem to do well on the southern beaches of Puget Sound. They also tend to have a brinier flavor profile.

The Olympia, known as *kloch kloch* by the Salish peoples, is the only oyster species native to the area, and this scrappy little mollusk leads a rough life of fighting tides. This gives Olympias a thick shell and an intensely packed flavor, including a coppery finish.

The popular Kumamoto oyster is beloved by beginners and connoisseurs alike for its petite size, mild saltiness, and fruity sweetness. While "Kumies" flourish in Japan's warmer waters, it is too cold for them to spawn in the Puget Sound area. Luckily, they can still be cultivated in the area; they grow best in Oakland Bay.

In contrast to the nonthreatening Kumamoto, the European flat is not for the faint of heart. It is related to the Olympia oyster but is much larger. It boasts a stronger metallic taste and tends to be very briny.

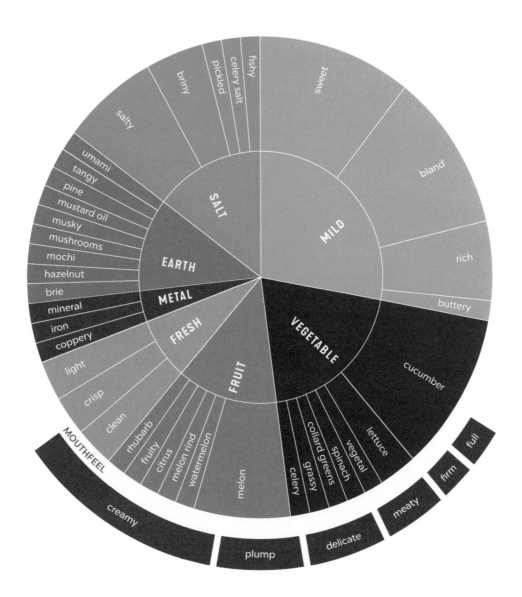

SALISH SEA OYSTER FLAVOR WHEEL

Flavor descriptions taken from various online oyster review websites providing species-specific tasting notes. See bibliography on page 158 for details.

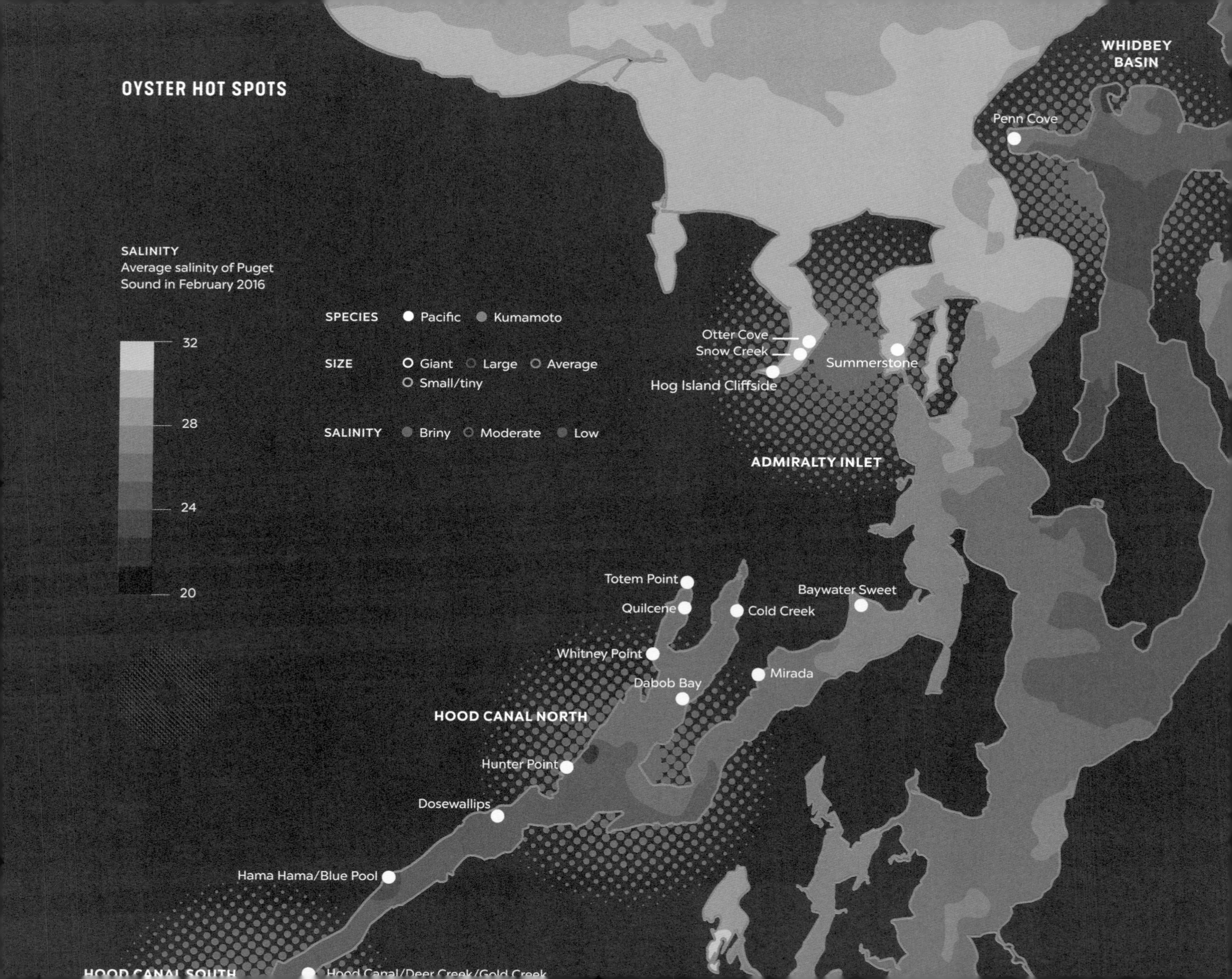

OYSTER HOT SPOTS

SALINITY
Average salinity of Puget
Sound in February 2016

32

28

24

20

SPECIES ● Pacific ● Kumamoto

SIZE ○ Giant ○ Large ○ Average
         ○ Small/tiny

SALINITY ● Briny ● Moderate ● Low

WHIDBEY
BASIN

Penn Cove

Summerstone

Otter Cove
Snow Creek
Hog Island Cliffside

ADMIRALTY INLET

Baywater Sweet

Cold Creek

Mirada

Totem Point

Quilcene

Dabob Bay

Whitney Point

HOOD CANAL NORTH

Hunter Point

Dosewallips

Hama Hama/Blue Pool

Hood Canal/Deer Creek/Gold Creek

HOOD CANAL SOUTH

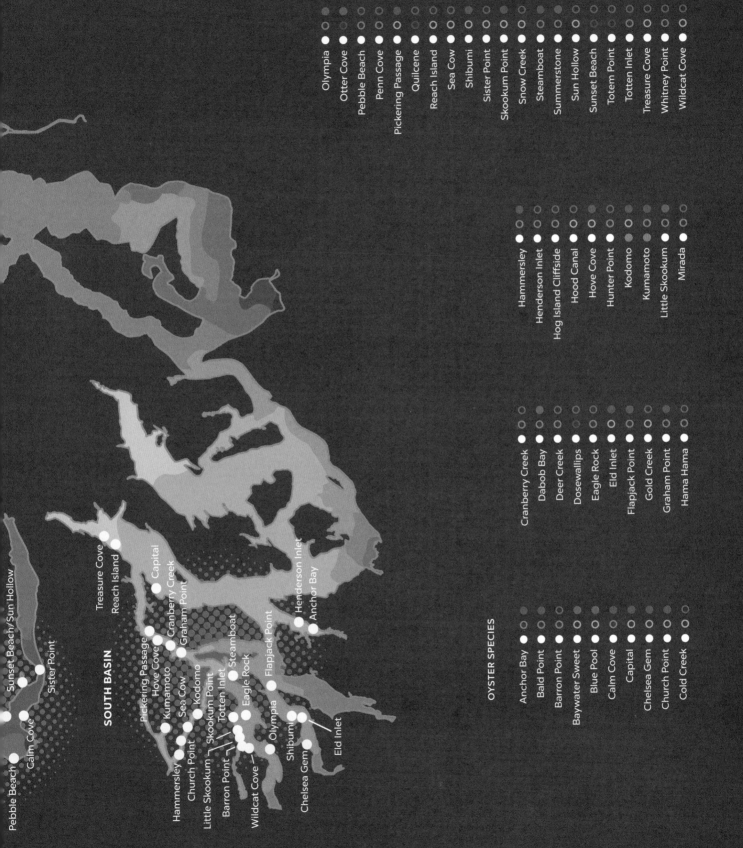

Olympia
Otter Cove
Pebble Beach
Penn Cove
Pickering Passage
Quilcene
Reach Island
Sea Cow
Shibumi
Sister Point
Skookum Point
Snow Creek
Steamboat
Summerstone
Sun Hollow
Sunset Beach
Totem Point
Totten Inlet
Treasure Cove
Whitney Point
Wildcat Cove

Hammersley
Henderson Inlet
Hog Island Cliffside
Hood Canal
Hove Cove
Hunter Point
Kodomo
Kumamoto
Little Skookum
Mirada

Cranberry Creek
Dabob Bay
Deer Creek
Dosewallips
Eagle Rock
Eld Inlet
Flapjack Point
Gold Creek
Graham Point
Hama Hama

OYSTER SPECIES

Anchor Bay
Bald Point
Barron Point
Baywater Sweet
Blue Pool
Calm Cove
Capital
Chelsea Gem
Church Point
Cold Creek

SOUTH BASIN

Pebble Beach
Calm Cove
Sunset Beach/Sun Hollow
Sister Point
Treasure Cove
Reach Island
Capital
Pickering Passage
Hove Cove
Cranberry Creek
Graham Point
Hammersley
Kumamoto
Church Point
Sea Cow
Little Skookum
Kodomo
Skookum Point
Barron Point
Totten Inlet
Steamboat
Eagle Rock
Wildcat Cove
Flapjack Point
Olympia
Shibumi
Chelsea Gem
Henderson Inlet
Anchor Bay
Eld Inlet

GUM WALL DISSECTION

Post Alley, which snakes through Pike Place Market, is home to the Market Theater Gum Wall, at coordinates N 47°60'84", W 122°34'05". This colorful specimen of public collective art features chewed gum stuck to the wall of the alleyway. It draws both locals and tourists, who come to leave their own sticky signatures.

The gum wall is now a Seattle landmark and tourist attraction, and it once contained twenty-two hundred pounds of chewed gum. At fifteen feet high and fifty feet long, the original wall was covered in over twenty years' worth of gum, measuring several inches thick in certain areas. TripAdvisor even "honored" the gum wall in 2009, naming it as the second germiest tourist attraction in the world. The tradition of applying gum to Post Alley's brick wall started in 1993 when bored Market Theater patrons, waiting hours in line for a late show, defiantly stuck their bubble gum on the wall. Theater staff cleaned the gum off twice before realizing that the gum enthusiasts refused to have their bubbles burst, and a local tradition was born. After twenty-two years, the gum wall was in rough shape, so in 2015 the Pike Place Market Preservation and Development Authority cleaned the wall for the first time, to prevent the buildup from further impacting the brick surface. The cleaning of this popular tourist attraction was announced on the gum wall's Facebook page, which stated: "Just like you, all that sugar can really mess up the surface of your bricks, er, teeth. I have to admit, after twenty years, I'm feeling a little icky, sticky and in desperate need of a good scrubbing to make me sparkle again." The removal took over 130 hours of intense steam cleaning. It was estimated that the wall contained 150 pieces of gum per brick, with over a million wads in total.

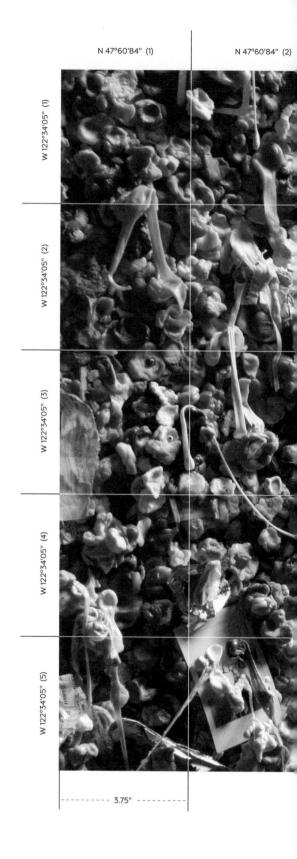

N 47°60'84" (1)   N 47°60'84" (2)

W 122°34'05" (1)

W 122°34'05" (2)

W 122°34'05" (3)

W 122°34'05" (4)

W 122°34'05" (5)

---------- 3.75" ----------

GUM WALL FLAVOR PROFILE

The adjacent graphic demonstrates our analysis of the gum found in a photographed sample of the wall in 2016. We explored the many color variations via surveying the photo and matched them to corresponding gum flavor profiles.

Mint

Spearmint

Bubble gum

Berry

Wintergreen

Peppermint

Watermelon

Cinnamon

Citrus

Mixed fruit

Polar Ice

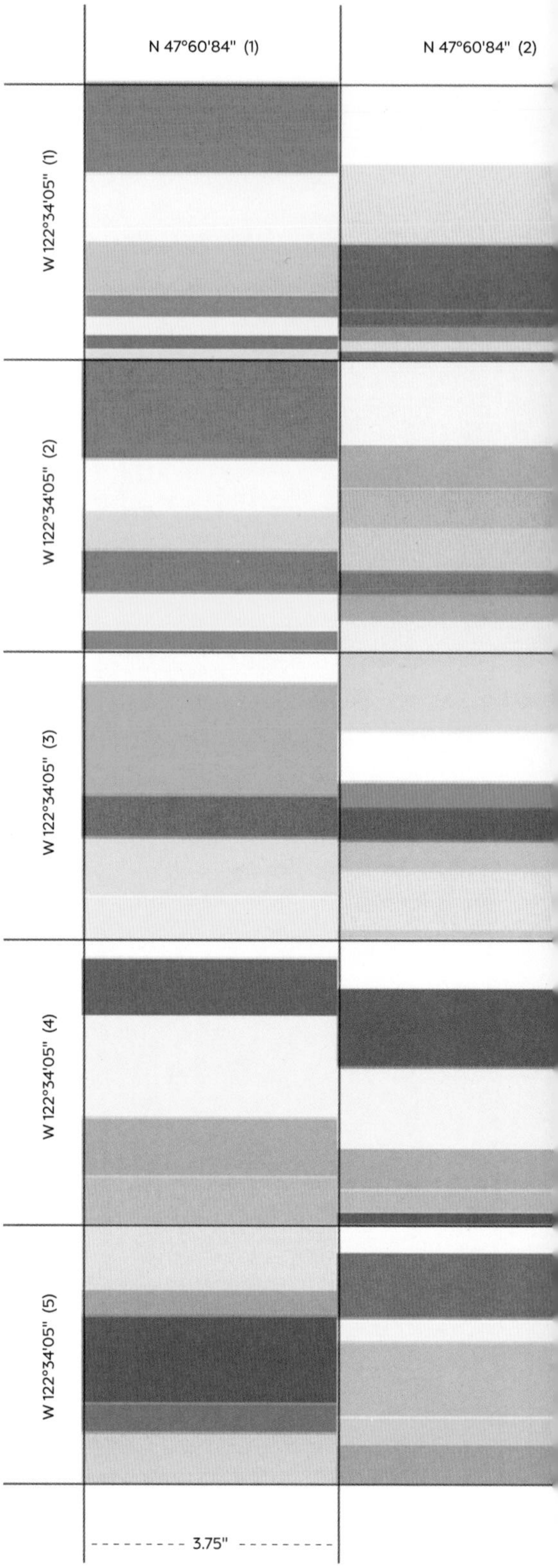

N 47°60'84" (1)

N 47°60'84" (2)

W 122°34'05" (1)

W 122°34'05" (2)

W 122°34'05" (3)

W 122°34'05" (4)

W 122°34'05" (5)

3.75"

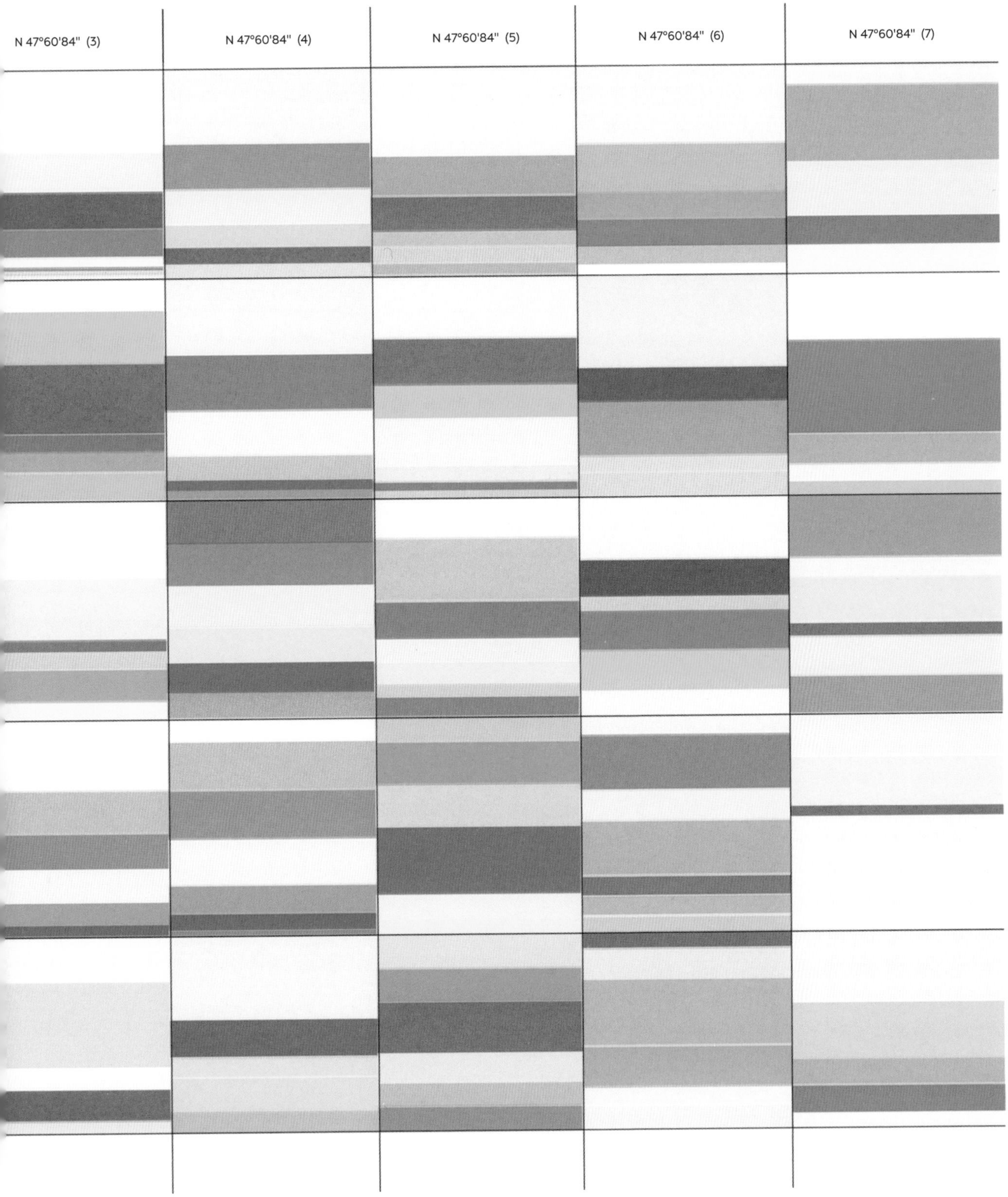
N 47°60'84" (3)
N 47°60'84" (4)
N 47°60'84" (5)
N 47°60'84" (6)
N 47°60'84" (7)

PIONEER SQUARE UNDERFOOT

Pioneer Square, Seattle's first neighborhood, has a history of cyclical growth and devastation, which has left behind fragments of its history within the urban fabric. The accumulation of these unique artifacts and infrastructural remnants, layered atop one another, is what makes this neighborhood so special.

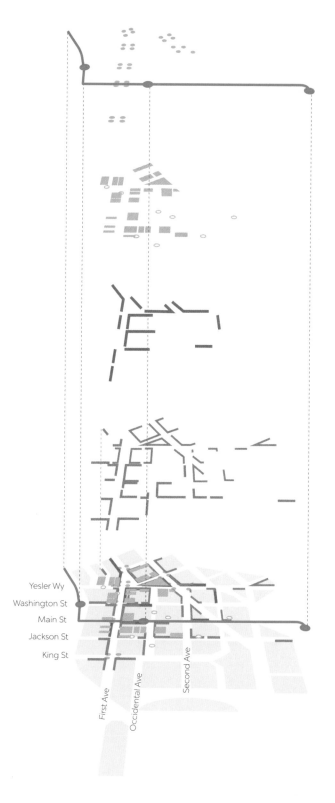

Pre-1850 — Seattle's Native Americans were the Duwamish and Suquamish. The location of Pioneer Square today was a seasonal village and the area was known as the "little crossing-over place."

1865 — The City of Seattle, named after Chief Seattle, was incorporated. The town plats were divided by Arthur Denny, Carson Benson, and Doc Maynard, and a planning dispute between the three men left its trace by way of the tangled intersections still found along Yesler Way today.

1889 — The Great Seattle Fire burned many blocks of Seattle's downtown and Pioneer Square neighborhoods. After the burning, the residents vowed to rise again and rebuild. Elevated streets were constructed to resolve issues of sanitation, creating today's many areaways under sidewalks. These underground spaces were often lit with glass prism blocks, which allowed natural light through.

1897 — During the Klondike Gold Rush, the city of Seattle was a lunching pad for many pioneers seeking new opportunities and bringing a population boom to the area.

1909 — The Iron Pergola, located in Pioneer Square Park served as a stop for the Yesler and James Street Cable Car company. A wrought iron gem with an underground bathroom, today the pergola serves as a popular public space in the neighborhood.

1914 — Seattle gained its first skyscraper: the Smith Tower. At forty-two stories, this was the tallest building west of Chicago and held that claim for nearly fifty years.

1970 — The Pioneer Square Preservation District was created, dedicating buildings within the boundary with important historical significance and specifying regulations for development.

1982 — The George Benson Waterfront Streetcar Line opened to riders along Pioneer Square and the Elliott Bay waterfront. This line closed in 2005.

2016 — The First Hill Streetcar opened, serving Seattle's Pioneer Square, International District, Capitol Hill, and First Hill neighborhoods.

Yesler Wy
Washington St
Main St
Jackson St
King St

First Ave
Occidental Ave
Second Ave

UNDERGROUND

In 1965, the Seattle Junior Chamber of Commerce held Know Your Seattle Day, and the first public Bill Speidel's Underground Tour hosted over five hundred people.

ON THE GROUND

The purple glass prism blocks in the neighborhood's sidewalks are skylights to the rooms below, which acted as important light sources in the 1800s, before electric lighting.

ABOVE GROUND

On the opening day of Smith Tower, over four thousand Seattle residents rode to the thirty-fifth floor to see the view of their city from above.

MOVING GROUND

The George Benson Waterfront Streetcar Line was named by National Geographic as one of the ten great trolley rides in 2007.

■ Areaways

■ Glass prism blocks

■ Historic buildings
◯ Historic markers

● Payphones
● Historic traffic lights
—● Waterfront streetcar line & station

TERRA-COTTA TIME CAPSULES

The University of Washington's Liberal Arts Quadrangle is a wonderful place to see the Collegiate Gothic style of architecture, which was prevalent in the first half of the twentieth century, and one of its great by-products: grotesques. Over one hundred of these realistic and symbolic sculptural figures adorn the buildings surrounding the Quad—created by artists who brought their own sensibilities, politics, and styles to the campus.

Grotesques differ from gargoyles in that they do not spout water. However, you can see a real gargoyle in action at the southwest entry to Gerberding Hall designed by artist and professor Dudley Pratt. For the grotesques on nearby Suzzallo Library, sculptor Allan Clark carved and cast in terra-cotta the likenesses of eighteen "great contributors to culture and learning." The cast of characters was selected by a committee that included then-president Henry Suzzallo, and legend has it that he vetoed a monkey clinging to Charles Darwin's leg at the last minute, which is why there is now an ill-defined bulge where the left leg should be.

Moving into the Quad itself, you see more work by Pratt at Smith Hall. With the help of several art students, Pratt pumped out one sculpture per day to complete his commission of twenty-eight grotesques in 1939. Most famous is the depiction of "power": one of four world philosophies posited by Pratt, and represented by a grenade-welding, gas-mask-wearing European soldier—a memento of wartime sentiments.

The most prolific grotesque artist commissioned by the university was Alonzo Victor Lewis—creator of the sculptures adorning Miller, Savery, and Raitt Halls. The latter building, erected in 1916, gets the most critical attention, for its depiction of "home economics" in the form of working women. These laboring ladies are cooking, cleaning, and taking care of babies while the sole male representative relaxes on the west side of the building, holding an inscribed tablet that some interpret as "laying down the law."

Though the artist's subject matter and symbolism are by no means representative of all viewpoints at their time of creation, the sculptures do serve as thought-provoking relics. The university has no plans to commission additional grotesques, so we are left to imagine how an artist today might represent higher education in the current era.

Left: Grotesques adorn Suzzallo Library at University of Washington's Seattle campus

1. Gargoyle, 1949
Dudley Pratt | Gerberding Hall

2. Charles Darwin, 1926
Allan Clark | Suzzallo Library

*Orange elements depicted in grotesques
are intended to highlight an interesting or
defining object in the sculpture. Charles
Darwin's monkey is imagined by the author
and not a part of the real grotesque.

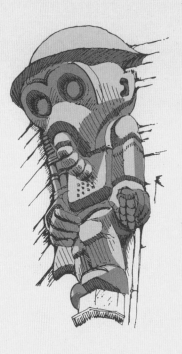

3. Hammer and Cog, 1932–1939
Dudley Pratt | Smith Hall

4. Chief Seattle, 1932–1939
Dudley Pratt | Smith Hall

5. Power, 1932–1939
Dudley Pratt | Smith Hall

6. Fish Teacher, 1922
Alonzo Victor Lewis | Miller Hall

7. Sweeping Woman, 1916
Alonzo Victor Lewis | Raitt Hall

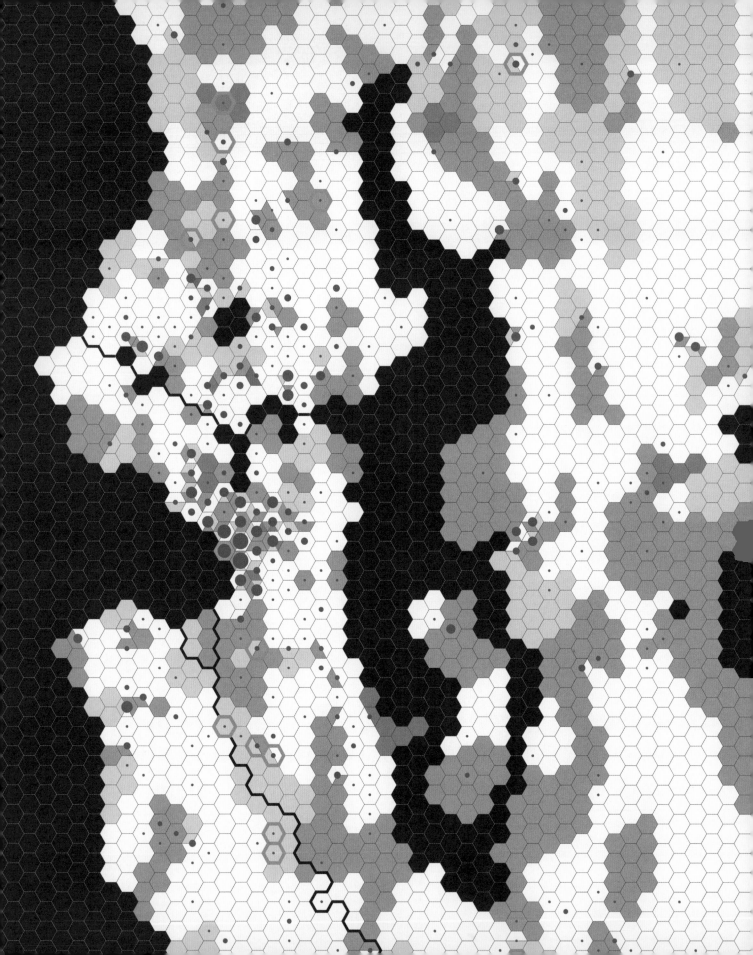

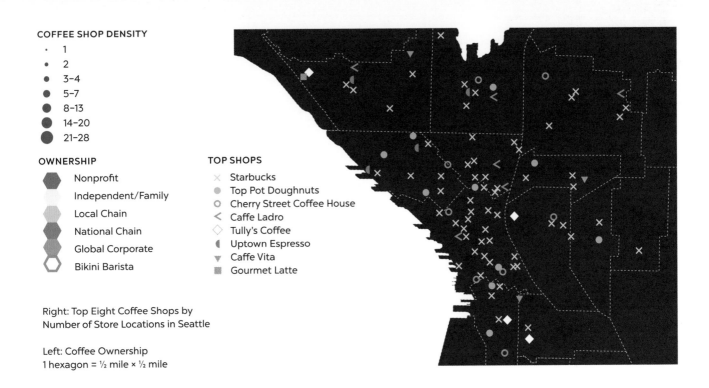

COFFEE SHOP DENSITY
· 1
· 2
· 3–4
· 5–7
· 8–13
· 14–20
· 21–28

OWNERSHIP
Nonprofit
Independent/Family
Local Chain
National Chain
Global Corporate
Bikini Barista

TOP SHOPS
✕ Starbucks
● Top Pot Doughnuts
○ Cherry Street Coffee House
◁ Caffe Ladro
◇ Tully's Coffee
◖ Uptown Espresso
▼ Caffe Vita
◼ Gourmet Latte

Right: Top Eight Coffee Shops by
Number of Store Locations in Seattle

Left: Coffee Ownership
1 hexagon = ½ mile × ½ mile

A DAMN FINE CUP OF COFFEE

Seattle is a destination city for any coffee aficionado. From roasters and equipment makers to coffeehouses and on-the-go kiosks, Seattle epitomizes coffee culture. Many of the city's present-day coffee enterprises can trace their roots to late 1960s and '70s counterculture establishments, places like the University District's storied Last Exit on Brooklyn (1967–2000) and Cafe Allegro (1975–present), Seattle's oldest espresso bar. Specially roasted coffee beans were sold to these coffeehouse communities by Pike Place Market businesses like the Good Coffee Company and a small Western Avenue joint offering beans, teas, and spices, and named after a Moby-Dick character: Starbucks.

Some forty years later, Seattle and its suburbs contain over a thousand coffee shops, more than a dozen coffee roasters, and many businesses related to coffee sourcing, logistics, and equipment. Starbucks has grown into a global powerhouse,

with over twenty-six thousand stores worldwide; the highest concentration per capita is in its hometown. Niche establishments compete alongside corporate chains and independent coffeehouses, the most controversial being "bikini barista" stands, where scantily clad women serve espresso to drive-through motorists.

The map at left shows regions of coffee-shop influence, categorized by ownership. Similar to a heat map, ownership is shown as a region around coffee-shop points, using the Thiessen polygon method to divide the regions of influence. The greatest concentrations of coffee shops are around Pike Place Market and the U District, reflections of the history and development of the city's coffee culture. This representation gives a broad sense of where certain ownership types flourish and clearly shows the dominance of independent shops around the greater Seattle region.

Pearl Lakes

One-Eyed Jack's

Sparkwood Mountain

Ghostwood
National Forest

Black Lake

Snoqualmie

Glastonbury Grove

White Tail Mountain

TWIN PEAKS: REAL + STRANGE

"We are like the dreamer who dreams and then lives inside the dream."
—"Eternal Stories from the Upanishads," Twin Peaks, Season 3, Episode 14

The towns of Snoqualmie, North Bend, and Fall City have again become pilgrimage destinations—this time for a new generation of *Twin Peaks* fans—after the 2017 installment of the popular TV drama that premiered in 1990. In the series, creator David Lynch explores the banal wonder and horror behind real and imagined landscapes, mapping metaphysical and existential despair with zeal at the foot of the North Cascades. While many of the show's landmarks (the Double R Diner) are real (Twede's Cafe) and just a short drive from Seattle, the fictional town of Twin Peaks has a geography of its own. Lynch made his own fictional map before he even began writing, and that map, along with many others, features prominently in the show. We've created a map in which the fictional and filmed geography collide, illustrating the show's most important places.

JACK RABBIT'S PALACE // OLALLIE STATE PARK

BLUE DIAMOND MOTEL // MT. SI MOTEL

DOUBLE R DINER // TWEDE'S CAFE
JAILHOUSE // BUICK BLDG, TOP FLOOR
MRS. TREMOND'S PAINTING // BENDIGO BLVD S & W MCCLELLAN ST

WELCOME TO TWIN PEAKS SIGN // SE REINIG RD

SPARKWOOD & 21 (LAURA FLEES JAMES'S BIKE INTO THE WOODS) // 396TH DR SE & SE REINIG RD
RONETTE'S BRIDGE // REINIG BRIDGE

PACKARD SAWMILL // WEYERHAEUSER MILL

TWIN PEAKS SHERIFF'S DEPARTMENT // DIRTFISH RALLY DRIVING SCHOOL

MO'S MOTOR & THE 324B10 UTILITY POLE // SE PARK ST & MEADOWBROOK WY
THE NEW FAT TROUT TRAILER PARK // TRAILER PARK BEHIND AUTO REPAIR OF SNOQUALMIE

TWIN PEAKS HIGH SCHOOL // MOUNT SI HIGH SCHOOL

LEO & SHELLEY JOHNSON'S HOUSE // PRIVATE RESIDENCE ON 372ND PL SE

LAURA & DONNA'S PICNIC // SNOQUALMIE POINT PARK

THE GREAT NORTHERN // SALISH LODGE

OPENING CREDITS // SNOQUALMIE FALLS

ELK'S POINT #9 BAR // JOE'S BAR & GRILL

BIG ED'S GAS FARM // INDOOR GARDEN
BOOKHOUSE BOYS HQ (EXTERIOR) // LAST FRONTIER SALOON

BANG BANG BAR // THE ROADHOUSE RESTAURANT & INN

North Bend

Fall City, WA

Above: Dots show sightings normalized by population of nearest town. Green areas are national and state parks and forests.

Right: Descriptions of Bigfoot. Gray indicates a visual description, orange an auditory description, and green indicates smell. Size indicates the most commonly reported description.

SASQUATCH SIGHTINGS

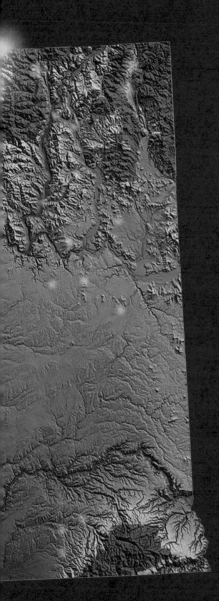

Bigfoot, Sasquatch, or Skunk Ape—whatever you call it, this creature is synonymous with Washington State. And while sightings may be most common at Sea-Tac gift shops, you have a better than average chance of seeing this creature deep in the Cascades—specifically in the forests surrounding Mount Rainier—than anywhere else in the world.

This information comes from the Bigfoot Field Researchers Organization. Since 1995, it has collected reports from all over the world, and the largest number come from Washington State (over six hundred sightings from as early as 1812).

In addition to location, many people filing reports describe in detail their "sighting" experience. Seeing a hairy apelike biped is the most common description, but many people also hear loud screams and deep howls and growls, and notice rotten skunky smells.

Spend some time reading the reports and you may find yourself a converted "squatcher."

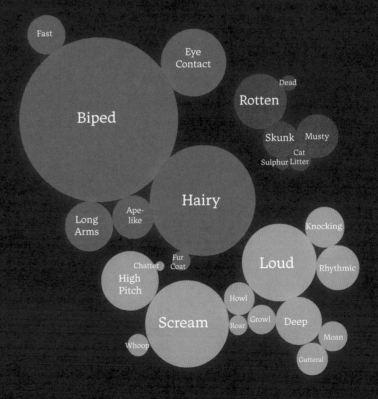

BITTER SEATTLE

Seattle's mild, wet climate produces an abundance of plant life, inviting residents to ponder how that plant life might best be put to use. And for millennia, one of the answers has been to extract the essence from these plants for medicinal purposes, or for pure enjoyment.

An excellent solvent for a wide variety of plants is alcohol, extracting not only flavors but also medicinal components. Perhaps the most versatile extract in daily life is bitters, highly concentrated, used with a light hand—and, yes, bitter. Adding a few dashes enhances the flavor of just about anything: cocktails, tea, seltzer water, even food. Dilute bitters at roughly a two-to-one ratio and you'll have an amaro, which can be enjoyed on its own as a digestif or mixed into cocktails. Soak the same plants in wine and you can make a vermouth. The important thing is to use botanicals with a strong bitter flavor as a foundation, and then mix them with other plants that balance the flavor profile.

To make bitters, people historically used plants that were local to their region. In Europe, colonialism introduced a wide variety of tropical botanicals that became popular additions, defining the flavors we generally expect in bitters. But there's no need to fetishize the great brands of Europe. You can make your own using locally wild plants. It's easy. And foraging for plants is a great way to explore where you live. No matter how urban, useful plants grow everywhere.

Making your own bitters will help you appreciate plants in a new way. Here in Seattle, we have excellent options for botanicals. The following plants will get you started. To find all of them, you may end up visiting all corners of the city, including some of Seattle's best urban parks, trails, and natural areas. Take a walk, and see what you come up with.

*Keep in mind that many of these plants have medicinal properties. If you have health concerns, or if you're pregnant or trying to become pregnant, you should consult your doctor before consuming them.

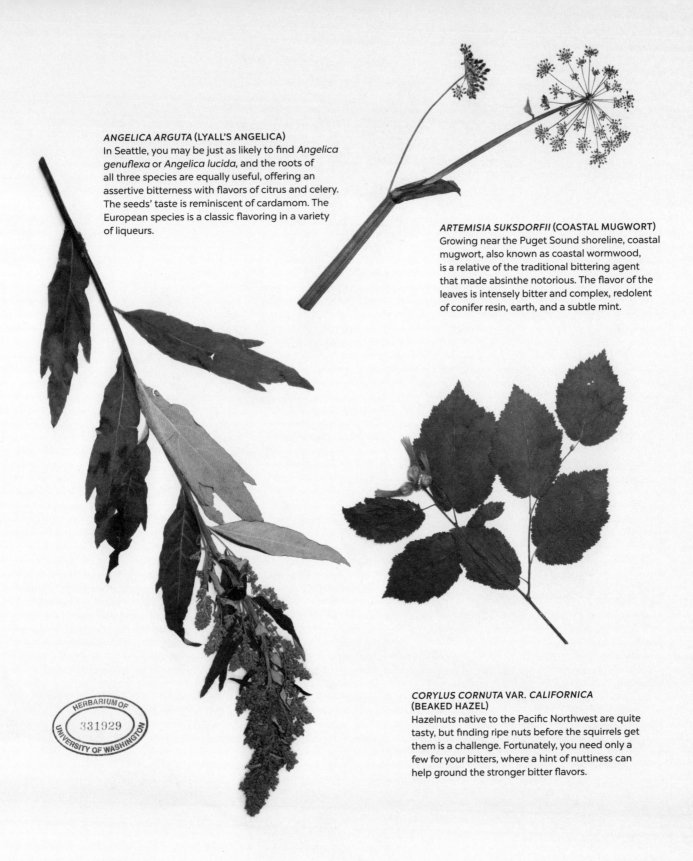

ANGELICA ARGUTA (LYALL'S ANGELICA)
In Seattle, you may be just as likely to find *Angelica genuflexa* or *Angelica lucida*, and the roots of all three species are equally useful, offering an assertive bitterness with flavors of citrus and celery. The seeds' taste is reminiscent of cardamom. The European species is a classic flavoring in a variety of liqueurs.

ARTEMISIA SUKSDORFII (COASTAL MUGWORT)
Growing near the Puget Sound shoreline, coastal mugwort, also known as coastal wormwood, is a relative of the traditional bittering agent that made absinthe notorious. The flavor of the leaves is intensely bitter and complex, redolent of conifer resin, earth, and a subtle mint.

CORYLUS CORNUTA VAR. CALIFORNICA (BEAKED HAZEL)
Hazelnuts native to the Pacific Northwest are quite tasty, but finding ripe nuts before the squirrels get them is a challenge. Fortunately, you need only a few for your bitters, where a hint of nuttiness can help ground the stronger bitter flavors.

ESCHSCHOLZIA CALIFORNICA (CALIFORNIA POPPY)

California poppy has been naturalized throughout Seattle for over a century. While this poppy is not a narcotic, it effectively eases anxiety and can be a mild sedative, at least with stronger doses. In bitters, the leaves offer a light, earthy bitterness that helps knit all the flavors together.

MAHONIA NERVOSA (DWARF OREGON GRAPE)

Easy to find in natural areas and even urban landscapes, dwarf Oregon grape is deservedly popular as a landscape ornamental. It's also a classic bitter tonic, which stimulates both the digestive system and liver. The roots are most useful, but don't shy away from experimenting with the leaves and fruit.

PRUNUS EMARGINATA (BITTER CHERRY)

Bitter cherry is a fast-growing native throughout Seattle. Although the name refers to the fruit, it's the inner bark of freshly cut limbs that is especially useful here. As you'd expect, the flavor is pleasantly fruity, but with assertive tannins and a subtle bitterness.

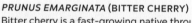

OPLOPANAX HORRIDUS (DEVIL'S CLUB)

Devil's club tastes like where it grows: dark, wet earth and moss. Related to ginseng, it also offers a complex bitterness with a sharp chile flavor. It's no longer common in Seattle, so you may have to explore some of the wetter urban forests to find it. Harvest the roots and don't be greedy.

SAMBUCUS NIGRA SSP. CERULEA (BLUE ELDERBERRY)
Blue elderberry can be found along regional trails throughout the city. Both the berries and the flowers are useful, so let the season determine which you use. Be sure the sweet-and-sour berries are fully ripe, and then press them and use only the juice, as some people can react poorly to the seeds.

SATUREJA DOUGLASII (YERBA BUENA)
This native evergreen ground cover is no longer common in Seattle, but you might well find it in cultivated landscapes. Yerba buena, with its delightfully sweet, minty flavor, has long been appreciated as a tea. It also works well in bitters, to round out the overall flavor profile.

SCUTELLARIA LATERIFLORA (BLUE SKULLCAP)
Blue skullcap leaves are another source of bitterness, yet not overwhelmingly so and with a grassy, earthy flavor that adds an interesting note to the overall mix. Skullcap is also a highly effective and safe nervine, if you're inclined to relax with a cocktail.

TARAXACUM OFFICINALE (COMMON DANDELION)
Having naturalized throughout the temperate world as a tenacious weed, dandelions deserve better appreciation, especially as an effective tonic. The leaves have a tangy bite, which belies a pure, sweet flavor. The roots, too, offer a sweet flavor, but one that's more complex, with a hint of vanilla. Roasting the roots brings out even more earthy complexity.

ISLANDS OF THE SALISH SEA

Seattle is one of many ports along the jagged edge of the Salish Sea, a rich marine ecosystem of waterways and islands that extends from Desolation Sound in British Columbia to the southern tip of Puget Sound. The islands that dot this region are made of tougher stuff, withstanding several ice ages, including the Fraser Glaciation—a 1.5-mile-thick sheet of ice that carved and gouged large swaths of land into the water bodies we know today as the Strait of Georgia, the Strait of Juan de Fuca, and Puget Sound.

While composed of resilient bedrock, all of the islands still bear the vestiges of the eroding forces that stripped them of preglaciation soils—the telltale scars of glacial striations, smooth, rounded surfaces, and the occasional head-scratching gift of a several-ton erratic, or boulder. Even now, the land continues to shrug off the burden of the long-removed glacial weight, in the form of isostatic uplift, subtly rebounding and rising from the sea by the smallest of increments.

Numbering in the hundreds, when counting the small uninhabited marine and wildlife refuges off the larger islands, the islands each have a compelling cultural and ecological history. Spieden Island in the San Juans, for instance, is billionaire-owned and uninhabited for most of the year. By a fluke of position and microclimate, this slim slip of land basks partially in the crook of Vancouver Island's rain shadow, leaving the eastern side of the island thickly forested and the sun-soaked south side barren, save for a few madrona trees clinging to deep crooks in the rocky hillsides.

In the 1960s, the island served as a hunting preserve for the rich, complete with exotic grazing animals and over two thousand species of game birds. Uproar from the local island communities of the San Juan archipelago and a *60 Minutes* special shut the dubious operation down; however, mouflon sheep from Corsica, fallow deer, also from Europe, and sika deer from Asia still roam the island.

Many of the islands, like Protection Island, play host to solitary individuals, who live all by their lonesome, often serving as caretakers of these rare enclaves. Named by explorer George Vancouver in 1792, Protection Island sits at the head of Discovery Bay, where intense winds buffet its unique shoreline spits and sandy bluffs, which make it ideal for 75 percent of Puget Sound's nesting marine bird population. Rhinoceros auklets, tufted puffins, pigeon guillemots, pelagic cormorants, and more all call Protection Island home in the summer months.

The sole residences on the island are two rustic A-frame cabins, the result of a failed eight-hundred-lot vacation development in the 1970s. In 1982, the federal government bought out most of the landowners (save two) and established it as a national wildlife refuge, making it off-limits to casual visitors.

Although there is one outlier that stands in stark contrast to the rest. At the head of the Duwamish River, Harbor Island is the largest artificial island in the United States. It was born of industry and fill from various dredging and regrading projects spanning the twentieth century. The island's inhabitants are colorful though mechanical. Enormous gantry cranes stand like lumbering giraffes at its shores, effortlessly hoisting containers from across the sea from one ship to the next, in what might be described as a never-ending confidence game of three-container monte.

Right: Deception Pass

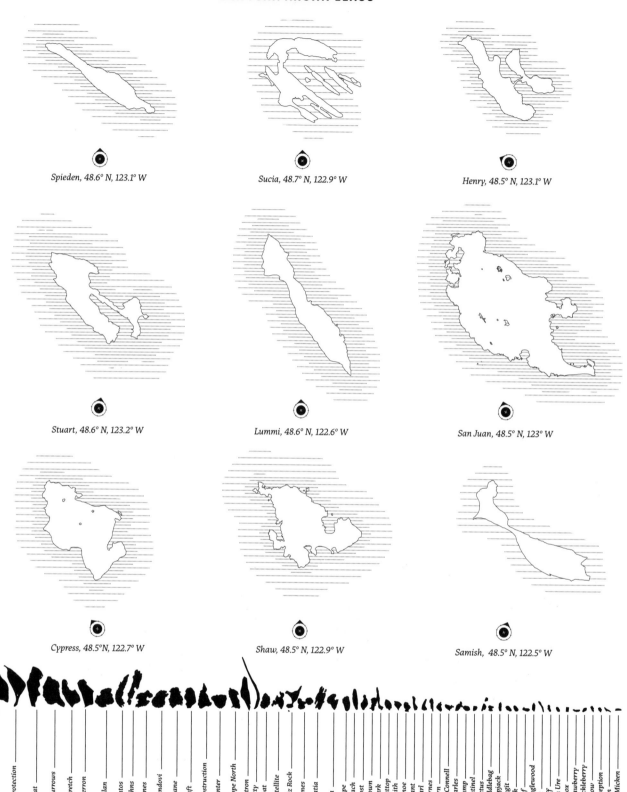

Spieden, 48.6° N, 123.1° W

Sucia, 48.7° N, 122.9° W

Henry, 48.5° N, 123.1° W

Stuart, 48.6° N, 123.2° W

Lummi, 48.6° N, 122.6° W

San Juan, 48.5° N, 123° W

Cypress, 48.5°N, 122.7° W

Shaw, 48.5° N, 122.9° W

Samish, 48.5° N, 122.5° W

Blake Protection Hat Burrows Stretch Herron Allan Patos Johns Jones Vendovi Crane Raft Obstruction Center Hope North Ketron Jetty Goat Satellite Eliz Rock James Matia Ika Hope Reach Frost Broun Clark Flattop Smith Canoe Grant Pearl Barnes Turn McConnell Charles Trump Sentinel Cactus Saddlebag Skipjack Skagit Jack Reef Tanglewood Rat Cliff Ben Ure Silcox Strawberry Huckleberry Yellow Deception Ram McMicken

Littered throughout Puget waters are numerous smaller landforms called islets and skerries. These obscure sea stacks often boast strange and sometimes hostile names (hello, Skull Island) thanks to generations of islanders and fisherfolk.

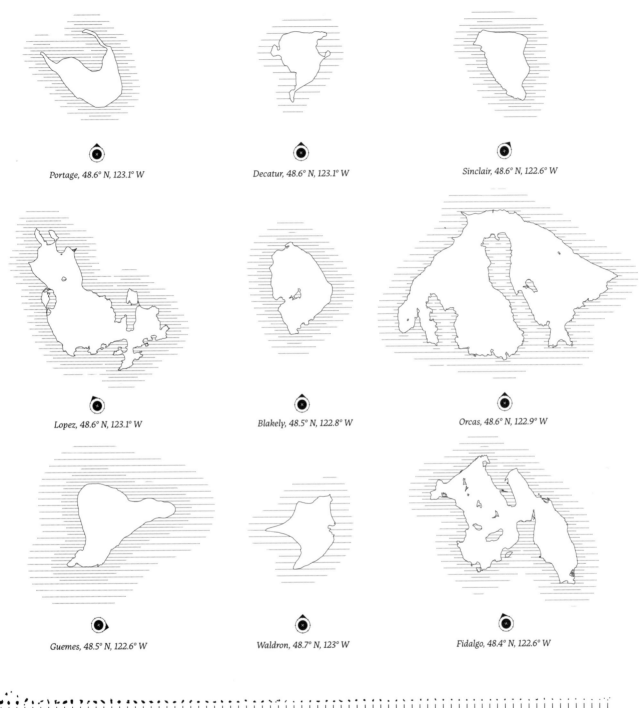

Portage, 48.6° N, 123.1° W

Decatur, 48.6° N, 123.1° W

Sinclair, 48.6° N, 122.6° W

Lopez, 48.6° N, 123.1° W

Blakely, 48.5° N, 122.8° W

Orcas, 48.6° N, 122.9° W

Guemes, 48.5° N, 122.6° W

Waldron, 48.7° N, 123° W

Fidalgo, 48.4° N, 122.6° W

Pass — Coupville — Dinner — Come — Chuckanut — Puffin — Strawberry — Vita Rocks — Minor — Lummi Rocks — Willow — Castle — Doe — Barnacle — Armitage — Young — North Peapod — Boulder — Reef Point — Tomkin — Deadman — Eagle — Alegria — Cutts — Bell — Deadman — Alec Rock — Dot — O'Neil — Flower — Iceberg — Victim — Goose — Crab — Hall — Battleship — Bird Rocks — Blind — Freeman — Halftide — Northwest — Indian — Skull Rock — Blind — Picnic — Lone Tree — Faun — Fortress — Little Deadman — Touhead — Ripple — Gossip — South Peapod — Peapod Rock — Rim — Swirl — Barren — Sisters — Posey — Black Rock — Lawson Rock — Harbor Rock — Northern Pacific Rock — Mummy Rocks — Williamson Rock — Nob — Richardson Rock — Whale Rocks — Guss — Double — Iowa Rock — Cemetery — Little Sister — Cayou — Twin Rocks — Low — Pointer — Secar Rock — Skull — Spindle Rock

PUGET SOUND ISLANDS

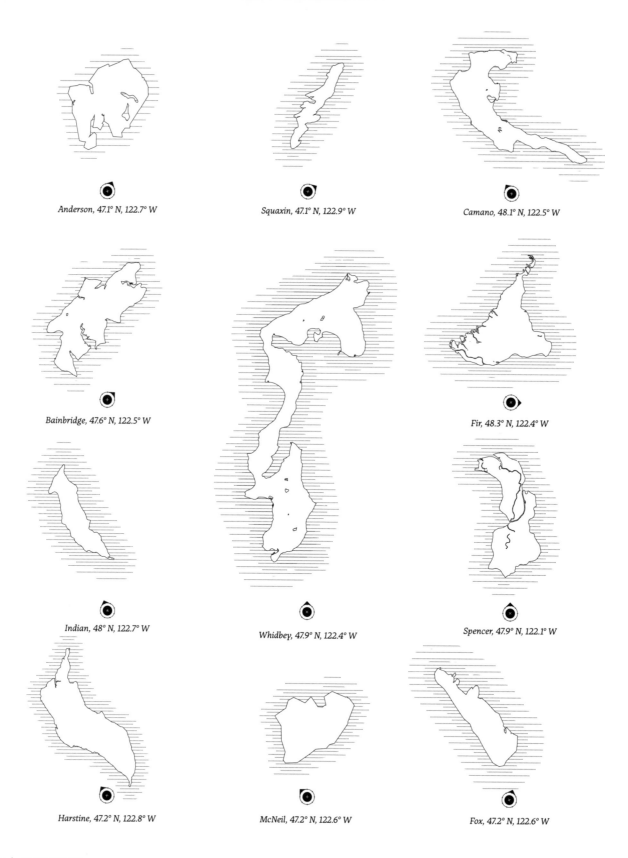

Anderson, 47.1° N, 122.7° W

Squaxin, 47.1° N, 122.9° W

Camano, 48.1° N, 122.5° W

Bainbridge, 47.6° N, 122.5° W

Fir, 48.3° N, 122.4° W

Indian, 48° N, 122.7° W

Whidbey, 47.9° N, 122.4° W

Spencer, 47.9° N, 122.1° W

Harstine, 47.2° N, 122.8° W

McNeil, 47.2° N, 122.6° W

Fox, 47.2° N, 122.6° W

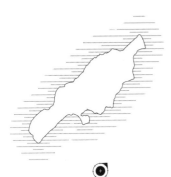

Vashon, 47.4° N, 122.4° W

Maury, 47.3° N, 122.4° W

HARBOR ISLAND
47.5° N, 122.3° W

THE CITY BEAUTIFUL

The citizens of Seattle have long supported the idea that their city's beauty derives from its many parks, gardens, beaches, and boulevards. From David Denny's gifting of Seattle's first park in 1883 to the 1968 Forward Thrust vote (a series of bond propositions, one of which was the largest parks and recreation issue bond ever passed in the United States)—Seattleites have consistently demonstrated the high priority they place on green space. This enthusiasm has attracted and produced preeminent landscape architects, whose contributions encircle and dot the city. The map on page 66 situates superb specimens of landscape architecture against the celebrated citywide system of parks and parkways designed by the Olmsted Brothers firm.

John Charles Olmsted recognized the rapid development of choice properties in gold rush Seattle and urged the city to purchase waterfront and hilltop lands to "secure and preserve for the use of the people . . . these advantages of water and mountain views." Over the next eight years, an enthusiastic citizenry taxed itself $3.5 million (or about $85 million in present-day dollars) to acquire lands and begin construction.

While the Olmsteds' open-space framework was an attempt to democratize the inherent beauty of Seattle, subsequent generations of designers faced new challenges and opportunities to uphold the city's emerald reputation. In the 1920s, master gardener Fujitaro Kubota envisioned a grand Japanese garden on a swampy property in the Rainier Beach neighborhood. Laws at the time prohibited Japanese Americans from purchasing land, and Kubota's internment during World War II set his work back several years. Despite these challenges, Kubota dedicated his life to the creation of this garden and was eventually able to purchase the property. In 1972, the Japanese government honored Kubota for his work on the garden. The land was purchased by the city in 1987 and is now a beloved public park.

A major challenge to the parks system came in the 1960s, when the trench needed to construct I-5 split Seattle in half. The path of the highway ran through part of the Olmsteds' Washington Park Arboretum, specifically through a twenty-five-year-old grove of Yoshino cherry trees. Despite the risk and expense, UW staff had the thirty cherries uprooted and transplanted into the Quad, along with over three hundred other trees in the freeway's path. The move was successful, and the spring blossoms are now seen by thousands each year.

Highway construction was also the impetus for Seattle's first land bridge. In 1976, local civic leader Jim Ellis came up with the idea to create a park above I-5, and landscape architect Lawrence Halprin was hired to design and execute the space. But the resulting Freeway Park wasn't designed as an escape from the urban hardscape and traffic. Halprin utilized concrete in the paving, walls, stairs, and fountains and maintained views down into the highway to emphasize the urban character of this park.

Similarly, Gas Works Park designer Richard Haag embraced the site's industrial history as a gasification plant to create a unique open space on the north shore of Lake Union. When the plant was abandoned in the 1960s, Haag's firm advocated preserving the factory remnants and retaining them as play features. The contaminated soil was piled and capped to form the central hill. The park was added to the National Register of Historic Places in 2013 and has inspired similar reclamation work around the world.

Seattle's Olympic Sculpture Park, owned and operated by the Seattle Art Museum and designed by Weiss/Manfredi and Charles Anderson Landscape Architecture, continues the tradition of both Halprin and Haag in that it bridges over several active freight rail lines and is the former brownfield site of oil and gas corporation Unocal. It also embraces the Olmstedian philosophy of providing accessible, free green space with views of water and mountains that reign supreme.

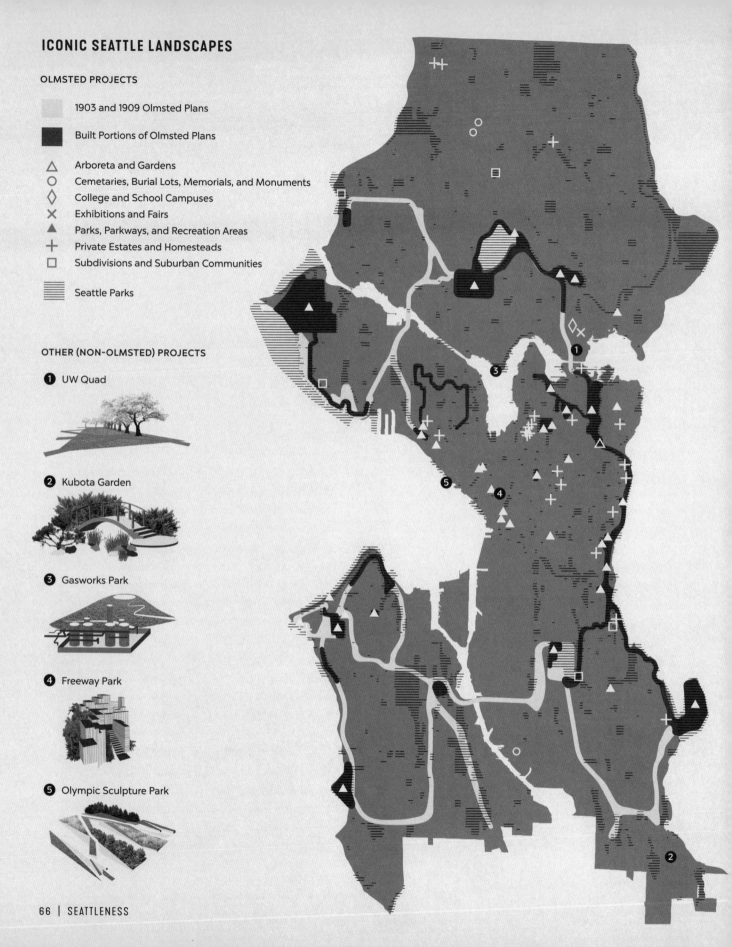

ICONIC SEATTLE LANDSCAPES

OLMSTED PROJECTS

1903 and 1909 Olmsted Plans

Built Portions of Olmsted Plans

△ Arboreta and Gardens
○ Cemetaries, Burial Lots, Memorials, and Monuments
◇ College and School Campuses
✕ Exhibitions and Fairs
▲ Parks, Parkways, and Recreation Areas
✛ Private Estates and Homesteads
☐ Subdivisions and Suburban Communities

Seattle Parks

OTHER (NON-OLMSTED) PROJECTS

1 UW Quad

2 Kubota Garden

3 Gasworks Park

4 Freeway Park

5 Olympic Sculpture Park

SIX DEGREES OF OLMSTED

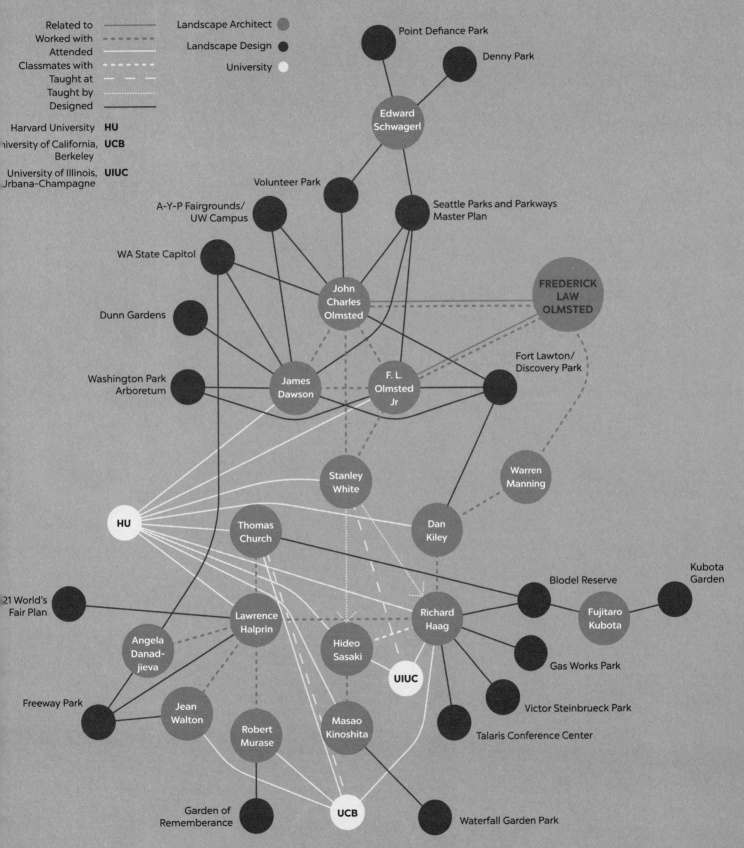

Related to
Worked with
Attended
Classmates with
Taught at
Taught by
Designed

Landscape Architect
Landscape Design
University

Harvard University — **HU**
University of California, Berkeley — **UCB**
University of Illinois, Urbana-Champagne — **UIUC**

Point Defiance Park
Denny Park
Edward Schwagerl

Volunteer Park
A-Y-P Fairgrounds/ UW Campus
WA State Capitol
Dunn Gardens
Washington Park Arboretum
Seattle Parks and Parkways Master Plan

John Charles Olmsted
FREDERICK LAW OLMSTED
Fort Lawton/ Discovery Park

James Dawson
F. L. Olmsted Jr
Warren Manning

Stanley White
Dan Kiley

HU
Thomas Church

Blodel Reserve
Kubota Garden
'21 World's Fair Plan

Lawrence Halprin
Richard Haag
Fujitaro Kubota

Angela Danadjieva
Hideo Sasaki
Gas Works Park

Freeway Park
UIUC
Victor Steinbrueck Park

Jean Walton
Robert Murase
Masao Kinoshita
Talaris Conference Center

Garden of Rememberance
UCB
Waterfall Garden Park

LEGENDARY LADIES

Seattleites owe much of their city's cultural wealth to the contributions and accomplishments of astounding women. From politics and education to dance and design, great women can be found in every facet of this city's history. Here we present nine extraordinary Seattle women who have helped shape history by pursuing with aplomb their passions and dreams and, in doing so, advancing against the odds into examples of excellence.

Their stories reflect a tradition of women's leadership that traces its roots to Seattle's founding. Reflecting upon his great-grandparents' labors to make a city, Brewster C. Denny noted that it really was "several generations of able, determined, often well-educated women who made so much of this place. . . . Women have provided not only the professional and business and public sector leadership but also the compassion, the vision, the courage, the nurturing sense, the values which a free people must hold and defend."

So here's to the ladies who helped make Seattle! And here's to the next generation of city builders!

BERTHA KNIGHT LANDES

October 1868–November 1943
Place of Influence: Civic Auditorium
47.623948° N, -122.350088° W

As the first woman to be elected mayor of a major US city, in 1926, Landes promised to clean up corruption and curb egregious behavior, like reckless driving and dancing. Construction of the Civic Auditorium (later the Seattle Opera House and now McCaw Hall) started during her tenure.

RUBY CHOW

June 1920–June 2008
Place of Influence: Ruby Chow's Restaurant
47.605882° N, -122.321652° W

Purchased in 1948 and lasting until 1979, Chow's restaurant was renowned in Seattle. Chow—restaurateur, activist, civic leader, and public servant—was an indomitable spirit in Seattle and an icon to Chinese Americans across the US. Her Ruby Chow's Restaurant was the locus of politics, engagement, and great food.

RUBY INOUYE SHU

November 1920–September 2012
Place of Influence: Shu Clinic
47.60082° N, -122.311311° W

Shu and her husband opened a clinic together in 1953 to practice family medicine. When she started working in 1949, Shu was the first female Japanese American physician in Seattle. An advocate for her community and a generous caregiver, she helped create nursing homes and delivered more than a thousand babies.

BONNIE "GUITAR" BUCKINGHAM

March 1923–present
Place of Influence: Dolton Records
47.625837° N, -122.344331° W

Bonnie Guitar and Bob Reisdorff co-owned the Dolton Records label from 1958 to 1960, cut several Billboard chart-leading hits, and launched groups called the Fleetwoods and the Ventures. From the 1950s to the '80s, Guitar topped the charts in country and pop with self-penned hits and her namesake instrument. Her label created Pacific Northwest talent, and she later became head of country music A&R for RCA Records.

ELIZABETH AYER

October 1897–August 1987
Place of Influence: Brookwood
47.744199° N, -122.377102° W

Ayers was the principal architect of the Brookwood mansion in the Highlands neighborhood, built in 1924. An architect who synthesized modern and traditional styles, she designed dozens of homes and buildings around Seattle. She was the first female architecture graduate from UW, and in 1930 was the first registered female architect in Washington.

ROBERTA BYRD BARR

January 1919–June 1993
Place of Influence: Lincoln High School
47.659936° N, -122.339842° W

Barr was the first female and black principal of a Seattle public school. As an educator, librarian, and TV talk show host, Barr surmounted challenges and passionately brought to the fore her belief in a better society through open dialogue and community action.

ZOË DUSANNE

March 1884–March 1972
Place of Influence: Zoë Dusanne Gallery
47.629545° N, -122.325765° W

An internationally acclaimed art collector and dealer, Dusanne opened Seattle's first modern art gallery in 1950 and helped promote the Northwest School of artists. While the gallery was short-lived, her advocacy matured art appreciation and awareness for Seattleites, ushering in a new sense of sophistication.

DOROTHY STIMSON BULLITT

February 1892–June 1989
Place of Influence: King Broadcasting
47.621357° N, -122.343613° W

Bullitt, a civic leader, broke barriers in 1947 when she purchased a fledgling radio station and turned it into a major media empire. She founded KING-FM and KING-TV, and helped influence quality broadcasting around the world.

HELENE MADISON

June 1913–November 1970
Place of Influence: Green Lake
47.680213° N, -122.328319° W

One of the greatest athletes in history, Madison got her start swimming in Green Lake (her family lived a block away) and returned there often. By the age of eighteen, she had broken every record in every distance in women's swimming, and held twenty-three world records, three Olympic golds, and numerous national championships.

PUTTING DOWN ROOTS

The Pacific Northwest can claim the densest ratio of tree trunk area to land acreage in North America. No wonder that Washington is called the Evergreen State. The native conifers that dominate the region's forests are tall, wide, and long-lived. Today, the world's largest Douglas fir (two hundred feet tall and fifty feet in circumference) is found on the Olympic Peninsula. While impressive, that pales in comparison to reports of the three-hundred- to four-hundred-foot-tall trees felled in the Seattle area during the logging era of the mid-1800s.

A striking example can be found in the history of Seattle's Ravenna Park. The privately owned ravine forest escaped the axe due to its wet and steep terrain, and so became one of the city's biggest tourist attractions at the start of the twentieth century. A 274-foot-tall Douglas fir named after Teddy Roosevelt got the most attention,

and it was the first tree that a local women's club reported missing after the city's parks department took over the land in 1913. Upon investigation, several other notable giants were found reduced to stumps at the hand of the new parks superintendent J. W. Thompson; he had profited from their sale as firewood.

So it may come as no surprise that there are very few native forest remnants in present-day Seattle. Seward Park harbors the city's largest Douglas fir standing today, at eighty-eight inches in diameter and nearly two hundred feet in height. The tree has "heritage tree" status, a designation initiated by Plant Amnesty and the city of Seattle to recognize individual trees of notable size, health, and meaning to community members. Most of the trees in the program are nonnative and deciduous, illustrating the trend of the urban canopy today.

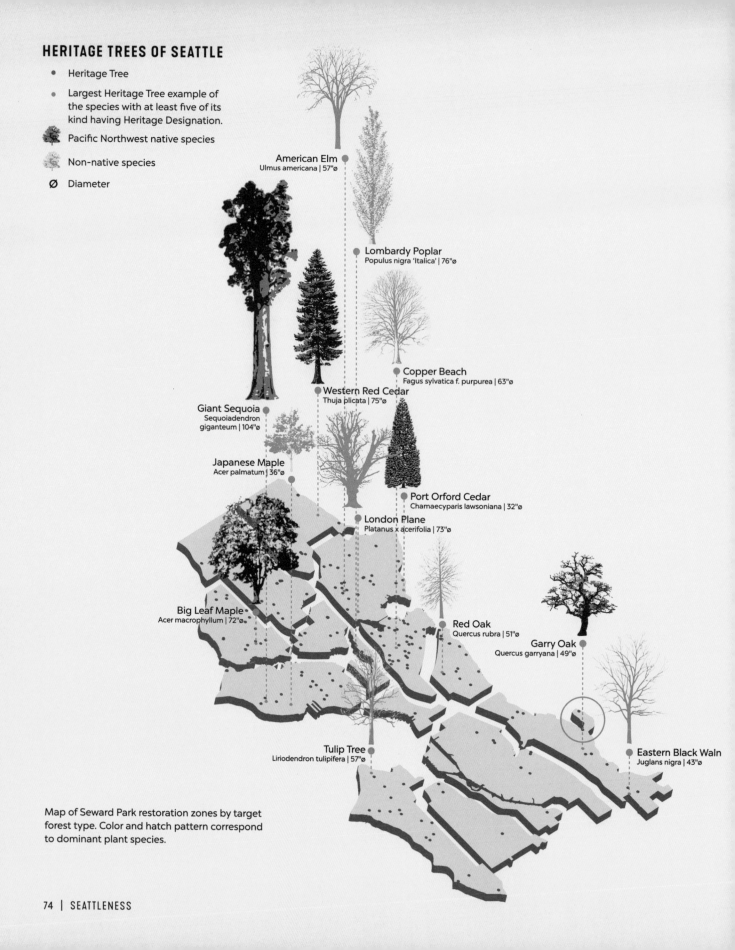

HERITAGE TREES OF SEATTLE

- Heritage Tree
- Largest Heritage Tree example of the species with at least five of its kind having Heritage Designation.
- Pacific Northwest native species
- Non-native species
- Ø Diameter

American Elm
Ulmus americana | 57"ø

Lombardy Poplar
Populus nigra 'Italica' | 76"ø

Copper Beach
Fagus sylvatica f. purpurea | 63"ø

Western Red Cedar
Thuja plicata | 75"ø

Giant Sequoia
Sequoiadendron giganteum | 104"ø

Japanese Maple
Acer palmatum | 36"ø

Port Orford Cedar
Chamaecyparis lawsoniana | 32"ø

London Plane
Platanus x acerifolia | 73"ø

Big Leaf Maple
Acer macrophyllum | 72"ø

Red Oak
Quercus rubra | 51"ø

Garry Oak
Quercus garryana | 49"ø

Tulip Tree
Liriodendron tulipifera | 57"ø

Eastern Black Waln
Juglans nigra | 43"ø

Map of Seward Park restoration zones by target forest type. Color and hatch pattern correspond to dominant plant species.

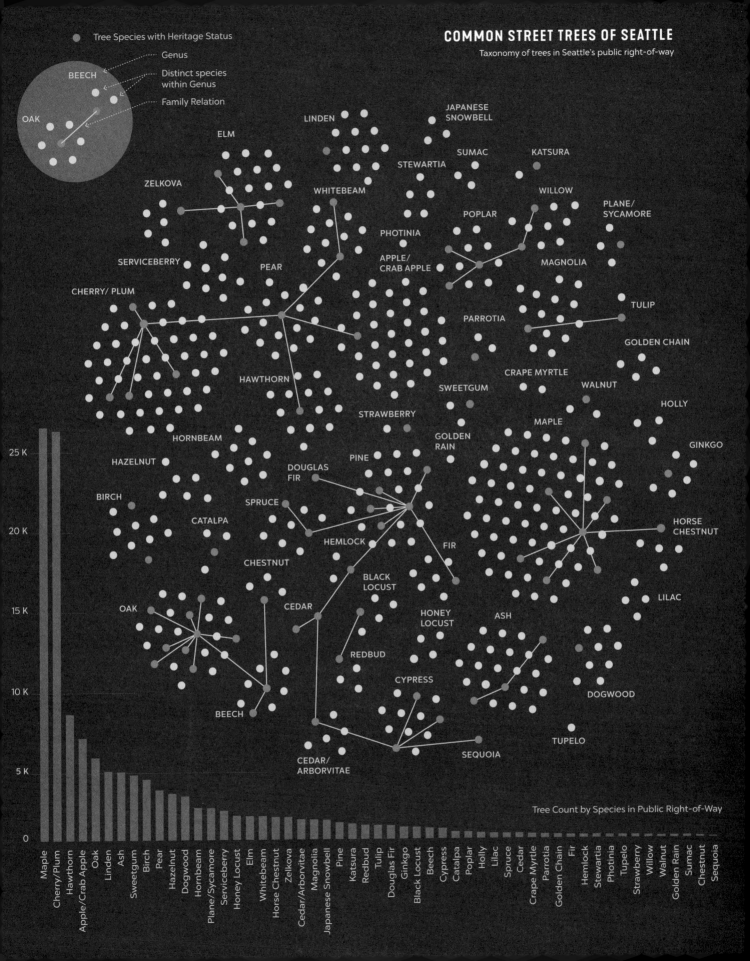

COMMON STREET TREES OF SEATTLE
Taxonomy of trees in Seattle's public right-of-way

Tree Species with Heritage Status
Genus
Distinct species within Genus
Family Relation

BEECH

OAK

Tree Count by Species in Public Right-of-Way

25 K

20 K

15 K

10 K

5 K

0

Map shows Seattle in 1903, just before the building of the new Central Library.

HUMBLE BEGINNINGS OF SEATTLE'S PUBLIC LIBRARY

For the past fifteen years, Seattle has ranked among the most literate cities in the United States, thanks in part to its robust library system. But the library, like many Seattle institutions, had humble beginnings.

In 1868, fifty citizens met at ❶ Yesler Hall and elected Sarah Yesler the first Seattle librarian and James McNaught library association president. The first library book was purchased in 1869, and the collection grew to 278 volumes and thirty national newspapers by 1873. But late fees and ice-cream-social fund-raisers weren't enough to keep the city library afloat, so in 1881 all 1,406 books were donated to the ❷ Territorial University (the precursor to the University of Washington).

Seven years later, dozens of prominent Seattle women came to the rescue to form the Ladies Library Association, backed by the owner of the *Seattle Post-Intelligencer* newspaper, Leigh S. J. Hunt, and lobbied to make the library an official city department. The library's collection grew to seven thousand volumes and moved in quick succession from the ❸ Occidental Building reading room to the ❹ Collins Building, across the street, and then two years later to the ❺ Rialto Building, and finally, in 1899, to the ❻ Yesler mansion, where the expanded twenty-five-thousand-volume collection was displayed in forty rooms.

All this movement spurred library boosters to seek a permanent home. Later in 1899, renowned philanthropist Andrew Carnegie was courted as a potential funding source. However, he declined, reasoning that Seattle was nothing more than a "hot air boomtown." Two years later, the Yesler mansion, along with twenty thousand books, burned to the ground and city librarian Charles Wesley Smith came under suspicion of arson.

But no arrest was made, and the fire ignited Carnegie's sympathy in the form of a $200,000 donation to build a new library on ❼ Fourth Avenue between Madison and Spring Streets, the location of Seattle's current Central Library.

SPL: VOLUMES I, II + III

1906

Architect: P. J. Weber

Cost: $200,000 (donation from Carnegie)

Size: 55,000 square feet

Number of Books: 80,000

Fun Fact: During construction, a large crack formed in the Madison Street wall, possibly caused by the concurrent construction of the Great Northern Railway tunnel running beneath downtown, the largest-diameter tunnel in the nation at the time.

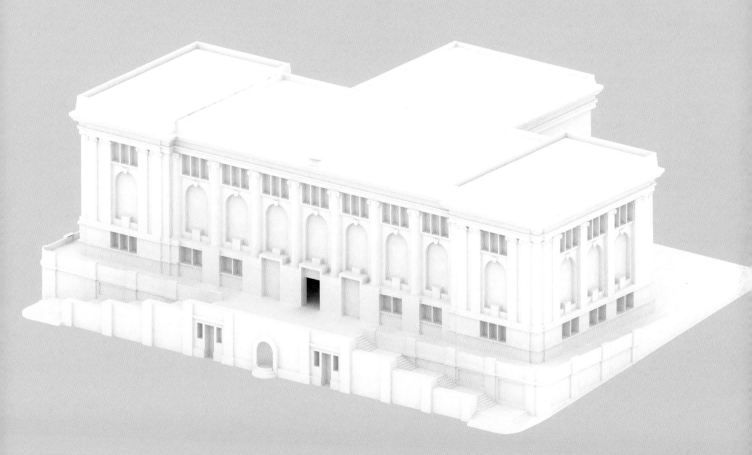

1960

Architects: Bindon & Wright; Decker, Christenson & Kitchin

Cost: $4,500,000

Size: 206,000 square feet

Number of Books: 1,000,000

Fun Fact: A drive-in service window was added to offset the lack of parking. Patrons who ordered books in advance could pick them up without having to get out of their cars.

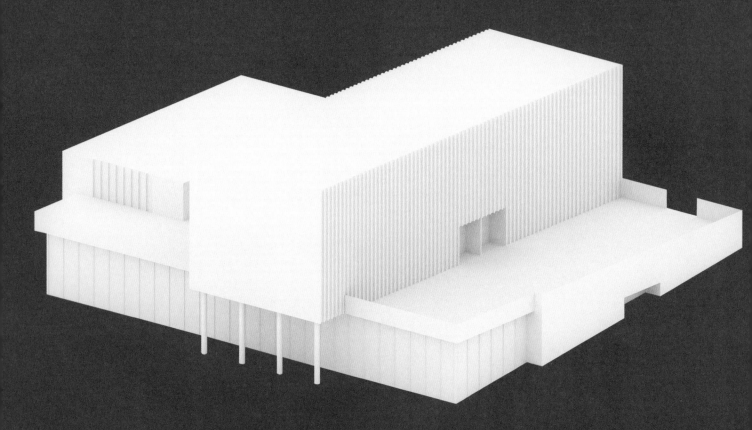

2004

Architects: OMA; LMN

Landscape Designers: Inside Outside; Jones & Jones

Cost: $165,900,000

Size: 360,000 square feet

Number of Books: 1,450,000

Fun Fact: The library's Books Spiral, designed to display the nonfiction collection in a continuous series of shelves without breaking up the Dewey Decimal System, goes all the way from the sixth floor to the ninth floor.

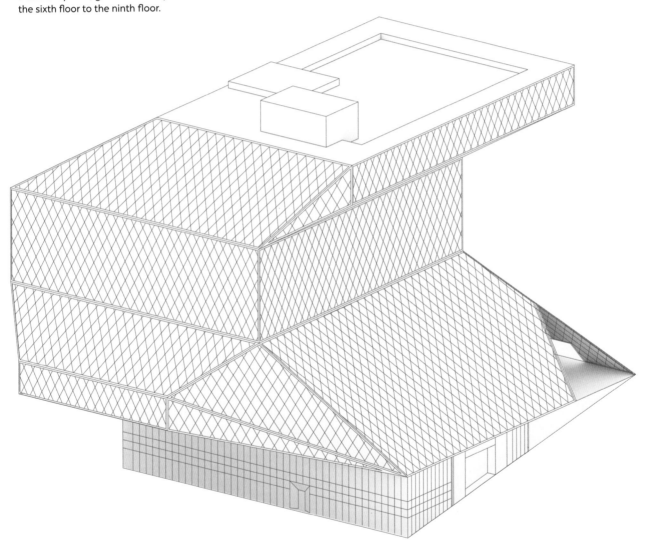

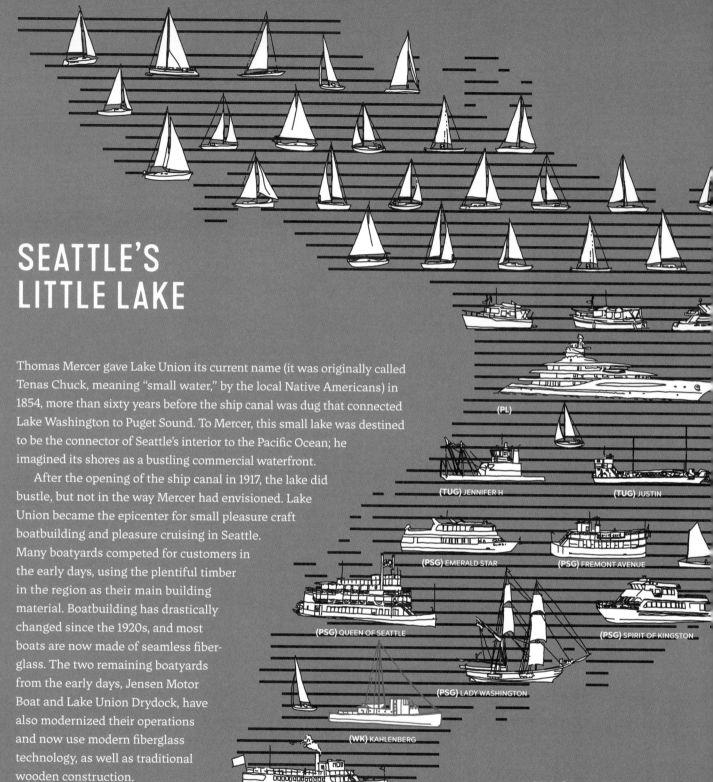

SEATTLE'S LITTLE LAKE

Thomas Mercer gave Lake Union its current name (it was originally called Tenas Chuck, meaning "small water," by the local Native Americans) in 1854, more than sixty years before the ship canal was dug that connected Lake Washington to Puget Sound. To Mercer, this small lake was destined to be the connector of Seattle's interior to the Pacific Ocean; he imagined its shores as a bustling commercial waterfront.

After the opening of the ship canal in 1917, the lake did bustle, but not in the way Mercer had envisioned. Lake Union became the epicenter for small pleasure craft boatbuilding and pleasure cruising in Seattle. Many boatyards competed for customers in the early days, using the plentiful timber in the region as their main building material. Boatbuilding has drastically changed since the 1920s, and most boats are now made of seamless fiberglass. The two remaining boatyards from the early days, Jensen Motor Boat and Lake Union Drydock, have also modernized their operations and now use modern fiberglass technology, as well as traditional wooden construction.

The Center for Wooden Boats on the south end of Lake Union provides exhibits, classes, and opportunities to sail in old boats.

(PL)

(TUG) JENNIFER H

(TUG) JUSTIN

(PSG) EMERALD STAR

(PSG) FREMONT AVENUE

(PSG) QUEEN OF SEATTLE

(PSG) SPIRIT OF KINGSTON

(PSG) LADY WASHINGTON

(WK) KAHLENBERG

(PSG) VIRGINIA V

(PSG) TREK

PSG = Passenger Vessel
TUG = Tugboat
WK = Shipwreck
SAR = Search and Rescue
PL = Pleasure Craft

(PL)

(SAR) FIRE RESCUE

(WK) JE BOYDEN

(WK) GYPSY QUEEN

(TUG) KOKUA

(TUG) MARINE RETRIEVER

(TUG) NAKALO

(TUG) SS PROPELLER

(PSG) CELEBRATIONS

(PSG) DUCK BOAT

(PSG) QUEEN ANNE'S REVENGE

(PSG) GOODTIME III

It also is leading an underwater archaeology project to document the uncounted vessels lying at the bottom of Lake Union and other bodies of water in the city. So far, the team has identified more than twenty vessels. Among these are a 1942 minesweeper named *Gypsy Queen*, a nineteenth-century tug called *J. E. Boyden*, and a US Navy gunboat named *Kahlenberg*. The stories of these ships and their many lives as military, civilian rescue, and fishing vessels are now part of the museum's shipwreck exhibit.

The map above shows examples of vessels commonly seen on Lake Union today. Fifty to sixty percent of all boat traffic is generated by passenger vessels, including Ride the Duck boats, Argosy Cruises, and every kid's favorite, the Fremont Sunday Ice Cream Cruise. An additional 15 to 25 percent of traffic comes from tugboats, many of which are owned by Fremont Tugboat Co., near Gas Works Park.

In the end, though, Lake Union is primarily a place for recreation. As the Tuesday evening Duck Dodge boat race (a.k.a. "Ultimate Beer Can Race") illustrates, this is the playground of pleasure seekers, sailors, and sunset cruisers in the heart of Seattle.

PINBALL WIZARDS

Pinball and Seattle go hand in hand these days. Since the inaugural Northwest Pinball and Arcade Show in 2008, game collectors and players have been expanding in the region. It's no surprise that pinball would thrive in Seattle; a healthy crop of tech workers and a long-established mechanical-tinkering culture, thanks to Boeing, are contributing factors. New locations and machines are popping up around the city, but some longtime pinball establishments have been here since the

1990s, before pinball's current vogue. Shorty's bar in the Belltown neighborhood is at the heart of the pinball resurgence, as is Add-a-Ball in Fremont, which hosts the biggest weekly pinball tournament in the country. Seattle is also home to top-ten world players, including Raymond Davidson and Cayle George, who came in first and second, respectively, at the 2017 IFPA World Pinball Championship, held in Copenhagen, Denmark.

NUMBER OF PINBALL MACHINES IN SEATTLE

2015

10

05

TOP 15 SEATTLE LOCATIONS

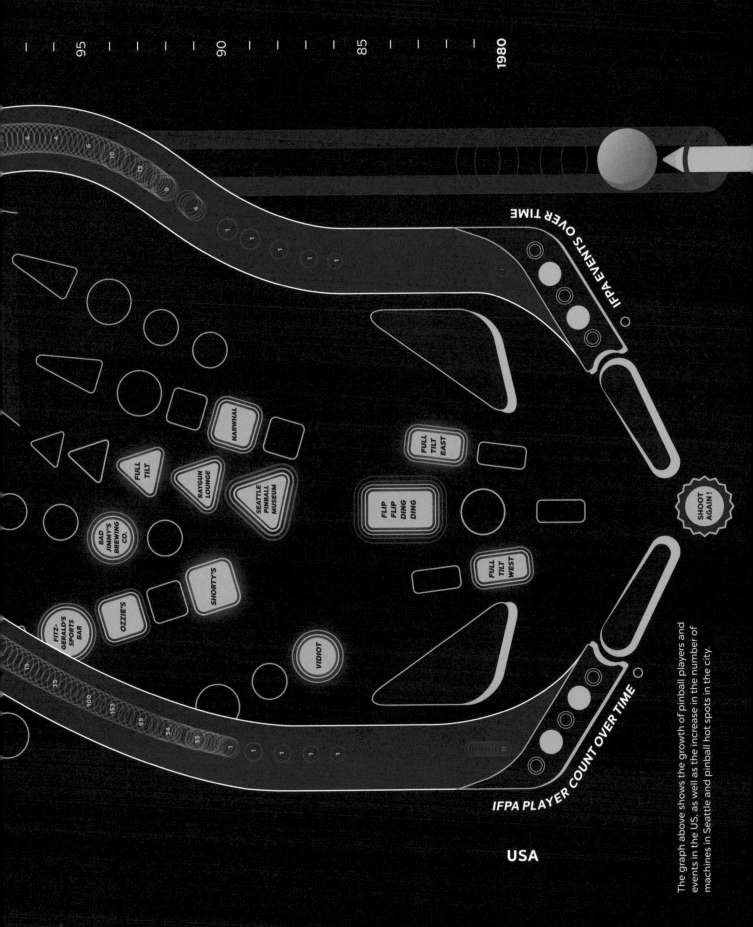

95 90 85 1980

IFPA EVENTS OVER TIME

SHOOT AGAIN !

NARWHAL

FULL TILT

RAYGUN LOUNGE

SEATTLE PINBALL MUSEUM

BAD JIMMY'S BREWING CO.

SHORTY'S

OZZIE'S

FITZ-GERALD'S SPORTS BAR

VIDIOT

FULL TILT EAST

FLIP FLIP DING DING

FULL TILT WEST

IFPA PLAYER COUNT OVER TIME

USA

The graph above shows the growth of pinball players and events in the US, as well as the increase in the number of machines in Seattle and pinball hot spots in the city.

I ♥ THE '90s

In the late 1980s through the '90s, an organic amalgam of heavy metal, punk rock, and distorted electric guitar rose out of Seattle and then ruled the world. The creation of "the Seattle sound," or grunge, informed the city's underground music scene and went hand in hand with the adjacent underground feminist punk Riot Grrrl movement, sparked just sixty minutes south in Olympia. Local bands such as the Fastbacks, Green River, the Gits, Mudhoney, TAD, Hammerbox, and Mother Love Bone (among many, many others) defined and evolved musical success on their own terms. This led to a chaotic, noisy, vital transformation of the music scene that changed the nation's mind-set about Seattle from that of a small sleepy second-tier coastal city to the home of a generation's breakout musical geniuses. With the rise of the colossally popular bands like Nirvana, Soundgarden, and Pearl Jam, the city became known for its grunge subculture, including an anticonsumerist "thrift-shop aesthetic" with oversize flannel shirts, ripped jeans, unkempt hair, and sturdy boots or Converse sneakers.

Like any pure creative movement, once it was clear the grunge sound connected with a generation, it was quickly manipulated, commodified, and marketed by outsiders (as chronicled in Doug Pray's excellent documentary, *Hype!*). After the meteoric rise of Nirvana and other bands, musicians from far-flung cities like Los Angeles and New York flooded into Seattle, appropriating a culture and community they didn't contribute to or even understand. For the rest of the world, the dynamic Seattle music scene was pigeonholed into one genre, even though the city has always had a vibrant and eclectic local music landscape. Thirty years later music still matters here, with KEXP public radio still dominating local tastes and the independent label Sub Pop Records still marketing and promoting Seattle's local bands, helping to propel them into international stardom.

The Seattle grunge movement rose out of punk rock rebellion and a sincere passion for music, was annoyed with and tried to prank its own popularity, became disillusioned in fame, and, in some instances, became self-destructive. Still, the impact of the Seattle sound in the 1980s and early '90s cannot be ignored. Grunge is part of Seattle's cultural flavor and many landmarks from this period in the city's history are revered, still visited by admiring fans today.

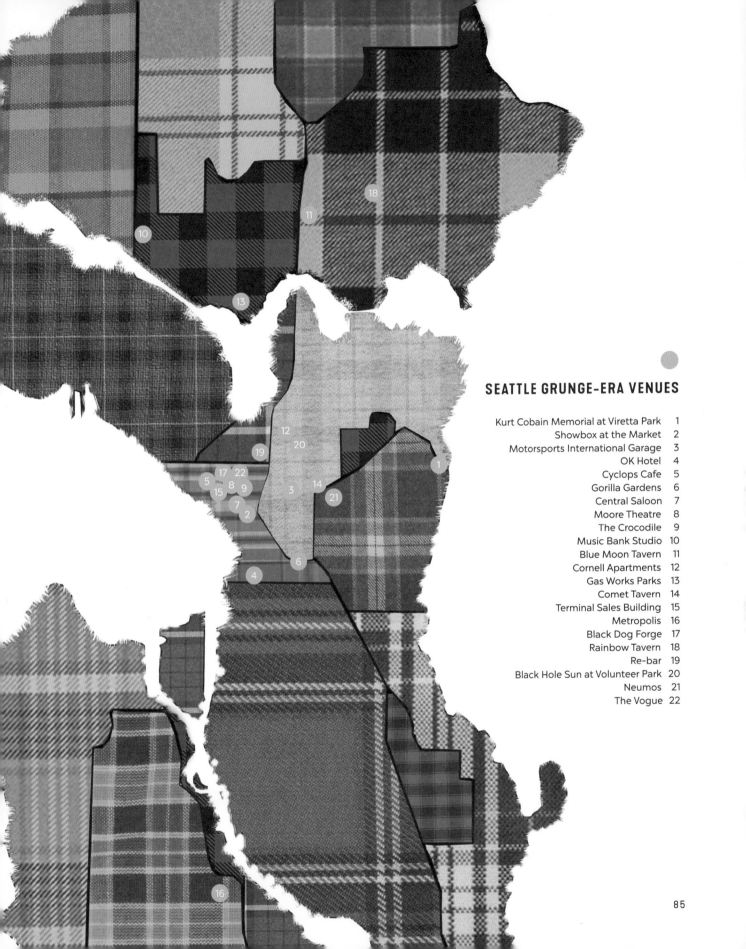

SEATTLE GRUNGE-ERA VENUES

LINES

The lines of a portrait, the drawn connections between
the past and present, relationships and networks.

Recent tunneling efforts with the boring machine, Bertha (B), have unearthed their own treasures, like a coil of prehistoric cedar rope.

During Seattle's reconstruction after the 1889 fire, the city ran out of money before new sidewalks were constructed at the same grade as the new buildings. Ladders—in some instances as tall as thirty-five feet—connected businesses aboveground and below, effectively creating what would come to be known as the Seattle Underground.

In the late 1890s, the wealthy machinist James Colman towed a shipwrecked vessel called the *Windward* inland. He quickly abandoned his salvage attempt, opting instead to build a brand-new building on top of it, near the waterfront. The ship's hull remains in the Colman Building's sub-basement to this day.

The marvel of its time, the Great Northern Tunnel was completed in 1905 and is still in operation.

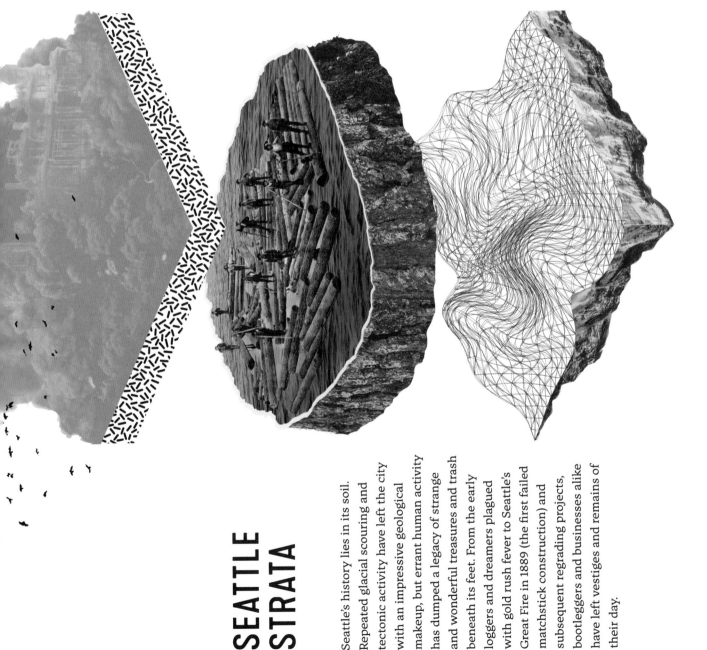

The Great Seattle Fire on June 6, 1889, destroyed over twenty-five blocks of mills and wharfs, including the Yesler-Leary Building and the famous Occidental Hotel. Not content merely to rebuild with fire-resistant materials like stone and brick, the city regraded and filled the area, raising city streets over twenty feet before beginning anew.

The last half of the nineteenth century was marked by radical manufactured landscapes that brought down swaths of great forest, tore into hills, and filled the city's tideflats with whatever people could find—dumped ballast, trash, rail ties, and forsaken gold rush accoutrements too heavy to carry north and ditched at the last moment.

During the Fraser Glaciation period, tendrils of glacial ice, known as the Puget Lobe, brought the weight of over three thousand feet of ice to bear on the area that would become Seattle, gracing the land with a mixed geological bag of compressed sand, gravel, and clay.

SEATTLE STRATA

Seattle's history lies in its soil. Repeated glacial scouring and tectonic activity have left the city with an impressive geological makeup, but errant human activity has dumped a legacy of strange and wonderful treasures and trash beneath its feet. From the early loggers and dreamers plagued with gold rush fever to Seattle's Great Fire in 1889 (the first failed matchstick construction) and subsequent regrading projects, bootleggers and businesses alike have left vestiges and remains of their day.

THE PLACES BETWEEN

Main streets and boulevards often claim the spotlight when it comes to urban pathways while less visible but equally important public spaces are being overlooked. Alleys provide for the smooth functioning of many urban processes critical to the functionality of any city; they amount to over 217,500 square feet of space in Seattle's dense downtown. An unseen dance of deliveries, moving logistics, and trash pickup occurs on the back side of buildings. This concealed choreography is vital to Seattle's economic flow.

Due to recent rapid growth and increased density, city agencies, researchers, and community groups are looking for opportunities to utilize alleys as public spaces, and forward thinkers are beginning to visualize the immense potential of these in-between spaces. Urban researchers have conducted studies on Seattle alleys over the years, gaining insights and producing new visions for these spaces.

The map to the right shows alleys in combination with public parks and plazas, illustrating the potential public right-of-way space that could be utilized as opportunities for other dedicated park and plaza space diminishes.

PUBLIC SPACE IN DOWNTOWN SEATTLE

(MEASURED IN ACRES)

4.9	9.0	0.8	4.8	0.6	5.2	0.1

Alleys

Olympic Sculpture Park (A)

Victor Steinbrueck Park (B)

Waterfront Park (C)

Occidental Square (D)

Freeway Park (E)

Westlake Park (F)

Alleys

Parks

Plazas

Privately Owned Public Open Spaces

Clay St

Vine St

Battery St

Blanchard St

Virginia St

Pine St

Union St

Seneca St

Madison St

Columbia St

James St

Yesler Way

Main St

King St

OUR FAIR CITY

Twice in the twentieth century, the twin spirits of boosterism and city pride prevailed upon Seattle civic leaders to successfully petition for and host a world's fair. Such fairs were well-known means to draw crowds from across the globe for the purpose of entertainment, education, and enticement. And so twice Seattle became, if briefly, the center of the world's attention and host to millions of visitors.

The first of the fairs was the Alaska-Yukon-Pacific Exposition—or the A-Y-P, for short—held from June 1 to October 16, 1909, on the grounds of the nascent and still forested University of Washington campus. It was, in part, a commemoration of the Klondike gold rush from twelve years earlier—an event that brought prospectors of all sorts to Seattle and other ways north, and which led to the city's first great boom. But the A-Y-P's main object was not the past but the future. It was to demonstrate to visitors (and investors) Seattle's potential greatness: a gateway for foreign goods (Japan, Canada, and the Hawaiian territories) and regional resources (lumber, coal, fish, etc.). To balance this emphasis on business, visitors were enticed by the pleasures of the Pay Streak, the raucous midway where exoticism was exploited in daily shows, and games, rides, foods, and wares were hawked to all passersby. Each day offered a new theme to attract different audiences, and civic groups across the region sponsored trips to visit the fair. In the final tally, more than 3.7 million people attended the A-Y-P: a financial and symbolic success for the Emerald City.

Fifty years later, the booster spirit once again roused leaders to successfully bid and plan for a second world's fair. Originally meant to be an anniversary celebration of the A-Y-P, the planners delayed the event two years and expanded the scope to focus on science and technology, hot Cold War topics, and prospects for Seattle. In a fairground about a mile from downtown, the Century 21 Exposition ran from April 21 to October 21, 1962.

The futuristic design and offerings were a concerted demonstration of progress and industry—particularly aerospace, transportation, communication, and energy. Even so, echoes of the A-Y-P abounded: President John F. Kennedy "opened" the fair with the same telegraph key that President William Howard Taft used to commence the A-Y-P. And like the 1909 fair, there were special days to attract regional and international audiences, and a midway—this time, called the Gayway—featuring rides, food, and performances (including Show Street, an adult section with risqué shows and topless women). But the big draws were the fantastical structures erected on-site: the Monorail, the Space Needle, Washington State Coliseum (later renamed KeyArena), and the United States Science Pavilion (now known as Pacific Science Center). Ten million people visited Century 21, including some famous folks: Prince Philip, Bobby Kennedy, John Glenn, Walt Disney, and Elvis Presley.

On the following pages, we compare Seattle's fairs in daily attendance, amusements, and offerings—a partial glimpse into the excitement of being present at these historic events. But the best way to understand the legacy of Seattle's two world's fairs is to visit the UW campus and Seattle Center. Both sites reflect their original fair plans: from UW's hub-and-spoke layout and unimpeded view of Mount Rainier, to Seattle Center's alleys, fountains, and iconic buildings.

ALASKA-YUKON-PACIFIC EXPOSITION

Both pages: Attractions and exhibits found at each fair, along with categories and locations

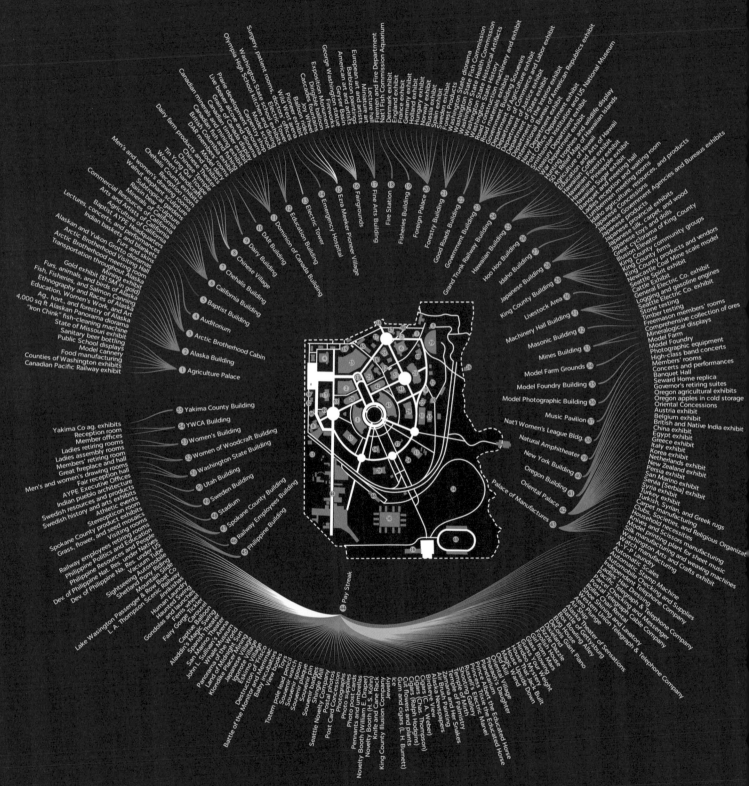

FUN FACT: THE PRESIDENTIAL FEAST

A dinner welcoming President Taft to the fair was far more decadent than the hot dogs and peanuts offered on the Pay Streak. The special feast included caviar on toast, followed by Nahcotta oysters and clear green turtle soup. Served for the main course were salmon, trout, julienne potatoes, sweetbreads, "larded mushrooms," roast mallard duck, hominy croquettes, and a "Rainier salad." For dessert: "ices" and "fancy cakes." And to finish off the meal, cheese and crackers, and coffee.

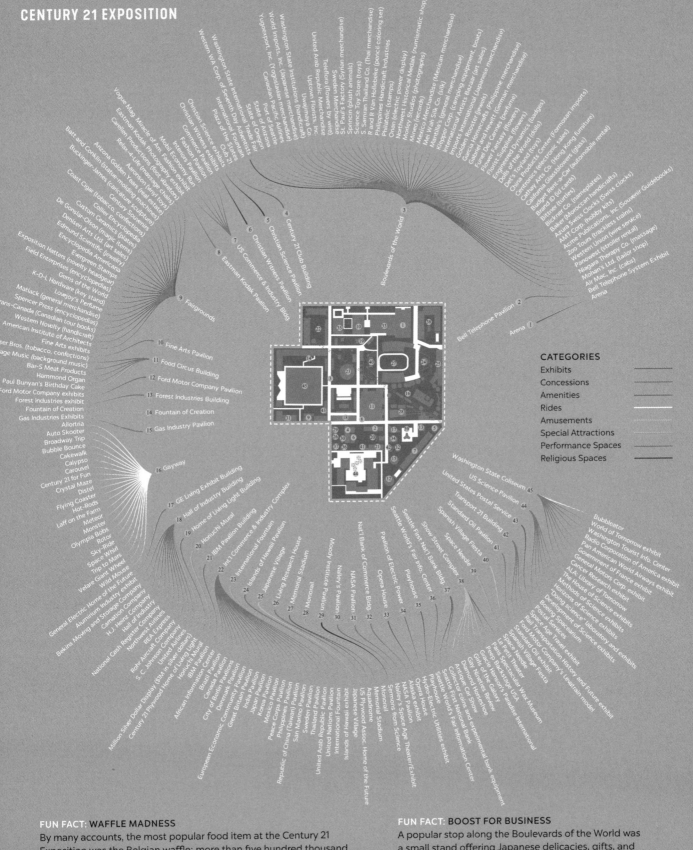

FUN FACT: WAFFLE MADNESS

By many accounts, the most popular food item at the Century 21 Exposition was the Belgian waffle; more than five hundred thousand were sold. Seattleites were delighted to learn that Smitty's Pancake House had purchased the recipe and would continue to sell these yeasty treats following the fair.

FUN FACT: BOOST FOR BUSINESS

A popular stop along the Boulevards of the World was a small stand offering Japanese delicacies, gifts, and kitchenware called Uwajimaya. It would go on to become the largest Asian supermarket in the Pacific Northwest after its major success at the fair.

ALASKA-YUKON-PACIFIC EXPOSITION

SEPTEMBER 30, 1909

Taft Day
President Taft's visit was celebrated with a parade, a banquet, and a speech to twenty-five thousand at the fair's amphitheater. For a special Alaska boostering event, the president also dressed in an Arctic Brotherhood parka and costume. He stayed at the newly opened Sorrento Hotel as its first guest.

JULY 23, 1909

**Ancient Order of United Workmen Day/
Pastry Cooks Day**
A Ford Model T driven by Bert Scott arrived in Seattle and was declared the winner of the transcontinental auto race sponsored by Robert Guggenheim. Scott drove 4,106 miles in twenty-three days. Henry Ford handed Scott the trophy. Scott and the Ford car were later disqualified for changing the engine midrace, in violation of the rules.

SEPTEMBER 11, 1909

New England Day
In celebration of the fifteen thousand New Englanders residing in Seattle, organizers staged a landing of the Mayflower Pilgrims—at the north end of Lake Union.

JULY 7, 1909

Woman Suffrage Day
The forty-first annual convention of the National American Woman Suffrage Association held final day activities at the fair. Among many prominent women attendees was Pauline Perlmutter Steinem, Gloria Steinem's grandmother.

AUGUST 9, 1909

Los Angeles Day
North Pacific International Lawn Tennis Association gathering

SEPTEMBER 12, 1909

Officials report an outbreak of typhoid in Seattle. (It was later associated with contaminated drinking water at the fair!)

AUGUST 16, 1909

Discovery Day
"To commemorate discovery of gold in the Klondike"

JUNE 1, 1909

Opening Day
Railroad magnate James J. Hill gave the keynote address at the opening ceremony.

SEPTEMBER 6, 1909

Seattle Day

SEPTEMBER 2, 1909

Smith Family Day
People with surname Smith (and variants, including Schmitz and Smythe) were invited for contests.

DAILY ATTENDANCE

140,000

120,000

100,000

80,000

60,000

40,000

20,000

0

June   July   August   September   October

CENTURY 21 EXPOSITION

OCTOBER 21, 1962

Closing Day
President Kennedy canceled his visit at the last minute, due to the Cuban Missile Crisis. The fair welcomed its ten millionth visitor, Earl Addis. Carl Sandburg read poems at the Opera House.

OCTOBER 13, 1962

Despite a major windstorm (sixty people died), thousands came to the fair; the big draw was a lumberjack show.

OCTOBER 6, 1962

The Royal Scots Greys and the Argyll and Sutherland High-landers, bagpipers and Highland dancers, played to packed Coliseum audiences.

SEPTEMBER 30, 1962

India Week
Joan Baez, twenty-one, performed barefoot at the Playhouse.

SEPT. 22, 1962

Ricky Nelson performs at the Arena; Neil Armstrong and Milton Thompson appear at NASA Pavilion; Henry Ford II (grandson of Henry Ford) visits the fair.

SEPTEMBER 15, 1962

Victoria, BC, Day
The main attraction was the performance of the Canadian Tattoo military band, the group's first-ever show outside of Canada.

SEPTEMBER 5, 1962

Virginia Day
Elvis Presley arrived for his first day of shooting *It Happened at the World's Fair*; it was also the first day of school in Seattle.

JUNE 19, 1962

Michigan Day/United Nations Day
Mrs. America, Lila Mason, visited from Detroit.

JUNE 22, 1962

A-Y-P Day
Dignitaries representing the 1909 fair visited, including President Taft's granddaughter.

AUGUST 9, 1962

Miami Day
Richard Nixon and family visited the fair. In honor of Miami Day, twenty-five hundred coconuts were handed out.

JULY 7, 1962

Alaska Day
Evangelist Billy Graham visited, as did Alaska governor William Egan and his wife, Neva. The US Navy's Blue Angels flew overhead.

MAY 5, 1962

Camp Fire Girls Day
Soviet cosmonaut Gherman Titov visited the fair. Ten thousand Camp Fire Girls dedicated the World's Fair flagpoles; twenty thousand people attended the ceremony.

MAY 10, 1962

New York Day
Astronaut John Glenn visited the fair.

MAY 19, 1962

Boy Scouts Day
Evalyn Van Vliet, twenty-eight years old, became the millionth visitor to the fair.

JUNE 1, 1962

HRH Prince Philip, Duke of Edinburgh and husband of Queen Elizabeth II, visited the fair.

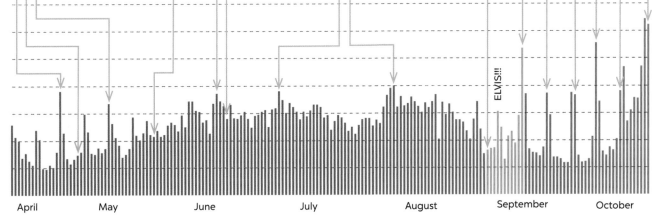

ELVIS!!!

April   May   June   July   August   September   October

STEEP STREETS

Seattle's intense topography offers amazing views of the breathtaking natural beauty that surrounds the city, but these vistas come with some travel caveats.

Seattle's downtown east-west streets have a range of slope percentages, but overall they can be categorized as steep! Though Seattle winters tend to be mild, the city does experience snow and ice on occasion, making these hills virtually impassable. Several of Seattle's most traveled thoroughfares boast a hill grade of over 15 percent. Hill grade is calculated by dividing the rise of the hill by the run, or length. According to data from the Seattle Department of Transportation, the streets of Madison, James, Cherry, Seneca, University, and Spring have slopes that range from around 10 to 20 percent. These hilly corridors pose a challenge to pedestrians, cyclists, and motorists alike. In fact, Seattle is so hilly there are now apps for residents to easily plot travel routes that avoid some of the city's most arduous hills. To combat these precipitous slopes, city planners have included infrastructure details, such as ribbed concrete, for easier traction and thoughtfully placed resting benches to help sooth those strained calves.

PINE STREET
175 ft elevation gain
Max slope 57.7%

PIKE STREET
190 ft elevation gain
Max slope 68.9%

UNION STREET
147 ft elevation gain
Max slope 32.9%

UNIVERSITY STREET
179 ft elevation gain
Max slope 61.7%

SENECA STREET
202 ft elevation gain
Max slope 71.9%

SPRING STREET
239 ft elevation gain
Max slope 38.3%

MADISON STREET
292 ft elevation gain
Max slope 64.0%

MARION STREET
275 ft elevation gain
Max slope 66.6%

COLUMBIA STREET
247 ft elevation gain
Max slope 54.8%

CHERRY STREET
193 ft elevation gain
Max slope 34.0%

JAMES STREET
154 ft elevation gain
Max slope 57.7%

JEFFERSON STREET
154 ft elevation gain
Max slope 57.7%

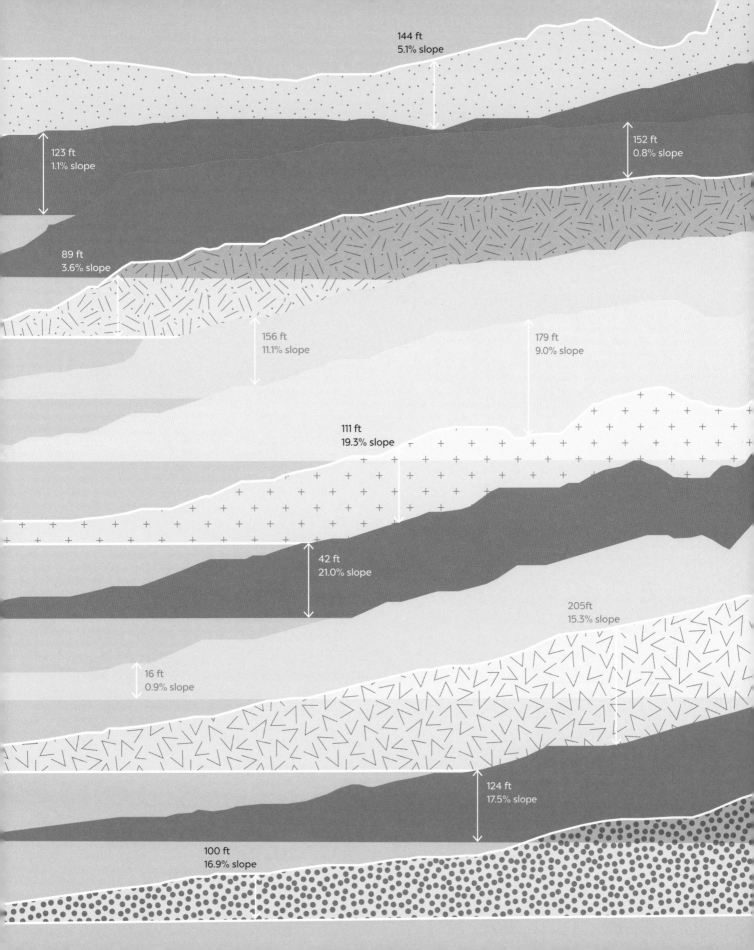

144 ft
5.1% slope

152 ft
0.8% slope

123 ft
1.1% slope

89 ft
3.6% slope

156 ft
11.1% slope

179 ft
9.0% slope

111 ft
19.3% slope

42 ft
21.0% slope

205ft
15.3% slope

16 ft
0.9% slope

124 ft
17.5% slope

100 ft
16.9% slope

JAZZ ON JACKSON

From 1920 to 1956, the hottest music scene in town was jazz on Jackson Street. Jazz exploded south of Yesler Way and east of Fifth Avenue primarily because of that area's proximity to Seattle's black community and its concentration of illicit speakeasies and clubs, which arose after the city passed Prohibition laws in 1916.

1 Russell "Noodles" Smith was an early entrepreneur, opening some of the first Prohibition clubs, starting in 1917. Most famous was the Black and Tan, which hosted great jazzmen like Duke Ellington and Charlie Parker. In 1919 Ragtime legend **2** Jelly Roll Morton stopped in Seattle to play with local pianist Oscar Holden and was inspired to write "Seattle Hunch" after losing big in a high-stakes poker game. Noodles Smith also recruited trumpeter **3** Herman Grimes, who is considered to be the greatest trumpet player from the Northwest. Several bands that came through tried to recruit him, but Grimes said, "I want to stay right here in Seattle."

Several restaurants and hotels were jazz-friendly in the largely Chinese and Japanese district west of Ninth Avenue, and during the Roaring Twenties, it was not uncommon for jazz musicians to tour Asia for extra money. Local bandleader **4** Palmer Johnson went to Shanghai for three years, arriving home just as the Great Depression hit the United States. It was also in the Jackson Street neighborhood that jazz great **5** Ray Charles got his start. He had a steady gig at the Black Elks Club, and it is there that producer Quincy Jones remembers seeing him play and being in awe of his performing and songwriting ability, which started their lifelong friendship.

During the Prohibition era, an unspoken agreement with police meant that payoffs kept most of the bootleg clubs from being shut down, but some weren't so lucky. **6** Doc Hamilton ran several popular speakeasies, the first out of his home on Union Street. After only a few years, police axed through three barred doors to find a cozy nightclub inside. Later, Hamilton opened his most famous establishment, the Barbecue Pit, frequented by Seattle socialites. Hamilton was eventually jailed and lost everything.

Farther north, along the Madison Street corridor, another cluster of jazz joints provided larger dance venues where many musicians got their start. **7** Quincy Jones and singer **8** Ernestine Anderson stepped onstage early at the East Madison YMCA, at the start of the bebop era. The Washington Social Club saw an eclectic group of musicians come through, from bluesman B. B. King to local virtuoso jazz pianist **9** Patti Bown.

By the 1950s, rock was entering the scene, centered on the Savoy Ballroom. The dance hall was famous for its house band, the **10** Dave Lewis Combo, touted as the Northwest's greatest rock 'n' roll band. It was also the venue where **11** Jimi Hendrix famously had his beloved guitar stolen.

Copper Kettle

Mardi Gras

Washington Social Club

23rd Ave

E Madison YMCA

Savoy Ballroom/Birdland

Elks Club

9

18th Ave

E Madison St

8

11th Ave

E Union St

Doc Hamilton's first speakeasy

11

E Spring St

Doc Hamilton's Barbecue Pit

6

THE NEGRO MUSICIANS' UNION
AFM LOCAL 493
1918 • 1958

7

Blue Note/Local 493 Union Hall

Jefferson St

3

14th Ave

Washington Hall

5

Fir St

Al's Lucky Hour

Blue Rose

Yesler Way

Entertainer's Club (original)

12th Ave S

Hilltop Tavern

Union/Marine Club

JFB
JAM FOR BREAKFAST

The Ebony

Evergreen Tavern

Congo Club

416 Club

Black Elks Club

Golden West Hotel

Main St

9th Ave S

Jackson St

Dumas Club

Alhambra/Black and Tan

2

2nd Ave S

4

Big Apple Club

Wah Mee Club

Bucket of Blood

Chinese Gardens

Ubangi Club

1

10

101

TLINGIT TOTEM

In Pioneer Square, a Tlingit totem pole towers sixty feet above the uneven cobblestone walk. The monument's upper carvings are dappled and at times partially obscured from view by the adjacent London plane trees that line the square. The totem pole bears a troubled legacy, having been razed and resurrected multiple times, hewed and burned and shipped across coastal waters, traveling distances of over six thousand miles back and forth between Alaska's Alexander Archipelago and Seattle. The illustrations at right diagrammatically detail the absurd dance and the vandalism marking the storied history of this beautiful cedar column.

The totem pole was originally carved in 1790 to commemorate the life and heritage of Chief of All Women, a noblewoman from the Ganaxadi Raven clan (also known by the surname Kinninook), after she drowned in the Nass River in British Columbia. It was likely carved using a short-handled "elbow" adze chisel, made of beaver teeth and elk horn, or possibly using iron blades salvaged from Japanese shipwrecks that had drifted ashore. This totem, which drew on ancient Tlingit mythology, stood for over a century before a group from the Seattle Chamber of Commerce, made up of clergymen, developers, and bankers, chopped it in half, rolled it down the island shore, and shipped it back to Seattle as a (stolen) gift to the city. A federal grand jury in Alaska quickly indicted eight of the men, charging them with theft of government property and a $20,000 tab for the stolen totem. Leveraging personal connections and wealth, the men dodged the charge and effectively paid a meager $500 fine.

Thirty-eight years later in Pioneer Square, an unknown arsonist set fire to the totem and successfully destroyed portions of the memorial. The remaining pieces were shipped to Ketchikan, Alaska, in the Tongass National Forest. Civilian Conservation Corps member and Tlingit carver Charles Brown, of the Nexadi clan, supervised the carving of the reproduction that stands in Pioneer Square today. With a price tag of $5,000, the new totem was strapped aboard the SS *Tanana* in one piece in April 1940 and shipped back to Seattle, arriving July 25 that same year.

1790 Totem is carved and erected in honor of Ganaxadi Tlingit noblewoman Chief of All Women.

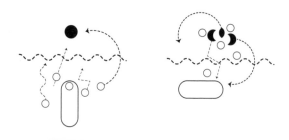

1899 Eight prominent Seattle Chamber of Commerce members encounter a Tlingit village on Tongass Island, Alaska. The tallest of its totems is cut down and loaded on the steamer *City of Seattle*.

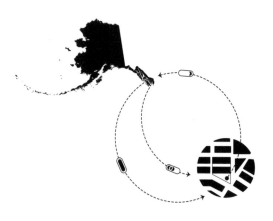

1899 The stolen totem is illegally gifted to Seattle and displayed in Pioneer Square.

1938 Irreparably damaged by arson, its charred remains are shipped back to Alaska's Saxman Totem Park in the Tongass National Forest.

1940 A replacement totem is carved and shipped back to Seattle.

LEGEND

● Totem   ⌐ Movement
∿ Shoreline   ○ SCC Members
▢ Steamer Ship   ✷ Pioneer Square

READING THE TOTEM

Each carving of the totem pole refers to specific legends, which have slight variation in Tlingit lore.

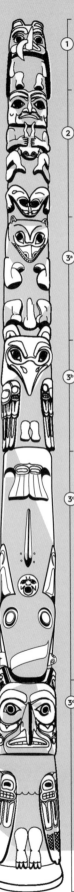

60'

1 RAVEN WITH MOON

Raven carries the moon in his mouth, freeing it and the sun and the stars by assuming the clever disguise of a hemlock needle.

2 WOMAN WITH FROG

A woman is tricked into marrying a frog and has two children who are also frogs.

The woman hatches a clever plan to be rescued through draining a dam and flooding the village where she lives. With the help of the woman's father, the family is rescued and the children become human.

3a MINK, RAVEN, ORCA, AND CHIEF OF ALL BIRDS

The last four portions of the totem relate a familiar tale that chronicles the account of Raven and Mink after they are swallowed whole by a whale as a means of transport across a strait. Along the way, the whale invites the two companions to partake of his blubber and insides, save for his heart.

3b Raven and Mink begin to eat the whale. Tiring of their jouney, they both eat the whale's heart, and the whale dies, washing ashore along the northern islands of British Columbia, known as Haidi Gwaii islands. Humans find the beached whale and cut a hole into it, freeing both Raven and Mink from the whale's stomach.

3c Once liberated, Mink jumps out first, covered in oil, and immediately rolls in rotten wood, thereafter giving his fur an oily brown appearance. Raven also emerges from the whale's stomach covered in oil with a slick and glossy appearance.

3d Raven and Mink proceed to walk around the islands where they stumble upon a house. The owner is Nasak Yale, otherwise known as Chief of All Birds. Raven is named chief of his tribe and, on a long walk, Raven tells Chief of All Birds about his journey and all that he's done. Unhappy, Chief of All Birds turns Raven into a bird and Mink into a semi-aquatic mammal.

0'

Waxwings by Jonathan Raban (2003): "Unlike most American cities that Tom knew, there was a here here, where herring gulls were a traffic hazard and all streets led down to the water, where the older buildings pursued a guileless infatuation with the architecture of Ancient Rome, and ungovernable greenery—bramble, vine, salal—rose up defiantly from every crevice and scrap of waste ground, as if to strangle the city fathers' vain Roman ambitions." *Truth Like the Sun* by Jim Lynch (2012): "Seattle reminded her of men she'd known who'd been told too many times how handsome they were." *Where'd You Go, Bernadette* by Maria Semple (2012): "All those ninnies have it wrong. The best thing about Seattle is the weather. The world over, people have ocean views. But across our ocean is Bainbridge Island, an evergreen curb, and over it the exploding, craggy, snow-scraped Olympics." *Still Life With Woodpecker* by Tom Robbins (1980): "Seattle where the clams were singing, Seattle where the trolls were hiding, Seattle where the blackberries were glistening, Seattle where the bloomers of the sky were drooping, Seattle the city that washed its hands with the incessancy of a proctologist, Seattle was far behind her, at memory's rest on a dank, deep mossy bed." *Indian Killer* by Sherman Alexie (1996): "Where water had once been a natural boundary, it now existed as an economic barrier. And in those places where natural boundaries between neighborhoods didn't exist, the engineers had quickly built waterways. So much water separating people." *Great Son* by Edna Ferber (1945): "On brilliant days she swept aside her concealing folds of gray chiffon and emerged a dazzling creature, her face and form glittering with a million jewels of ice and snow. Then all Seattle turned its eyes up to her; they paused in the busy canyons of the downtown streets; they faced her, blinking, from the hills; they peered from their windows and they called to each other, 'Look! Look! Rainier's out!'" *Great Son* by Edna Ferber (1945): "It was fantastic, it was thrilling, it was absurd, it was majestic, it could have been the most beautiful city in the world—it might yet be, one day." *Oxygen* by Carol Cassella (2008): "The streets wind down past galleries and bookstores where hip young musicians and artists share sidewalks with unshaven men whose mongrel dogs wear signs asking for spare change or spare jobs, down to the piers where Seattle meets the sea. The deepening sky has lifted Mount Rainier right up off the horizon, a melting scoop of ice cream suspended in the city smog." *We Interrupt This Broadcast* by K.K. Beck (1997): "Why should Seattle try to be world class? If people wanted world-class culture they should go to New York or London or Rome or Paris, for Christ's sake. Franklin saw no need for Seattle to have world-class baseball teams or convention centers, either. It was a vulgar conceit of newcomers to the area, and Caroline, as the descendant of pioneers, should know better." *Benedict Hall* by Cate Campbell (2013): "Frank's first impression of Seattle was of grayness. Sky, streets, mist-shrouded buildings, all were painted in drab shades. Automobiles mingled with horse-drawn carriages and slow-moving oxcarts. Walkers carried umbrellas and wore boots against the dampness of the streets. As Frank turned down Yesler, a streetcar clanged by, its scarlet paint the sole spot of color." *A Sudden Light* by Garth Stein (2014): "'Don't you want to see this?' the father says, finally, desperately, tapping the boy's shoulder and indicating the glory of Seattle all around them. The boy lifts his eyes and looks around. Bridges, lakes, bland buildings, radio towers, floatplanes, mountains, trees. He's seen it." *Boneshaker* by Cherie Priest (2009): "Seattle used to be an uncomplicated trading town fed and fattened by gold in Alaska, and then it had dissolved into a nightmare city filled with gas and the walking dead."

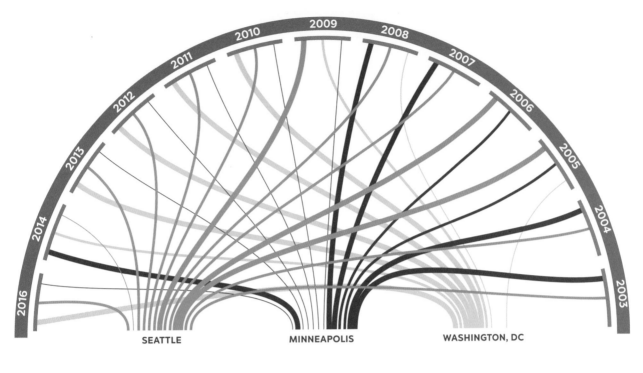

SEATTLE MINNEAPOLIS WASHINGTON, DC

LITERARY SEATTLE

From its murky dockside warehouses and misting cedar slopes to its high-rise surfaces and foghorn bridge bellows, Seattle is an evocative place in which to set a novel. Writers need not reach deep to snatch an interesting persona from the city's wellspring of yore, nor look far to find, in its corners and under its covers, an intriguing issue to explore.

Seattle can also be an effective place in which to write a novel: there are hundreds of coffee shops, dozens of libraries and bookstores (Elliott Bay Book Company, Third Place Books, Queen Anne Book Company, Phinney Books, Twice Sold Tales, Open Books, et al.), and a few supportive writing resource centers (Hugo House, UW Department of English). Indeed, Seattle is home to several best-selling writers and surely some soon-to-be best-selling writers.

In these visualizations, we examine how the city is described by novelists and what topics they talk about when they talk about Seattle. We drew from a range of genres, eras, and authors, our boundaries being fiction and published books only, and, of course, the size of these pages. There are dozens of superb Seattle novels and novelists, and, unfortunately, we could not fit them all. Nonetheless, we hope this selection inspires readers and writers alike to explore Seattle in these books and more.

Above: Seattle has ranked in the top-three most literate cities from 2003 to 2016, according to Central Connecticut State University's annual study. Rankings are based on six key indicators of literacy: number of bookstores, educational attainment, internet resources, library resources, periodical publishing resources, and newspaper circulation.

Left: Select quotations from books about, inspired by, or set in Seattle.

NOVEL NICHES

Novels are arranged by genre and linked to subject matter.

DRAMA

Hotel on the Corner of Bitter and Sweet | 2009 | Jamie Ford
No-No Boy | 1956 | John Okada
Five Flavors of Dumb | 2010 | Antony John
How the Mistakes Were Made | 2011 | Tyler McMahon
Your Heart Is a Muscle the Size of a Fist | 2016 | Sunil Yapa
Waxwings | 2003 | Jonathan Raban
Long for This World | 2003 | Michael Byers
Set This House in Order | 2003 | Matt Ruff
A Sudden Light | 2014 | Garth Stein
Aquarium | 2015 | David Vann
Adios, Nirvana | 2010 | Conrad Wesselhoeft
Don't Breathe a Word | 2012 | Holly Cupala
Starbird Murphy and the World Outside | 2014 | Karen Finneyfrock
Oxygen | 2008 | Carol Wiley Cassella
Truth Like the Sun | 2012 | Jim Lynch

SCI-FI/FANTASY

Hold Me Closer, Necromancer | 2010 | Lish McBride
City at the End of Time | 2008 | Greg Bear
Slaves of Sleep | 1939 | L. Ron Hubbard
Life on the Preservation | 2013 | Jack Skillingstead
Gravity's Rainbow | 1973 | Thomas Pynchon
Wizard of the Pigeons | 1986 | Megan Lindholm
Boneshaker | 2009 | Cherie Priest
Blueprints of the Afterlife | 2012 | Ryan Boudinot
Goodbye for Now | 2012 | Laurie Frankel
Black Hole | 2005 | Charles Burns
Medusa | 2003 | Skye Kathleen Moody

HISTORICAL FICTION

Madison House | 2005 | Peter Donahue
The Fences Between Us | 2010 | Kirby Larson
Seattle Green | 1987 | Jane Adams
Fatal Induction | 2012 | Bernadette Pajer
The Bones and the Book | 2012 | Jane Isenberg
Seattle | 1986 | Charlotte Paul
Great Son | 1945 | Edna Ferber
Benedict Hall | 2015 | Cate Campbell

Woodland Park Zoo
1999 WTO Protests
West Seattle
Timber Industry
Port of Seattle
Pioneer Square
Native Americans
Medical Industry
Houseboats
Billionaires
A-Y-P Exposition
Serial Killers
1962 World's Fair
Pike Place Market
Chinatown/ID
Seedy Seattle
Seattle Sports
Japanese Internment
Immigrants
Grunge/Rock Scene

NOIR/THRILLER

Indian Killer | 1996 | Sherman Alexie
Morning Glory | 2013 | Sarah Jio
Sayonaraville | 2003 | Curt Colbert
The Rainy City | 1985 | Earl W. Emerson
Trouble in Rooster Paradise | 2015 | T. W. Emory
The Bum's Rush | 1997 | G. M. Ford
Disclosure | 1994 | Michael Crichton
Nerve | 2012 | Jeanne Ryan

MYSTERY

Her Final Breath | 2015 | Robert Dugoni
Red Jade | 2010 | Henry Chang
We Interrupt This Broadcast | 1997 | K. K. Beck
Assault and Pepper | 2015 | Leslie Budewitz
Second Watch | 2003 | Lowen Clausen
Doghouse | 2014 | L. A. Kornetsky
Murder Strikes a Pose | 2014 | Tracy Weber

ROMANCE

Fifty Shades of Grey | 2011 | E. L. James
Blindsided | 2015 | Jami Davenport
Solstice | 2010 | Kate Christie
See Jane Score | 2003 | Rachel Gibson
Invisible Lives | 2006 | Anjali Banerjee
Pastries | 2003 | Bharti Kirchner
Delicious | 2006 | Susan Mallery

HUMOR

Still Life with Woodpecker | 1980 | Tom Robbins
Ed King | 2012 | David Guterson
Terroryaki! | 2011 | Jennifer K. Chung
Where'd You Go, Bernadette | 2012 | Maria Semple
Microserfs | 1995 | Douglas Coupland

WOMEN'S FRIENDSHIPS

Lizzy and Jane | 2014 | Katherine Reay
The Lost Art of Mixing | 2013 | Erica Bauermeister
Broken for You | 2004 | Stephanie Kallos
Blossom Street Brides | 2014 | Debbie Macomber
Firefly Lane | 2008 | Kristin Hannah

Dystopian Seattle
Boeing Company
Ballard
Homelessness
Gold Rush Era
Queen Anne
Tech Industry
Culinary Seattle
Teenagers
Professional Women

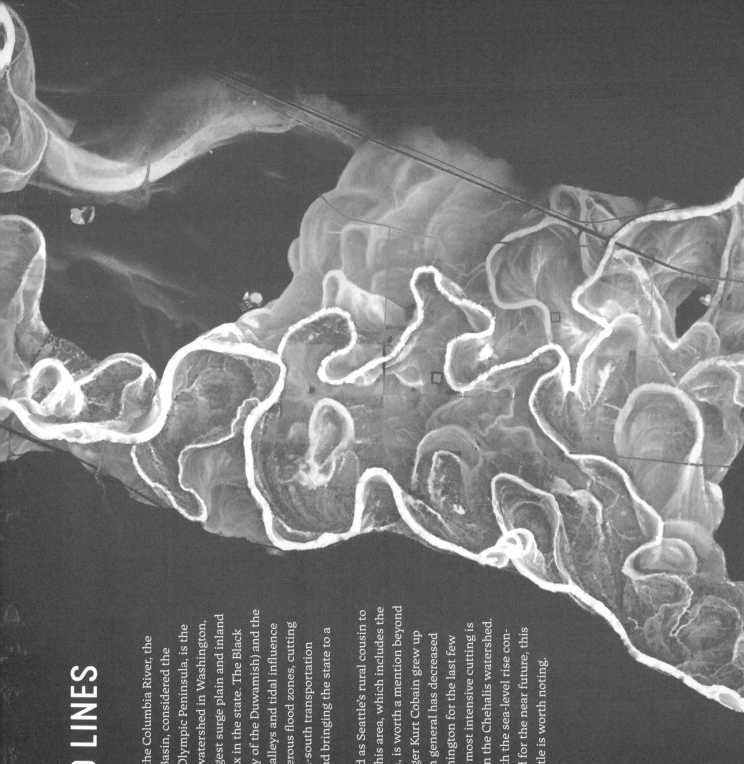

FLOOD LINES

Second only to the Columbia River, the Chehalis River Basin, considered the gateway to the Olympic Peninsula, is the second-largest watershed in Washington, boasting the largest surge plain and inland wetland complex in the state. The Black River (a tributary of the Duwamish) and the Chehalis's low valleys and tidal influence can create dangerous flood zones, cutting off critical north-south transportation routes like I-5 and bringing the state to a standstill.

Often ignored as Seattle's rural cousin to the southwest, this area, which includes the city of Aberdeen, is worth a mention beyond the fact that singer Kurt Cobain grew up there. Logging in general has decreased in Western Washington for the last few decades, but the most intensive cutting is still happening in the Chehalis watershed. When paired with the sea-level rise conditions predicted for the near future, this neighbor of Seattle is worth noting.

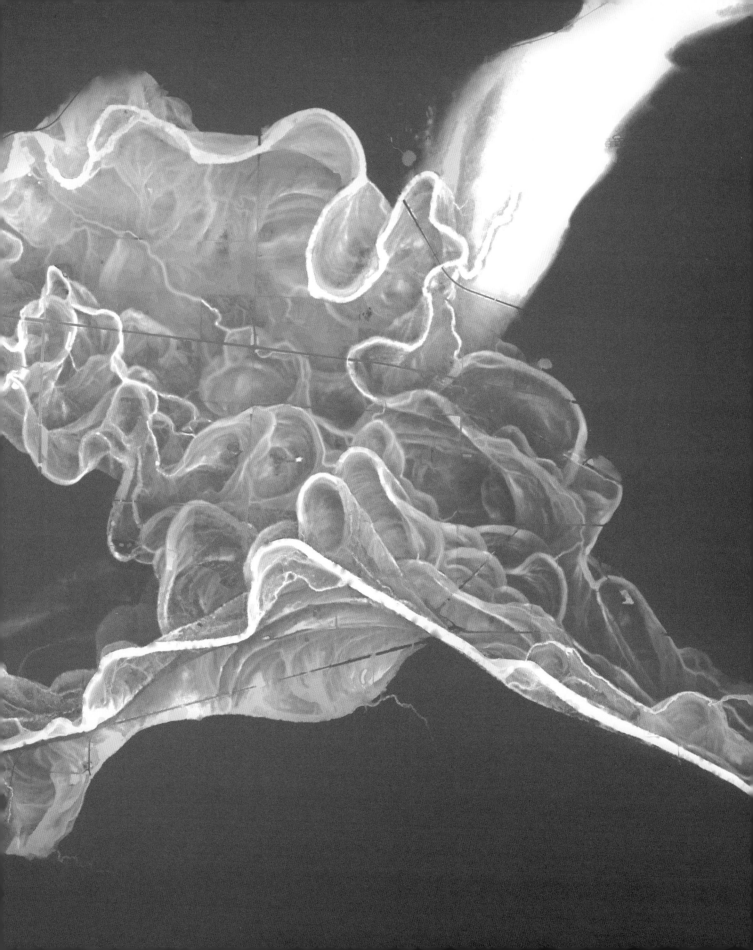

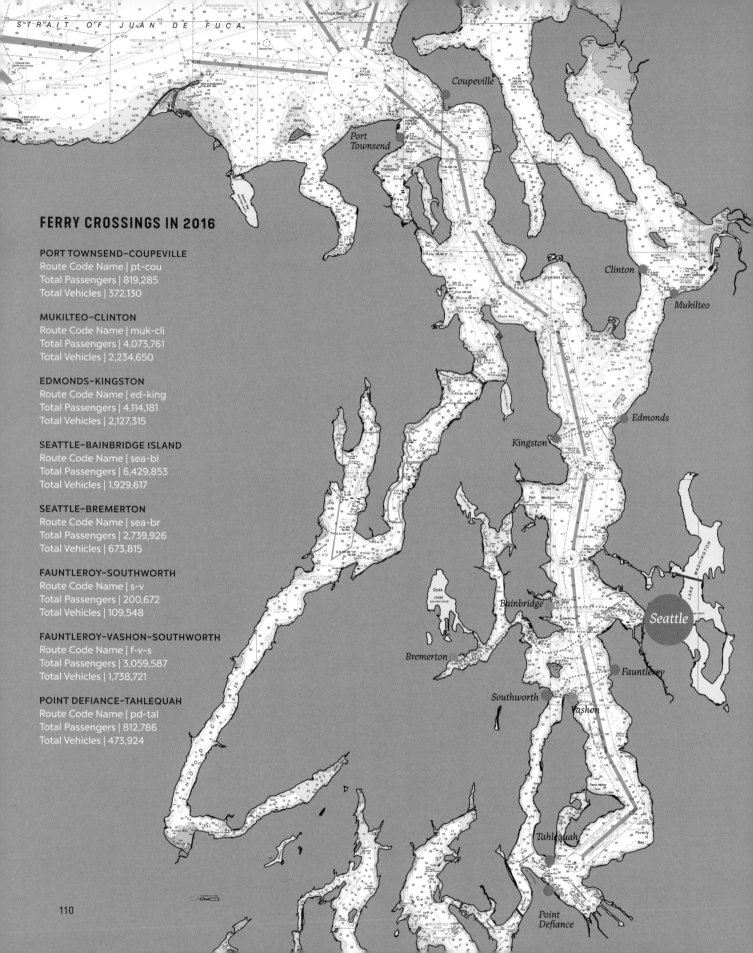

FERRY CROSSINGS IN 2016

PORT TOWNSEND–COUPEVILLE
Route Code Name | pt-cou
Total Passengers | 819,285
Total Vehicles | 372,130

MUKILTEO–CLINTON
Route Code Name | muk-cli
Total Passengers | 4,073,761
Total Vehicles | 2,234,650

EDMONDS–KINGSTON
Route Code Name | ed-king
Total Passengers | 4,114,181
Total Vehicles | 2,127,315

SEATTLE–BAINBRIDGE ISLAND
Route Code Name | sea-bi
Total Passengers | 6,429,853
Total Vehicles | 1,929,617

SEATTLE–BREMERTON
Route Code Name | sea-br
Total Passengers | 2,739,926
Total Vehicles | 673,815

FAUNTLEROY–SOUTHWORTH
Route Code Name | s-v
Total Passengers | 200,672
Total Vehicles | 109,548

FAUNTLEROY–VASHON–SOUTHWORTH
Route Code Name | f-v-s
Total Passengers | 3,059,587
Total Vehicles | 1,738,721

POINT DEFIANCE–TAHLEQUAH
Route Code Name | pd-tal
Total Passengers | 812,786
Total Vehicles | 473,924

FERRIED AWAY

The best views of the Seattle skyline can be seen from the top deck of the Bainbridge Island or Bremerton ferry. As the vessel recedes from the terminal at Colman Dock, passengers witness the enormity of the downtown port, the varied topography of the city, and the beautiful expanse of the waterfront and its abundant activity. More than six million people ride these routes every year. Some are daily commuters; others, weekend adventurers; and many others still, tourists taking in one of the city's prime attractions.

Here, we examine the Washington State Ferries (WSF) system, which came into being in 1951 when the state took over the vessels and routes from a private ferry company. Though originally intended only to convey passengers and vehicles until cross-sound bridges were built, WSF has since grown into the largest ferry system in North America and among the top five in the world. The current fleet of twenty-two vessels, divided into seven classes, services ten routes across Puget Sound, from Tacoma in the south to Anacortes in the north. In 2016, WSF carried more than twenty-four million people and ten million vehicles across these waters.

For well over a century, ferries have helped connect communities around the Salish Sea, and today they remain the only public means of travel to Vashon Island and the San Juan Islands. This limited connection will likely persist, at least if islanders have anything to say about it. As writer Timothy Egan once noted in a *New York Times* article about residents' reaction to a possible Vashon Island bridge, "The only word that can scare up a harsher image than 'California' is 'bridge.'"

WASHINGTON FERRIES BY CLASS
TOTAL VESSEL TYPES PER EACH CLASS

Kwa-di Tabil

Super

Evergreen State

Jumbo

Olympic

Jumbo Mark II

Issaquah

KWA-DI TABIL
Total Ships in Class: 3
Max Passengers: 748
Max Vehicles: 64
Length: 273' 8"
Horsepower: 6,000
Speed: 15 knots
Ships in Fleet:
Chetzemoka, 2010
Kennewick, 2011
Salish, 2011

ISSAQUAH
Total Ships in Class: 6
Max Passengers: 1,200
Max Vehicles: 124
Length: 328'
Horsepower: 5,000
Speed: 16 knots
Ships in Fleet:
Cathlamet, 1981 (rebuilt 1993)
Chelan, 1981 (rebuilt 2005)
Issaquah, 1979 (rebuilt 1989)
Kitsap, 1980 (rebuilt 1992)
Kittitas, 1980 (rebuilt 1990)
Sealth, 1982

SUPER
Total Ships in Class: 4
Max Passengers: 2,000
Max Vehicles: 144
Length: 382' 2"
Horsepower: 8,000
Speed: 20 knots
Ships in Fleet:
Elwha, 1967 (rebuilt in 1991)
Hyak, 1967
Kaleetan, 1967 (rebuilt in 2005)
Yakima, 1967 (rebuilt in 2005)

EVERGREEN STATE
Total Ships in Class: 2
Max Passengers: 1,061
Max Vehicles: 87
Length: 310' 2"
Horsepower: 2,500
Speed: 13 knots
Ships in Fleet:
Klahowya, 1958 (rebuilt 1995)
Tillikum, 1959 (rebuilt 1994)

JUMBO MARK II
Total Ships in Class: 3
Max Passengers: 2,499
Max Vehicles: 202
Length: 460' 2"
Horsepower: 16,000
Speed: 18 knots
Ships in Fleet:
Puyallup, 1999
Tacoma, 1997
Wenatchee, 1998

OLYMPIC
Total Ships in Class: 4
Max Passengers: 1,500
Max Vehicles: 144
Length: 362' 3"
Horsepower: 6,000
Speed: 17 knots
Ships in Fleet:
Chimacum, 2017
Samish, 2015
Suquamish, 2018
Tokitae, 2014

JUMBO
Total Ships in Class: 2
Max Passengers: 2,000
Max Vehicles: 188
Length: 440'
Horsepower: 11,500
Speed: 18 knots
Ships in Fleet:
Spokane, 1972 (rebuilt in 2004)
Walla Walla, 1973 (rebuilt in 2003)

AVERAGE ANNUAL WEEKDAY TRAFFIC

▪ FREMONT BRIDGE

Year Built: **1917**
2016 Openings: **5,497**
Vessel Clearance: **30'**
Fun Fact: In 1974, local residents voted on the unique paint colors of the Fremont Bridge, one of the most frequently opened drawbridges in the world. The winning colors: Fremont orange and canal blue.

54,500

33,900

▪ BALLARD BRIDGE

Year Built: **1917**
2016 Openings: **3,885**
Vessel Clearance: **44'**
Fun Fact: This Chicago-style double-leaf trunnion bascule bridge is opened by the release of a concrete counterweight, powered by a one-hundred-horsepower motor. If the motor fails, it would take six hours to open one leaf by hand.

DAILY BRIDGE OPENINGS IN 2016

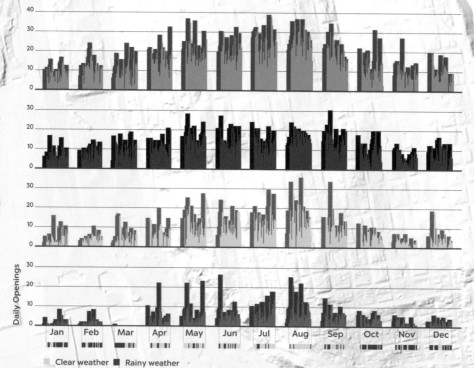

Fremont Bridge
Ballard Bridge
University Bridge
Montlake Bridge

Daily Openings

Jan | Feb | Mar | Apr | May | Jun | Jul | Aug | Sep | Oct | Nov | Dec

Clear weather   Rainy weather

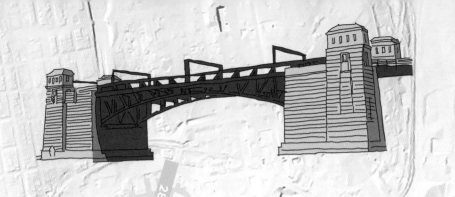

28,500

57,400

UNIVERSITY BRIDGE

Year Built: 1919
2016 Openings: 2,708
Vessel Clearance: 42' 6"
Not-So-Fun Fact: Originally paved with timber trestles, the University Bridge was the first to use steel-mesh technology in the US when it was remodeled in 1933. The original slippery surface caused 182 accidents and six deaths per year.

MONTLAKE BRIDGE

Year Built: 1925
2016 Openings: 1,486
Vessel Clearance: 46'
Fun Fact: The Montlake Bridge, near the UW stadium, came later due to several failures to win bond measure votes. Proponents referred to the bridge as the Montlake-Stadium Bridge in hopes that it would convince some football fans who were otherwise disinclined to spend public money on the wealthy part of town.

BRIDGING THE GAP

Seattle boasts 150 bridges within its city limits; ten are listed in the National Register of Historic Places, two are the longest floating bridges in the world, and one is the most frequently opened bascule bridge in the United States, the Fremont Bridge, spanning the Lake Washington Ship Canal. When the city completed the canal and the nearby Ballard Locks, the level of Lake Washington dropped nine feet, raising Lake Union and the new canal twenty feet above sea level. This much wider waterway required new bridges. City engineer Arthur Dimock recommended a Chicago-style double-leaf trunnion bascule bridge, which uses large counterweights, rotating around a heavy pin called a trunnion, to open and close the leaves, resulting in the Fremont, Ballard, University, and Montlake Bridges. One of the reasons these bridges open so regularly is that maritime traffic is given right-of-way, so the bridges open on demand despite car traffic.

CITY MICROCLIMATES

When someone mentions Seattle, most people immediately think of one word: rain. Seattle is in an oceanic
climate zone situated within a temperate wet forest
biome. This means cool, wet winters and mild, dry
summers. The city is known for its notoriously wet and
cloudy weather, so it may come as surprise that in a list of
major US cities Seattle ranks only forty-fourth for annual
precipitation, experiencing an average of around thirty-
eight inches per year. While it may rain significantly
fewer inches annually than other US cities, it does rain
more often. The area experiences 152 rainy days a year,
creating Seattle's famous misty ambience. The lack of
heavy downpours is due to the Olympic rain shadow. As
moisture-laden air is forced upward when it meets the
Olympic Mountains, it condenses and is released. This
creates the rain shadow, and Seattle's cloudy, rainy days.

Seattleites longing to escape the slow, steady drizzle of
the winter months won't have too much luck. However, if
they know a little about Seattle's microclimates, they may
be able to find some reprieve. Microclimates are docu-
mented patterns of rainfall variations within Seattle's city
limits. Rain amounts can vary literally from neighborhood
to neighborhood. Seattle's very hilly topography creates
miniature rain shadows, so the lee sides of these large
hills typically enjoy less annual rainfall and even a little
more sunshine. Though it's probably still a good idea to
keep that umbrella on hand.

Rainfall data shows the average from 2000 to 2005

▓ 32"   ░ 34"   ■ 36"   ▒ 38"   ▓ 40"

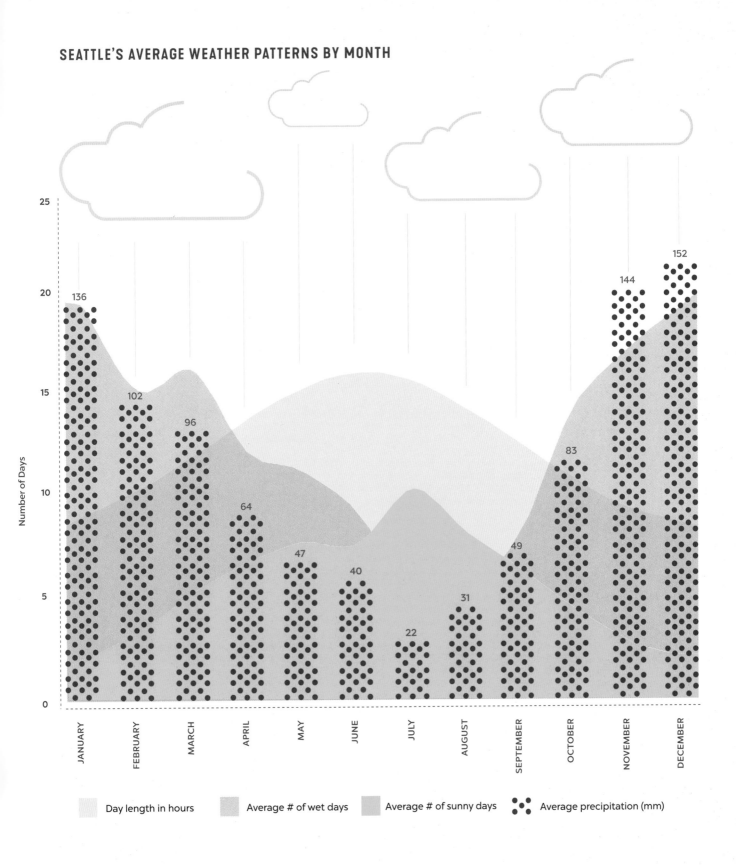

SEATTLE'S AVERAGE WEATHER PATTERNS BY MONTH

Number of Days

136 102 96 64 47 40 22 31 49 83 144 152

JANUARY FEBRUARY MARCH APRIL MAY JUNE JULY AUGUST SEPTEMBER OCTOBER NOVEMBER DECEMBER

Day length in hours   Average # of wet days   Average # of sunny days   Average precipitation (mm)

SEATTLE FLOWS

Buoy data from NOAA collected at the entrance
to the Ballard Locks and the Strait of Juan de Fuca
chart surface water movement in the form of
tides and currents along an X, Y, and Z axis. Using
Processing, an open-source graphical programming
language, we've graphed these changing vectors to
create this flow field.

The Ballard Locks crouch on the head of Salmon
Bay, maintaining the freshwater levels of Lake
Washington and Lake Union that swell twenty-two
feet above Puget Sound's sea level. The eighteen-
mile-wide Strait of Juan de Fuca, which separates
British Columbia and Washington, sits exposed at
the entrance to the Pacific Ocean. In comparison
to the strait, which is subject to rampant fluxes
of oceanic wave energy resulting in the scribbled
mass of powering lines at far right, the sequestered
locks location on the left offers a more consistent
and calmer context.

BALLARD LOCKS ENTRANCE

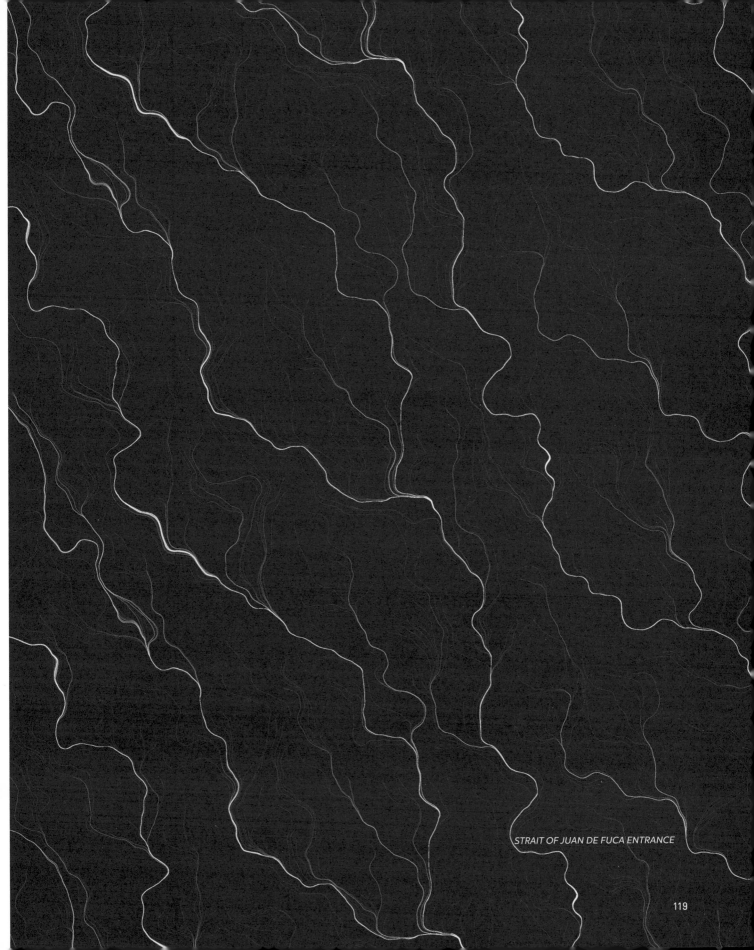

STRAIT OF JUAN DE FUCA ENTRANCE

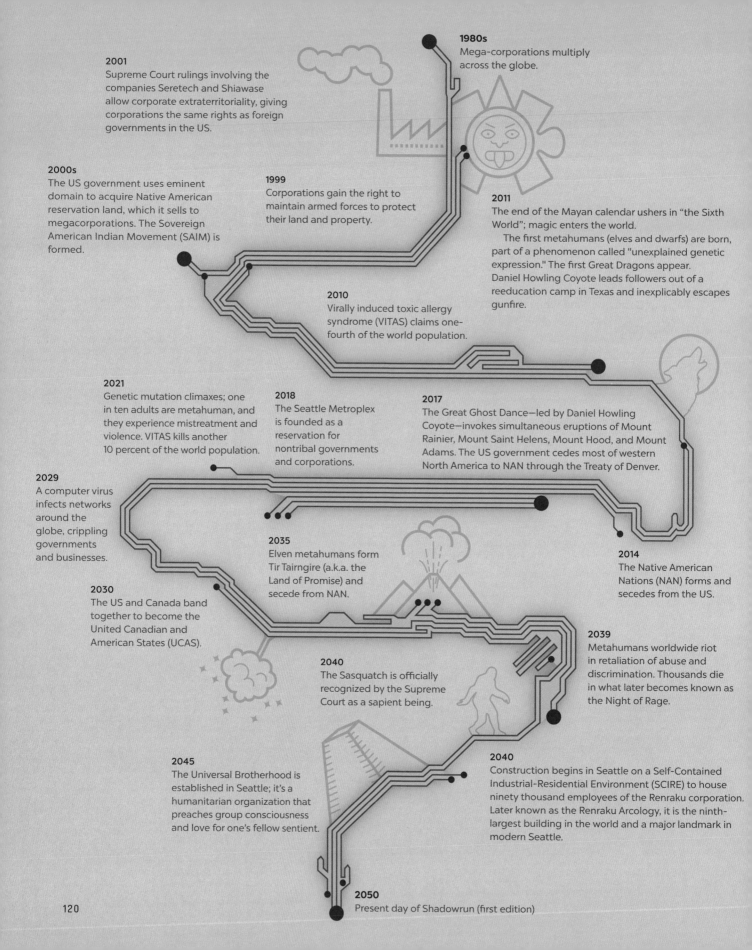

1980s
Mega-corporations multiply across the globe.

2001
Supreme Court rulings involving the companies Seretech and Shiawase allow corporate extraterritoriality, giving corporations the same rights as foreign governments in the US.

2000s
The US government uses eminent domain to acquire Native American reservation land, which it sells to megacorporations. The Sovereign American Indian Movement (SAIM) is formed.

1999
Corporations gain the right to maintain armed forces to protect their land and property.

2011
The end of the Mayan calendar ushers in "the Sixth World"; magic enters the world.
   The first metahumans (elves and dwarfs) are born, part of a phenomenon called "unexplained genetic expression." The first Great Dragons appear. Daniel Howling Coyote leads followers out of a reeducation camp in Texas and inexplicably escapes gunfire.

2010
Virally induced toxic allergy syndrome (VITAS) claims one-fourth of the world population.

2021
Genetic mutation climaxes; one in ten adults are metahuman, and they experience mistreatment and violence. VITAS kills another 10 percent of the world population.

2018
The Seattle Metroplex is founded as a reservation for nontribal governments and corporations.

2017
The Great Ghost Dance—led by Daniel Howling Coyote—invokes simultaneous eruptions of Mount Rainier, Mount Saint Helens, Mount Hood, and Mount Adams. The US government cedes most of western North America to NAN through the Treaty of Denver.

2029
A computer virus infects networks around the globe, crippling governments and businesses.

2035
Elven metahumans form Tir Tairngire (a.k.a. the Land of Promise) and secede from NAN.

2014
The Native American Nations (NAN) forms and secedes from the US.

2030
The US and Canada band together to become the United Canadian and American States (UCAS).

2039
Metahumans worldwide riot in retaliation of abuse and discrimination. Thousands die in what later becomes known as the Night of Rage.

2040
The Sasquatch is officially recognized by the Supreme Court as a sapient being.

2040
Construction begins in Seattle on a Self-Contained Industrial-Residential Environment (SCIRE) to house ninety thousand employees of the Renraku corporation. Later known as the Renraku Arcology, it is the ninth-largest building in the world and a major landmark in modern Seattle.

2045
The Universal Brotherhood is established in Seattle; it's a humanitarian organization that preaches group consciousness and love for one's fellow sentient.

2050
Present day of Shadowrun (first edition)

SHADOW OF SEATTLE

Shadowrun was made for Seattle. This postapocalyptic cyberpunk fantasy RPG (role-playing game) is one of the most popular ever created. Now in its twenty-ninth year, Shadowrun has spawned over fifty books, card games, tabletop games, and video games, and has an international following (especially in Germany). And while this near-future world of cybernetic fantasy and magic spans the globe, Seattle takes a central role as the setting for international espionage and eponymous "shadowruns," in which players attempt to steal high-tech secrets from the rivals of their corporate overlords.

So why Seattle? When the game was created by the company FASA in 1989, Microsoft (based in the Seattle suburb of Redmond) had just gone public, the grunge scene (dubbed "the Seattle sound") was gaining national popularity, and many of the "megacities" in the United States (New York, LA, Chicago) were on the decline. Paired with the brooding atmosphere created by Seattle's rainy winters, there could be no better setting for a high-tech neonoir conspiracy.

The game creators also capitalized on some of Seattle's other cultural assets—namely, the influence of Japanese immigrants on the city and the relatively strong presence of Native American culture in the greater Puget Sound and the Pacific Northwest. There is a seemingly endless web of Yakuza (Japanese mafia) storylines in Shadowrun that have developed throughout the years, and there is no denying the geopolitical influence of Native peoples on this future world.

Over the past thirty years, the foundations of Shadowrun have been built upon by fans and players to become a complex world worth exploring.

Left: Timeline of Shadowrun world

TROLL At over nine feet tall, trolls are the rarest of the metahumans, and have the unique ability to see in the infrared specrum, helping them to navigate in the dark.

ELF Elves showed up in 2011, sporting pointy ears and extreme longevity. They have formed their own sovereign nation called Tir Tairngire just south of Seattle.

DWARF Like elves, dwarves were first born to human mothers through the transformation know as "unexplained genetic expression" (UGE). They are also immune to most diseases.

ORK Orks grow much faster than humans, reaching maturity between the ages of twelve and fourteen. They are larger and stronger than humans, if not slightly more dull.

PIXIE A pixie's most recognizable characteristic is their wings—like a dragonfly's and three feet wide. They have an ability to see into the astral plane and are very good at hiding.

HUMAN Humans represent the first metatype and existed for thousands of years before the "awakening". They still represent the majority population in most places.

SHADOW MAP

EVERETT
The district was hit hard by the crash of 2064, losing nearly all digital records. Megacorporations now own most of the land, and organized crime syndicates control the rest. Add Everett's border status with Salish-Shidhe lands and you have a smugglers' paradise.

DOWNTOWN SEATTLE
This is the heart of the Metroplex, a dense forest of shiny skyscrapers and home to the Renraku Arcology; one of the largest structures in the world. Traffic is a nightmare, whether you're dodging drones, navigating moving sidewalks, or surviving an air taxi ride.

BELLEVUE
Borders are heavily patrolled in this elite district. CEOs shuttle to their downtown offices in armored airships, and large domes loom over neighborhoods to keep out the smog. In 2060, nearby Cougar Mountain was leveled to make space for new development.

SNOHOMISH
The breadbasket of the Metroplex. This is where GMO farms, aquaculture, and bio-enhanced livestock that feed the rich are based. Also in Snohomish is the Crash Zone—the location of a fatal airship crash that leveled the Metroplex Reformatory and let loose hundreds of prisoners who now control the area.

THE REDMOND BARRENS
The power plant meltdown of 2013 left this district contaminated with radiation and pushed most inhabitants west. The computer crash of '29 eliminated the remaining businesses, leaving behind a wasteland. The epicenter of the meltdown is called Glow City. Also in the Redmond Barrens is Rat's Nest, a municipal garbage-dump home to thousands of squatters living off Metroplex refuse.

RENTON
Alongside the malls and country clubs in this residential district, supremacist groups and metahuman gangs clash. Bored teens can be found abusing simsense chips and drugs in parks and basements.

AUBURN
Lahars from Mount Rainier leveled most of Auburn back in 2017, opening up a land grab for megacorporations, the biggest of which is Federated Boeing. The land, mostly used for heavy industry, is humming nonstop.

EVERETT

French W.
Ranch

Crash Zone

SNOHOMISH

Rat's Nest

Federated
Boeing

REDMOND

Glow City

OUTREMER

SEATTLE

BELLEVUE

RENTON

COUNCIL
ISLAND

TACOMA

Tacoma's busy port and high-tech nanofactories dominate the district, making it a well-protected bastion of blue-collar industry. And while efforts have been made to clean up the historically polluted port, the "Tacoma aroma" persists.

FORT LEWIS

Home to the Seattle Metroplex Guard, McChord Airfield, and the UCAS Army Pacific Command, Fort Lewis also houses a state-of-the-art full-scale mock-up of Seattle Center, used for training in AR-simulated urban warfare.

POPULATION DISTRIBUTION

- Human
- Elf
- Dwarf
- Ork
- Troll
- Pixie / Other

SAFETY RATINGS

AAA: 24-7 patrol; immediate response

AA: 24-7 patrol; less frequent than AAA but prompt response

A: Frequent street patrol presence; no astral or drone response

B: Commercial-level A rating

C: Infrequent patrols and poorly maintained panic button booths

D: Commerical-level C rating

E: Areas are not patrolled; response only to headline-making violence

Z: Total anarchy

- Military Base
- Lahar flow zone from eruption of Mt. Rainier
- Area of active radiation

PUYALLUP BARRENS

Mount Rainier also decimated Puyallup, covering the district in ash and producing toxic acid rain, which is still falling fifty years later. The eruption left a tract called Hell's Kitchen, known to be a magical hot spot and attracting shamans from across the region.

SPLIFFS + SCHEMAS

In Seattle, in general, it can be said that the sites of protest and celebration are Westlake Park and Seattle Center, respectively. So it was at the latter, one month after Washington voters approved passage of Initiative 502, where hundreds of people gathered with marijuana in hand to praise the end of the plant's prohibition. Granted, they were in violation of I-502, which outlaws public consumption, but after seventy-five years of proscription, it was hard to resist the enthusiasm, and only warnings were issued. Besides, Washingtonians would have to wait another twenty-one months before the first legal weed stores were open for business. The first pot shop in Seattle was Cannabis City, which opened its doors (at "high noon") on July 8, 2014. Within three days, it had completely sold out its entire stock: eleven pounds of weed.

According to I-502, adults age twenty-one and older are allowed to purchase up to one ounce of bud, sixteen ounces of solid edibles, seventy-two ounces of liquid edibles, and seven grams of concentrates. Only state-licensed establishments may grow and sell these substances. In King County, which includes Seattle, there are more than one hundred marijuana retailers (at this writing), and the variety of products and paraphernalia available may astound. Consumers can purchase marijuana-infused cookies, lozenges, nuts, coffees, juices, balms, and lubricants, not to mention the myriad concentrates, including oils, extracts, hashes, waxes, and shatter.

And, of course, consumers may also purchase dried bud, or flower. Of these, the selection is immense. Using online marijuana-locater guides, we counted more than thirteen hundred varieties, called strains, available for purchase in King County. When we saw strain names like Alaskan Thunder Fuck and Blueberry Cheesecake, we thought it would be fun and interesting to perform a semantic analysis of these strains. First, we split apart the names into their constituent terms (e.g., "blueberry" and "cheesecake"). Then we separated them into common classifications, or facets, such as "flavor" and "effect." The facets of the most frequently used terms are visualized on the adjacent page. We then clustered terms according to common themes and meanings, such as "space" and "cold." What emerges is a view into the creative and curious world of legal cannabis. Enjoy!

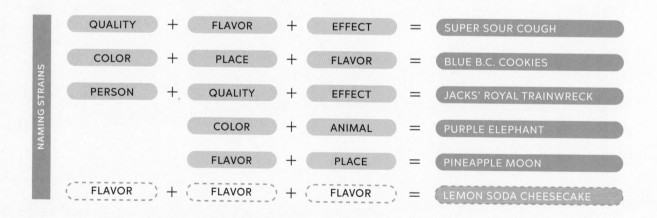

NAMING STRAINS

QUALITY + FLAVOR + EFFECT = SUPER SOUR COUGH

COLOR + PLACE + FLAVOR = BLUE B.C. COOKIES

PERSON + QUALITY + EFFECT = JACKS' ROYAL TRAINWRECK

COLOR + ANIMAL = PURPLE ELEPHANT

FLAVOR + PLACE = PINEAPPLE MOON

FLAVOR + FLAVOR + FLAVOR = LEMON SODA CHEESECAKE

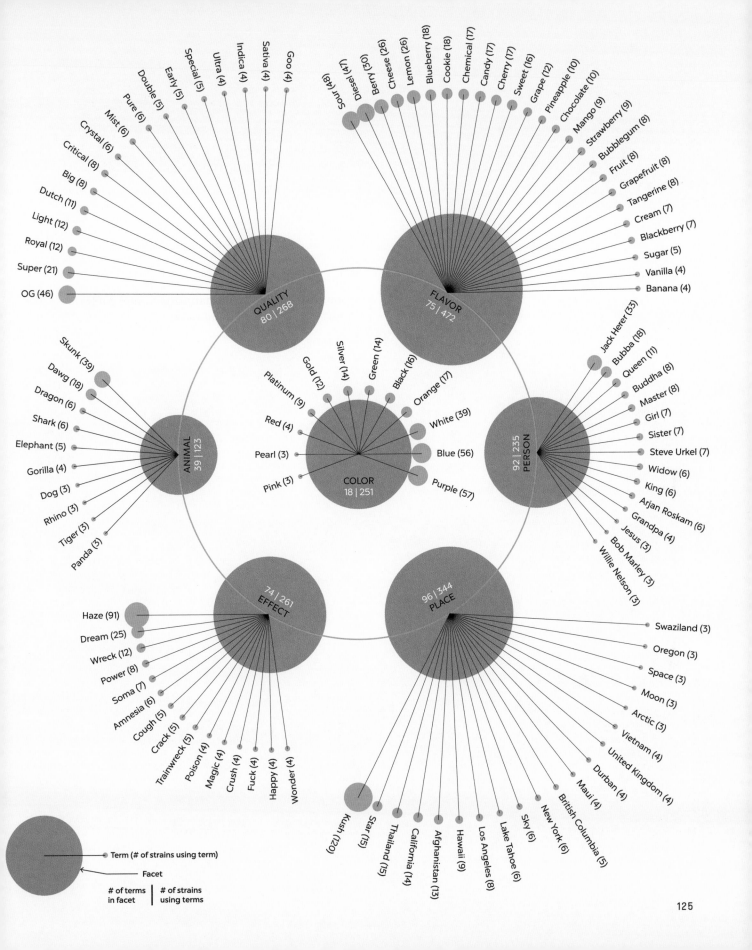

QUALITY
80 | 268

Goo (4)
Sativa (4)
Indica (4)
Ultra (4)
Special (5)
Early (5)
Double (5)
Pure (6)
Mist (6)
Crystal (6)
Critical (8)
Big (8)
Dutch (11)
Light (12)
Royal (12)
Super (21)
OG (46)

FLAVOR
75 | 472

Sour (48)
Diesel (47)
Berry (30)
Cheese (26)
Lemon (26)
Blueberry (18)
Cookie (18)
Chemical (17)
Candy (17)
Cherry (17)
Sweet (16)
Grape (12)
Pineapple (10)
Chocolate (10)
Mango (9)
Strawberry (9)
Bubblegum (8)
Fruit (8)
Grapefruit (8)
Tangerine (8)
Cream (7)
Blackberry (7)
Sugar (5)
Vanilla (4)
Banana (4)

ANIMAL
39 | 123

Skunk (39)
Dawg (18)
Dragon (6)
Shark (6)
Elephant (5)
Gorilla (4)
Dog (3)
Rhino (3)
Tiger (3)
Panda (3)

COLOR
18 | 251

Platinum (9)
Gold (12)
Silver (14)
Green (14)
Black (16)
Orange (17)
Red (4)
White (39)
Pearl (3)
Blue (56)
Pink (3)
Purple (57)

PERSON
92 | 235

Jack Herer (33)
Bubba (18)
Queen (11)
Buddha (8)
Master (8)
Girl (7)
Sister (7)
Steve Urkel (7)
Widow (6)
King (6)
Arjan Roskam (6)
Grandpa (4)
Jesus (3)
Bob Marley (3)
Willie Nelson (3)

EFFECT
74 | 261

Haze (91)
Dream (25)
Wreck (12)
Power (8)
Soma (7)
Amnesia (6)
Cough (5)
Crack (5)
Trainwreck (5)
Poison (4)
Magic (4)
Crush (4)
Fuck (4)
Happy (4)
Wonder (4)

PLACE
96 | 344

Swaziland (3)
Oregon (3)
Space (3)
Moon (3)
Arctic (3)
Vietnam (4)
United Kingdom (4)
Durban (4)
Maui (4)
British Columbia (5)
Sky (6)
New York (6)
Lake Tahoe (6)
Los Angeles (8)
Hawaii (9)
Afghanistan (13)
California (14)
Thailand (15)
Star (15)
Kush (120)

Term (# of strains using term)
Facet
# of terms in facet | # of strains using terms

125

CANNABIS CLUSTERS

The individual terms from over 1,300 marijuana-strain names were split up and regrouped by like meaning. The resulting clusters reveal marijuana's preoccupations.

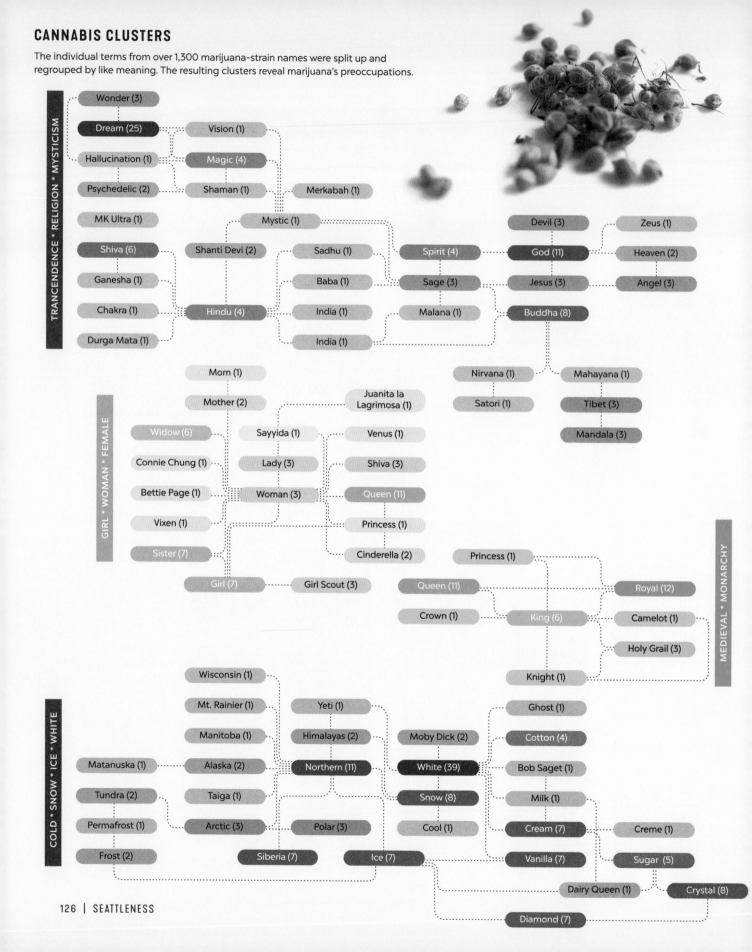

TRANCENDENCE * RELIGION * MYSTICISM

Wonder (3)
Dream (25) — Vision (1)
Hallucination (1) — Magic (4)
Psychedelic (2) — Shaman (1) — Merkabah (1)
MK Ultra (1) — Mystic (1)
Shiva (6) — Shanti Devi (2) — Sadhu (1) — Spirit (4)
Ganesha (1) — Baba (1) — Sage (3)
Chakra (1) — Hindu (4) — India (1) — Malana (1)
Durga Mata (1) — India (1)

Devil (3) — Zeus (1)
God (11) — Heaven (2)
Jesus (3) — Angel (3)
Buddha (8)

Nirvana (1) — Mahayana (1)
Satori (1) — Tibet (3)
Mandala (3)

GIRL * WOMAN * FEMALE

Mom (1)
Mother (2) — Juanita la Lagrimosa (1)
Widow (6) — Sayyida (1) — Venus (1)
Connie Chung (1) — Lady (3) — Shiva (3)
Bettie Page (1) — Woman (3) — Queen (11)
Vixen (1) — Princess (1)
Sister (7) — Cinderella (2)
Girl (7) — Girl Scout (3)

Princess (1)
Queen (11)
Crown (1) — King (6) — Royal (12)
Camelot (1)
Holy Grail (3)
Knight (1)

MEDIEVAL * MONARCHY

COLD * SNOW * ICE * WHITE

Wisconsin (1)
Mt. Rainier (1) — Yeti (1) — Ghost (1)
Manitoba (1) — Himalayas (2) — Moby Dick (2) — Cotton (4)
Matanuska (1) — Alaska (2) — Northern (11) — White (39) — Bob Saget (1)
Tundra (2) — Taiga (1) — Snow (8) — Milk (1)
Permafrost (1) — Arctic (3) — Polar (3) — Cool (1) — Cream (7) — Creme (1)
Frost (2) — Siberia (7) — Ice (7) — Vanilla (7) — Sugar (5)
Dairy Queen (1) — Crystal (8)
Diamond (7)

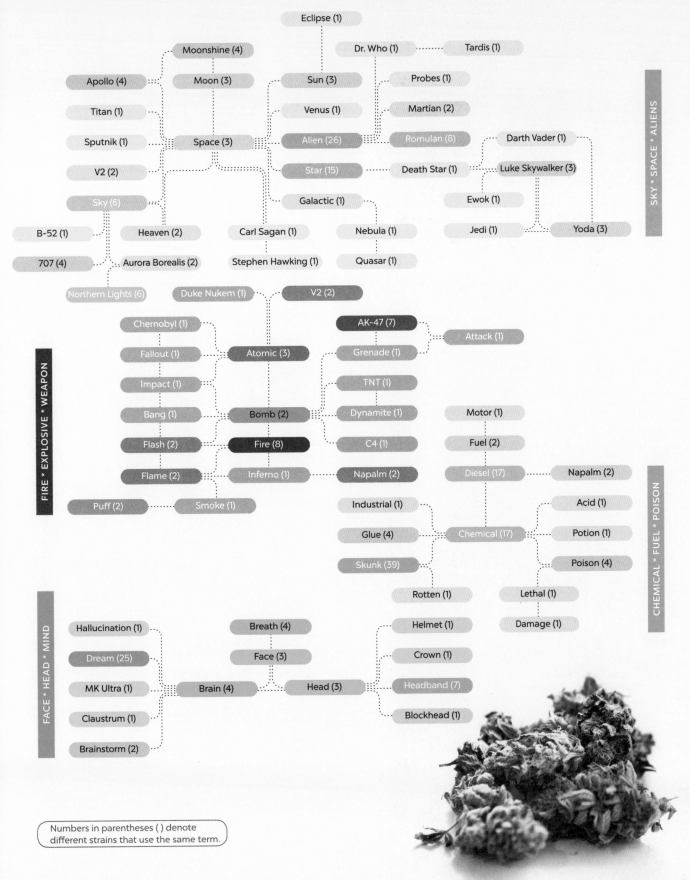

Eclipse (1)

Moonshine (4)

Dr. Who (1) ┄┄┄┄ Tardis (1)

Apollo (4) ┄┄ Moon (3) Sun (3) Probes (1)

Titan (1) Venus (1) Martian (2)

Sputnik (1) Space (3) Alien (26) Romulan (8) Darth Vader (1)

V2 (2) Star (15) ┄┄ Death Star (1) Luke Skywalker (3)

Sky (6) Galactic (1) Ewok (1)

B-52 (1) Heaven (2) Carl Sagan (1) Nebula (1) Jedi (1) Yoda (3)

707 (4) Aurora Borealis (2) Stephen Hawking (1) Quasar (1)

Northern Lights (6) Duke Nukem (1) V2 (2)

Chernobyl (1) AK-47 (7) Attack (1)

Fallout (1) Atomic (3) Grenade (1)

Impact (1) TNT (1)

Bang (1) Bomb (2) Dynamite (1) Motor (1)

Flash (2) Fire (8) C4 (1) Fuel (2)

Flame (2) Inferno (1) Napalm (2) Diesel (17) Napalm (2)

Puff (2) Smoke (1) Industrial (1) Acid (1)

Glue (4) Chemical (17) Potion (1)

Skunk (39) Poison (4)

Rotten (1) Lethal (1)

Damage (1)

Helmet (1)

Hallucination (1) Breath (4) Crown (1)

Dream (25) Face (3) Headband (7)

MK Ultra (1) Brain (4) Head (3)

Claustrum (1) Blockhead (1)

Brainstorm (2)

Numbers in parentheses ( ) denote
different strains that use the same term.

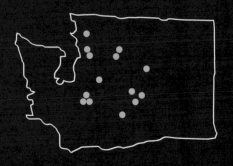

2015 WASHINGTON STATE EARTHQUAKES

MAGNITUDE

	1	2	3	4	5
Mt. Vernon			●		
Darrington			●		
Darrington (2)			●		
Morton			●		
North Bend			●		
Morton (2)			●		
Grand Coulee				●	
Ellensburg			●		
Yakima			●		
Mt. Vernon (2)			●		
Morton (3)			●		
Ellensburg (2)			●		
Ellensburg (3)				●	
Kirkland			●		
Forks			●		

SEISMIC SEATTLE

The greater Seattle metropolitan area is no stranger to fault activity. The city is located in the Cascadia subduction zone, an active fault zone that stretches from Canada to California, and the faults here seem to be flexing their muscles. In December of 2015, a magnitude 4.8 earthquake with an epicenter eleven miles northeast of Victoria, BC, jostled Washington residents. It was the largest quake to shake the area since the magnitude 4.9 that struck in 2004. More recently, a magnitude 4.2 quake hit in February 2017, and in both early 2016 and early 2017, thousands of small earthquakes were recorded. But don't panic; this isn't too out of the ordinary, as the area has been regularly experiencing these quake "swarms" every fourteen months since the 1990s.

In addition to monitoring Seattle's traditional seismic scene, the Pacific Northwest Seismic Network (PNSN) has installed seismometers in various locations of CenturyLink Field to measure the ability of Seahawks fans to rock the bedrock. PNSN has been measuring the seismic activity caused by the notoriously raucous fans since 2011, when a post-touchdown celebration, now known as the Beast Quake, unexpectedly registered on a seismograph located a block away from the stadium. As powerful as the Beast Quake was, it was sidelined when the Dance Quake struck CenturyLink Field in January of 2015, during the Packers-Seahawks NFC championship game. PNSN seismologists measured the largest seismic activity yet affiliated with a football game when Seahawks fans started dancing and stomping in unity after a go-ahead touchdown and two-point conversion late in the game. This earthshaking boogying must have energized the home team, since Seattle beat Green Bay in overtime, 28–22.

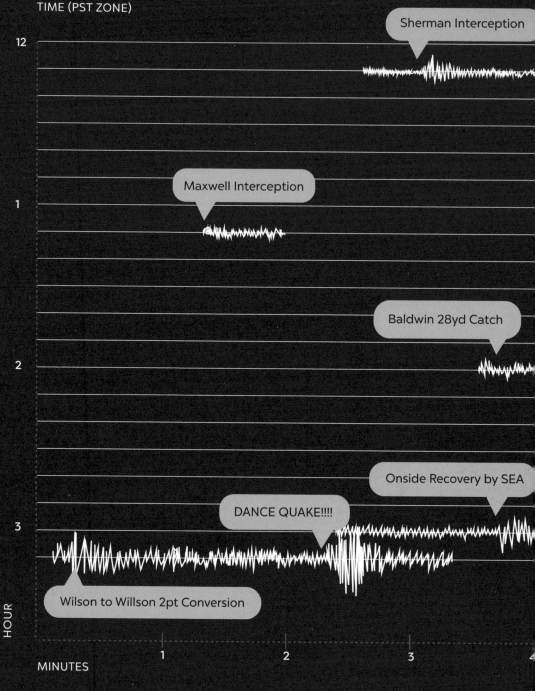

GREEN BAY PACKERS VS. SEATTLE SEAHAWKS
NFC CHAMPIONSHIP GAME, JANUARY 2015

PACIFIC NORTHWEST SEISMIC NETWORK
HAWK-O-GRAM (HWK1)

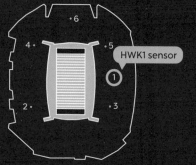

CENTURYLINK FIELD
Seahawk Stadium's Pacific
Northwest Seismic Network
sensor locations

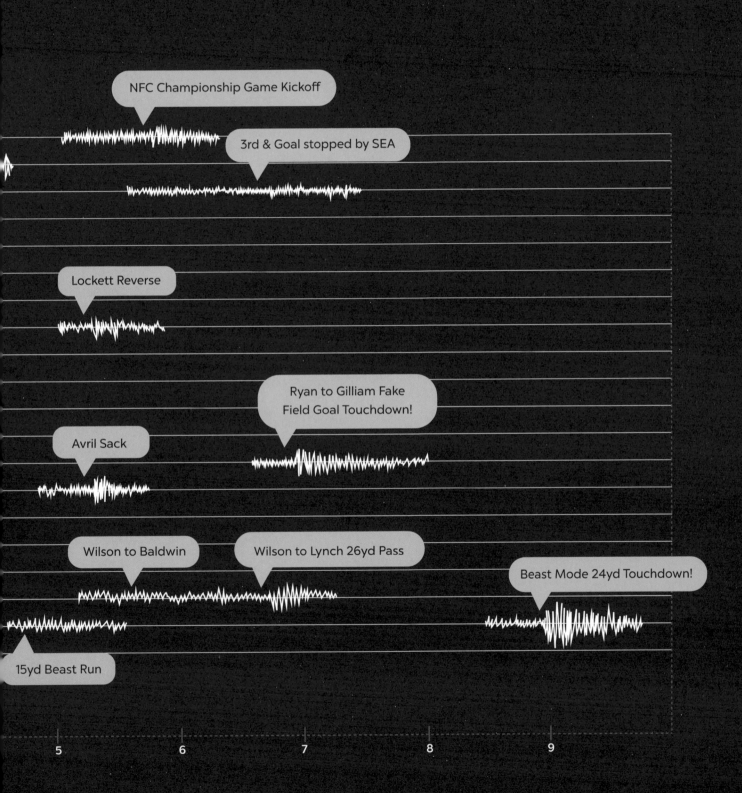

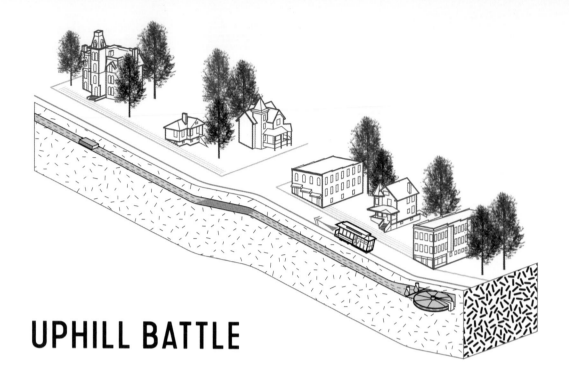

UPHILL BATTLE

Seattle's hills are its bane and its beauty. Turn-of-the-century real-estate promoters likened the city's topography to the legendary seven hills of Rome, naming Beacon, Denny, First, Second, Capitol, Yesler, and Queen Anne Hills as the Northwest city's noteworthy icons. Unlike the mythical King Romulus, who was said to have founded Rome at the top of Palatine Hill, Seattleites started at sea level and found many interesting ways to ascend the slopes.

The streetcar and cable-car system was one way, at first utilizing horsepower, then electric power and cables, to pull people uphill. Technologies such as the counterbalance pulled carloads of people up steep inclines like Queen Anne Avenue by releasing a sixteen-ton counterweight along a miniature underground rail tunnel. Another famous counterbalance pulled passengers up a steep one-block-long slope to the famous Washington Hotel, one of the casualties of the Denny Regrade.

Seattleites also used their own legs to power up those hills. As rail lines expanded into new neighborhoods, hillside dwellers needed access to these transit networks. Stairs of that time were generous and sturdy, reflecting the gold rush capital that was flooding the city. Many stairs of this era can still be found on the south slope of Queen Anne Hill.

In the 1920s and '30s, streetcars were being overtaken by automobiles, and the city-owned rail lines were bankrupted by the mandated nickel fares. Many lines were dismantled, and the remnants use to build more stairs (perhaps to take the place of a cheap trolley ride for pedestrians). Today you can see staircases from this era constructed from the concrete sleepers that ran under the tracks, and handrail posts made from the steel tracks themselves.

This all makes for interesting walking tours around the city, and several Seattleites have taken it upon themselves to map these routes for the enjoyment of urban explorers. Jake and Cathy Jaramillo wrote a thorough guide called *Seattle Stairway Walks*, which takes you up and down 14,286 steps. Architect and Queen Anne resident Thomas Horton mapped all the stairs in his neighborhood; he shares those maps along with details of stair typology on his website Queen Anne Public Stairs: QAStairs.com.

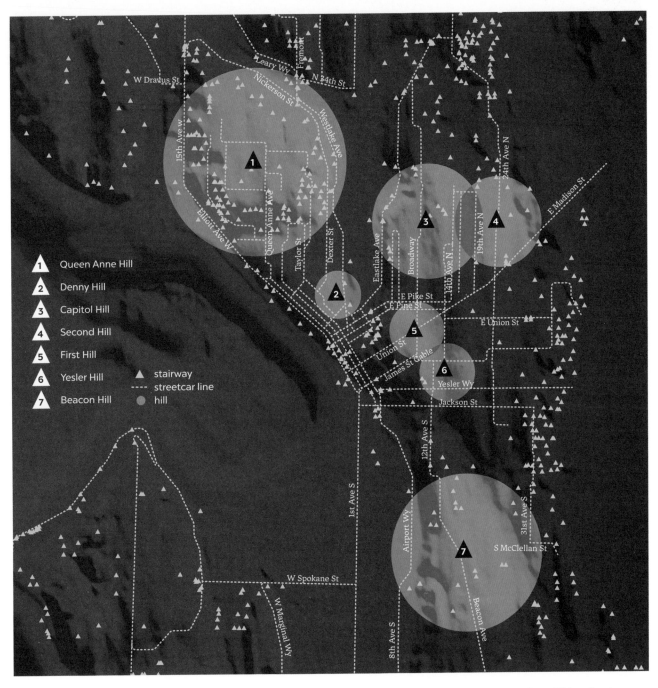

1	Queen Anne Hill
2	Denny Hill
3	Capitol Hill
4	Second Hill
5	First Hill
6	Yesler Hill
7	Beacon Hill

▲ stairway
- - - streetcar line
● hill

Above: Map shows streetcar lines from 1930 and staircases present today overlaid on the seven hills of Seattle.

Left: This diagram shows a cutaway of Queen Anne counterbalance, which operated 1898 to 1940. A sixteen-ton counterweight pulled the trolley uphill. Several sandbags were located at the bottom of the tunnel as a cushion in case a cable snapped.

HILLS + STAIRS

SECOND
CAPITOL
FIRST — YESLER
QUEEN ANNE
DENNY

DENNY HILL ①

Staircase: Washington Hotel
Year Built: Early 1900s
Steps: Over 200

Construction of the Washington Hotel was started by Arthur Denny and later finished by James Moore on the southeastern slope of Denny Hill. During the first stages of the regrade, Virginia Street was dug down one hundred feet below the hotel's entrance, essentially cutting off access. But Moore built a one-block-long counterbalance-powered trolley and adjoining staircase to reconnect the hotel to Third Avenue. The hotel was originally a Victorian showpiece but was left abandoned for over ten years after the crash of 1893. When the hotel was finally reopened in 1903 by Moore, its first guest was President Theodore Roosevelt. The hotel was demolished three years later and Denny Hill ultimately flattened.

▲ Seattle staircase
 Featured staircase
 *Staircase that has been demolished or closed

QUEEN ANNE HILL ②

Staircase: Comstock and Sixth
Year Built: 1905
Steps: 45

These are the oldest stairs in Seattle.

QUEEN ANNE HILL ③

Staircase: Boston Street Haunted
Year Built: Early 1900s
Steps: Unknown

Local lore says that a woman walking down these wooden stairs fell to her death on the way to meeting her fiancé. Years later, another woman walking down this staircase heard a voice warning her to turn back; the stairs suddenly crumbled, and she narrowly escaped.

CAPITOL HILL ④

Staircase: Howe Street
Year Built: 1911
Steps: 388

This is the longest staircase in Seattle, made up of thirteen flights and rising 160 feet. Many houses have their own private paths that lead to the stairs, and there is a "secret garden" (Streissguth Gardens) waiting at the top of the hill as a reward for making the climb.

SECOND HILL ⑤

Staircase: Crescent
Year Built: Unknown
Steps: 103

Part of Interlaken Park, these wooden stairs were created as part of the Olmsted Brothers' 1903 master plan for Seattle. Interlaken Boulevard had been used as a major bike and pedestrian thoroughfare since 1890, connecting Second Hill with the Lake Washington waterfront.

BEACON

9

8

FIRST HILL 6

Staircase: Freeway Park
Year Built: 1976
Steps: 612

Designed by Lawrence Halprin and Angela Danadjieva, this stepped park was created to connect downtown to First Hill after the I-5 trench separated the two in the early 1970s. It was the first park to bridge over a highway.

YESLER HILL 7

Staircase: Tenth Avenue Hillclimb
Year Built: 2016
Steps: 80

This new staircase and accessible ramp, designed by GGLO, connects the Chinatown–International District and Little Saigon with Yesler Terrace. The hillclimb features a bike runnel and an extensive stormwater treatment system integrated into the planting.

BEACON HILL 8

Staircase: Katie Black's Garden
Year Built: 1914
Steps: 23

This staircase leads to a small Japanese-style garden built by early settler Katie Black. The garden was purchased by the city's parks department in 1990 and is now open to the public.

BEACON HILL 9

Staircase: Cheasty Greenspace
Year Built: 2009
Steps: 73

This green space was originally part of the 1903 Olmsted park plan. Steps were built through the restored green space in 2009 to connect the neighborhood with a new light-rail running along Martin Luther King Jr. Way South.

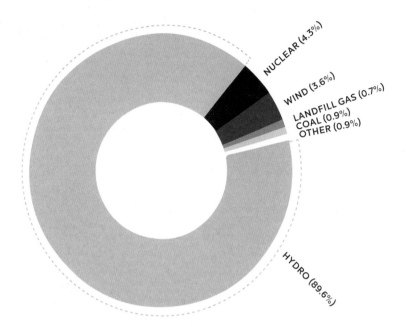

NUCLEAR (4.3%)

WIND (3.6%)

LANDFILL GAS (0.7%)

COAL (0.9%)

OTHER (0.9%)

HYDRO (89.6%)

CURRENT POWER

When it comes to Washington State, a river definitely runs through it: there are over 70,400 breathtaking miles of rivers, streams, tributaries, and creeks. One of the most strikingly beautiful rivers in the state is the Columbia River; it is seventeen million years old and winds through the mountains and desert in dramatic fashion.

Washington's rivers, while scenic, serve as more than just eye candy. In recognizing the awesome power of these waters to carve paths through mountains, a bright idea was born: turn this natural force into a renewable energy source. Washington puts its rivers to work; there are over 1,160 dams in the state (darn, that's a lot of dams!), and hydroelectric power accounts for 69 percent of Washington's total energy usage. This is the highest of any state. Even more impressive, Seattle gets 90 percent of its energy from hydropower. The city's public utility company, Seattle City

Light, owns seven dams on four different rivers. The state's largest and oldest hydroelectric dam is the Grand Coulee Dam, located on the Columbia about four hours east of Seattle. This concrete giant generates twenty-one billion kilowatt-hours annually, enough to supply 2.3 million households with power for a full year.

Another impressive Washington river is the 150-mile-long Skagit. The Skagit River Hydroelectric Project supplies 25 percent of Seattle's electric power with its three dams: Gorge, Diablo, and Ross. All of this wild white-water energy benefits more than just the locals; one-third of the total hydroelectric power in the United States is generated along the Columbia Basin. Alas, all that electricity has come at the expense of wild salmon runs.

Above: Seattle's power supply

Left: Winter at Grand Coulee Dam

SEATTLE CITY LIGHT
HYDROPOWER

N

Puyallup

Palouse

Klickitat

Pend Oreille

Yakima

Rock Creek

Okanogan

Snake

Boundary Dam

*Bonneville, designated a National
Historic Landmark District in 1987*

Grand Coulee Dam
(Largest hydro plant in US)

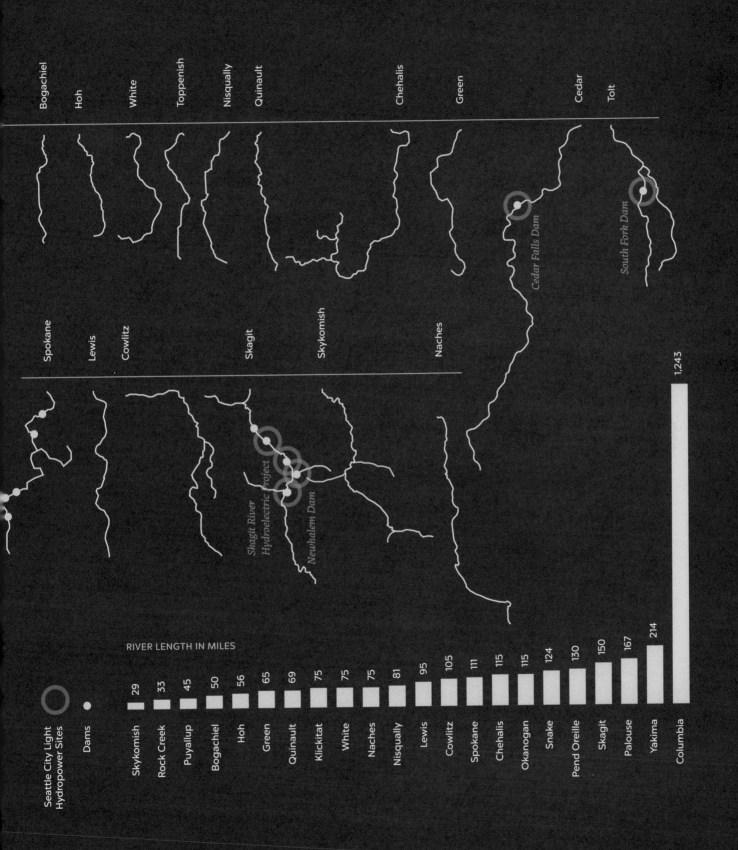

Bogachiel
Hoh
White
Toppenish
Nisqually
Quinault
Chehalis
Green
Cedar
Tolt

Spokane
Lewis
Cowlitz
Skagit
Skykomish
Naches

Cedar Falls Dam

South Fork Dam

*Skagit River
Hydroelectric Project*

Newhalem Dam

1,243

RIVER LENGTH IN MILES

Seattle City Light
Hydropower Sites

Dams

Skykomish	29
Rock Creek	33
Puyallup	45
Bogachiel	50
Hoh	56
Green	65
Quinault	69
Klickitat	75
White	75
Naches	75
Nisqually	81
Lewis	95
Cowlitz	105
Spokane	111
Chehalis	115
Okanogan	115
Snake	124
Pend Oreille	130
Skagit	150
Palouse	167
Yakima	214
Columbia	1,243

ACTOR LINES

From its majestic forests and views of towering peaks to its vital urban landscape and glistening waters, the visually stunning city of Seattle offers a perfect backdrop for feature films and television series of all genres. The scenery seems to lend itself to any plotline, from horror to drama to romantic comedy, and it has a star-studded history to prove it. The city's film career began in 1933 with *Tugboat Annie*, featuring actress Marie Dressler as a scrappy skipper, and has since included a number of popular films and television shows. More than sixty years later, the iconic romcom *10 Things I Hate About You* featured several of Seattle's most recognizable landmarks, including Gas Works Park. Of course, it would be blasphemous to mention local romcoms and leave out the 1993 classic *Sleepless in Seattle* (the houseboat remains a tourist attraction). Yet another well-known project filmed near Seattle is the genre-defying cult classic series *Twin Peaks*. The towns featured (see page 51) are frequently visited by *Twin Peaks* fans longing to perhaps catch a vapory glimpse of Laura Palmer in the mists of Snoqualmie Falls or taste-test Special Agent Dale Cooper's favorite "damn fine cup of coffee" and cherry pie.

MOVIES AND TV SHOWS FILMED IN SEATTLE

1933	Tugboat Annie
1963	It Happened at the World's Fair
1977	MacArthur
1980	The Changeling
1982	An Officer and a Gentleman
1987	Harry and the Hendersons
1987	House of Games
1988	The Chocolate War
1989	Three Fugitives
1989	The Fabulous Baker Boys
1989	Say Anything
1990	Twin Peaks
1991	Dogfight
1991	My Own Private Idaho
1992	Singles
1993	Bill Nye the Science Guy
1993	Sleepless in Seattle
1993	Little Buddha
1994	Disclosure
1995	Mad Love
1998	The Real World
1999	10 Things I Hate About You
2001	Rock Star
2002	The Ring
2005	Grey's Anatomy
2009	Man v. Food
2006	Expiration Date
2007	Battle in Seattle
2007	88 Minutes
2009	World's Greatest Dad
2013	21 & Over
2013	Touchy Feely
2013	Matt's Chance
2014	Laggies
2014	Beta Test

BAINBRIDGE ISLAND

Disclosure

MacArthur

BREMERTON

An Officer and a Gentleman

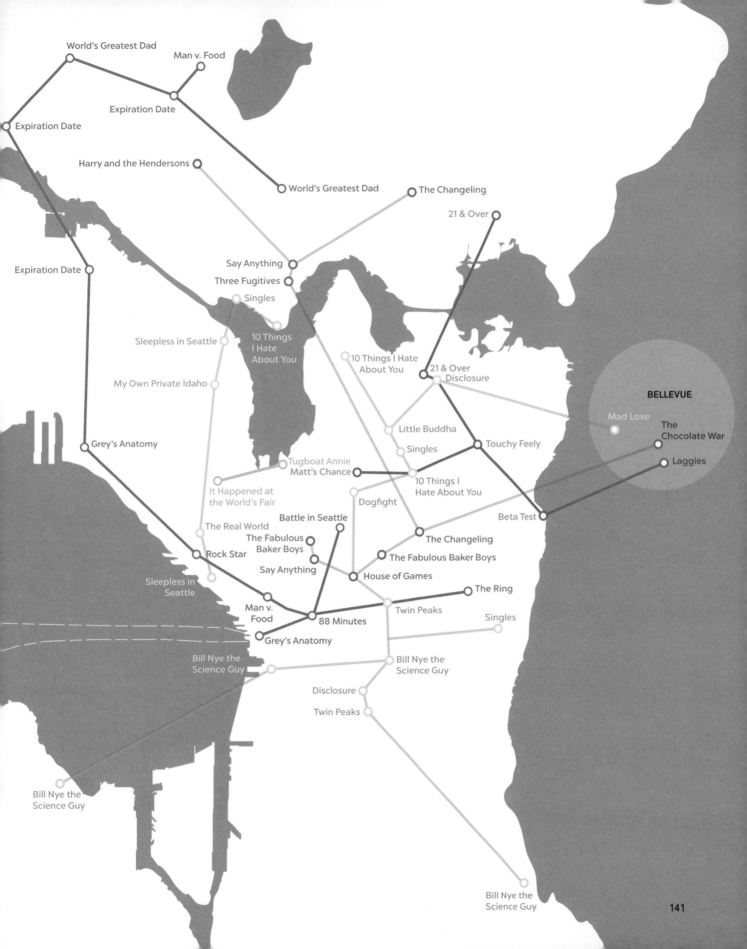

WELCOME TO SEATTLE

Washington is growing. From 2010 to 2016, the state grew 8.5 percent compared to California's 5.4 percent and New York's 2 percent. Even more impressive is Seattle's growth of a whopping 15.7 percent—a much higher number than big cities like New York and Los Angeles, which both saw about 5 percent growth during that time. So where do all these people come from, and why are they coming? Thanks to the University of Minnesota IPUMS-USA birthplace data set, we can look back over the last 150 years to find trends and interesting anomalies.

The gold rush era and the building of transcontinental railroads attracted East Coasters and Midwesterners alike at the turn of the twentieth century, with Minnesotans topping the list of new residents as the era culminated in the 1909 world's fair. The 1950s and '60s saw a boom as Boeing and the aerospace industry took hold in the region, culminating with a world's fair focused on space-age technology. This is when the scales tipped toward newcomers from western and southern states like California, Texas, and Hawaii. Today, the population influx is greatly influenced by Amazon's hiring frenzy, bringing in many more people from outside the United States than has been seen in recent decades.

Within the city of Seattle, the top five places that new residents moved from between 2015 and 2016 were Los Angeles, Phoenix, San Diego, Portland, and Chicago. The recent population boom has created a scarcity of housing, which is increasing prices far beyond the pace of median incomes. Between 2016 and 2017, Seattle's average home price increased by 13.4 percent, landing at $750,000. Compare that to Phoenix's average price of $190,000 and you may wonder when Seattleites will start moving south. And while Seattle has seen the highest wage increases in the country during that time, they rose only 4.8 percent—still not keeping pace.

So how does Seattle measure up in other ways? On the following pages, we look at demographic census data for three cities of similar size to Seattle, situated in different parts of the country. A city by the numbers is clearly not the whole story, but it's an interesting jumping-off point for more exploration.

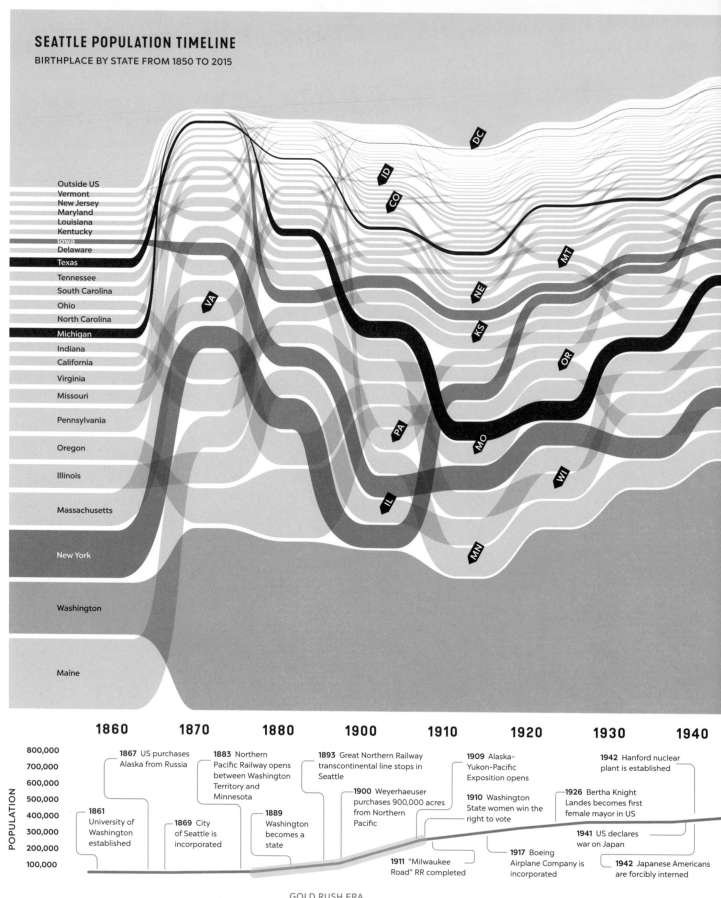

SEATTLE POPULATION TIMELINE
BIRTHPLACE BY STATE FROM 1850 TO 2015

Outside US
Vermont
New Jersey
Maryland
Louisiana
Kentucky
Iowa
Delaware
Texas
Tennessee
South Carolina
Ohio
North Carolina
Michigan
Indiana
California
Virginia
Missouri
Pennsylvania
Oregon
Illinois
Massachusetts
New York
Washington
Maine

1860   1870   1880   1900   1910   1920   1930   1940

POPULATION

800,000
700,000
600,000
500,000
400,000
300,000
200,000
100,000

1867 US purchases Alaska from Russia

1883 Northern Pacific Railway opens between Washington Territory and Minnesota

1893 Great Northern Railway transcontinental line stops in Seattle

1909 Alaska-Yukon-Pacific Exposition opens

1942 Hanford nuclear plant is established

1900 Weyerhaeuser purchases 900,000 acres from Northern Pacific

1910 Washington State women win the right to vote

1926 Bertha Knight Landes becomes first female mayor in US

1861 University of Washington established

1869 City of Seattle is incorporated

1889 Washington becomes a state

1917 Boeing Airplane Company is incorporated

1941 US declares war on Japan

1911 "Milwaukee Road" RR completed

1942 Japanese Americans are forcibly interned

GOLD RUSH ERA

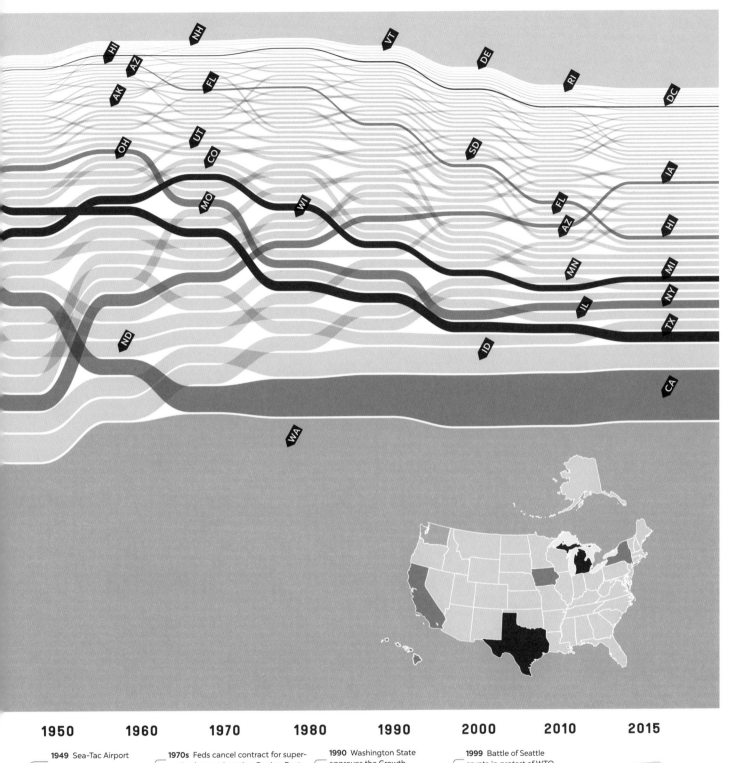

HI NH AZ VT DE RI DC
AK FL IA
OH UT CO SD FL HI
MO WI AZ MN MI
ND IL NY
ID TX
CA
WA

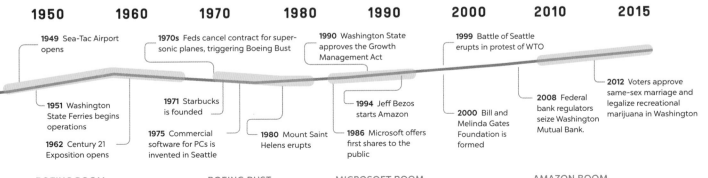

1950   1960   1970   1980   1990   2000   2010   2015

1949 Sea-Tac Airport opens

1970s Feds cancel contract for super-sonic planes, triggering Boeing Bust

1990 Washington State approves the Growth Management Act

1999 Battle of Seattle erupts in protest of WTO

1951 Washington State Ferries begins operations

1971 Starbucks is founded

1994 Jeff Bezos starts Amazon

2008 Federal bank regulators seize Washington Mutual Bank.

2012 Voters approve same-sex marriage and legalize recreational marijuana in Washington

1962 Century 21 Exposition opens

1975 Commercial software for PCs is invented in Seattle

1980 Mount Saint Helens erupts

1986 Microsoft offers first shares to the public

2000 Bill and Melinda Gates Foundation is formed

BOEING BOOM   BOEING BUST   MICROSOFT BOOM   AMAZON BOOM

PEOPLE IN THE CITY

While Seattle is exceptional in its recent growth, there are many other ways in which it stands out. These charts compare Seattle to three other cities of similar size (about seven hundred thousand people) in different regions of the United States. In many ways, Seattle is most similar to Washington, DC. Both have more than the average number of highly educated, unmarried twenty- and thirtysomethings born in another state who are fairly wealthy and well employed.

However, they differ significantly in racial makeup; Seattle is majority white while both DC and Detroit are majority African American and El Paso is majority Hispanic. More foreign-born Seattleites come from Asian countries—China being the most frequently represented—than foreign-born residents of the other cities.

This data comes from the US Census Bureau's 2015 American Community Survey. It is a macro-level snapshot in time and clearly misses some of the important nuances of Seattle's character, which are explored in other parts of the book.

 SEATTLE, WA

AGE

Under 5 years
5 to 9 years
10 to 14 years
15 to 19 years
20 to 24 years
25 to 34 years
35 to 44 years
45 to 54 years
55 to 59 years
60 to 64 years
65 to 74 years
75 to 84 years
85 years and over

BIRTH
Inside/Outside State

State of residence
Different state

BIRTH
Inside/Outside US

Native-born population
Foreign-born population

Naturalized U.S. citizen
Not a U.S. citizen

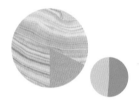

FOREIGN BIRTHPLACE

Europe
Asia
Africa
Oceania
Latin America
Northern America

RACE

White
Black or African American
American Indian/Alaska Native
Asian
Native Hawaiian/Pacific Islander
Other race

Hispanic or Latino (of any race)
Not Hispanic or Latino

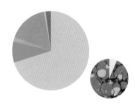

MARRIAGE

Never married
Married
Separated
Widowed
Divorced

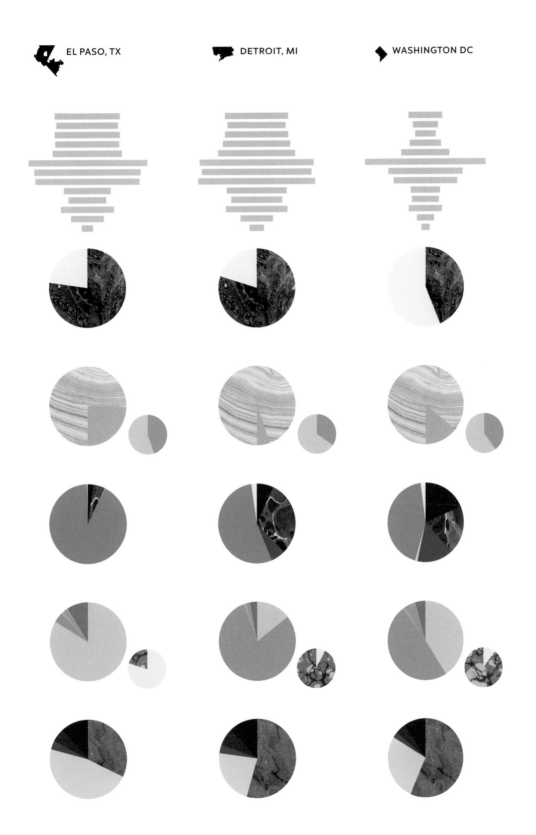

EL PASO, TX DETROIT, MI WASHINGTON DC

 SEATTLE, WA

INCOME

Less than $10,000	22,160
$10,000 to $14,999	10,981
$15,000 to $24,999	20,991
$25,000 to $34,999	22,540
$35,000 to $49,999	32,748
$50,000 to $74,999	46,235
$75,000 to $99,999	35,702
$100,000 to $149,999	49,142
$150,000 to $199,999	25,332
$200,000 or more	30,852

poverty

EMPLOYMENT

In labor force
Not in labor force

Employed
Unemployed

RENT VS OWN

Owner occupied & Average home value
Renter occupied & Average monthly rent

Home Value

$1,185

$452,800

EDUCATION

Less than 9th grade
9th to 12th grade, no diploma
High school graduate
Some college, no degree
Associate's degree
Bachelor's degree
Graduate or professional degree

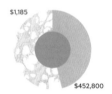

TRANSPORTATION

Car, truck, or van (single occupant)
Car, truck, or van (carpool)
Public transportation
Walks
Other means
Works at home

SAME-SEX HOUSEHOLDS

Male partners
Female partners

 EL PASO, TX    DETROIT, MI   ◆ WASHINGTON DC

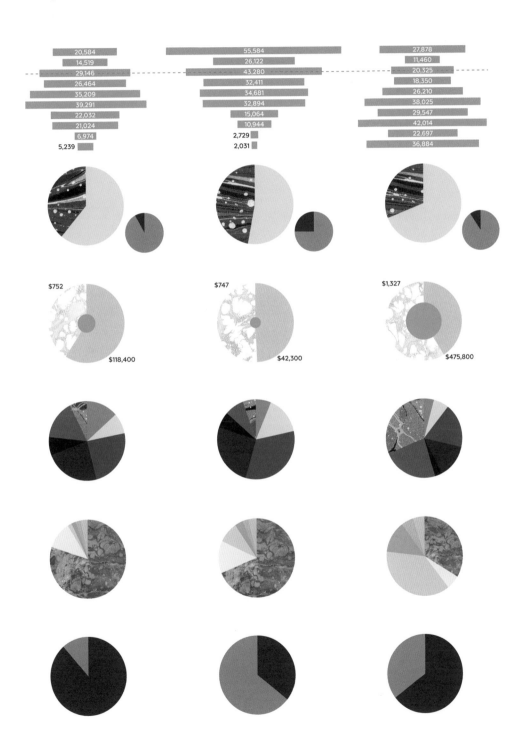

EL PASO, TX	DETROIT, MI	WASHINGTON DC
20,584	55,584	27,878
14,519	26,122	11,460
29,146	43,280	20,325
26,464	32,411	18,350
35,209	34,681	26,210
39,291	32,894	38,025
22,032	15,064	29,547
21,024	10,944	42,014
6,974	2,729	22,697
5,239	2,031	36,884

$752 — $118,400 $747 — $42,300 $1,327 — $475,800

SEATTLE BY ANY OTHER NAME

What's in a (nick)name? Seattle has been known as the Emerald City since the 1980s, but recently some have expressed that this moniker doesn't fully describe the city's current vibe. It has also been known as Jet City, Rain City, and the City of Flowers, but some Seattleites don't think these quite fit the bill either. The blog of Seattle-based real-estate company Estately decided to throw in its two cents and offer a few new nickname ideas, including City of Swass, in honor of Seattle rapper Sir Mix-a-Lot's debut album, and Highest City at Sea Level (pun very much intended).

While the future of the city's nickname may be uncertain, Seattle's neighborhood names seem to be standing the test of time. When the Denny party settled in the area in 1851, unique neighborhoods began to identify themselves, and they have evolved with the city through the decades. The origins of Seattle's neighborhood names is varied and diverse. Ballard is named after Captain William Ballard, who had to take full responsibility of the then-unwanted land plot after losing a coin toss to his business partner. Guess the joke's on the other guy. The Queen Anne neighborhood sits on a glacial hill and is named for the architectural style of the homes first built there. Seattle's oldest established neighborhood, Pioneer Square, was the city's original downtown. Each Seattle neighborhood has a feel and culture as unique as the history behind its name, and while the names stay the same, these bustling districts continue to grow and evolve.

SEATTLE NICKNAMES – – – – – – – – – Years in use

Neighborhood Name – – – – – – – A

A Selected Neighborhood year name established

Phinney Ridge
Pinehurst
Pioneer Square
PITTSBURGH – – – – – – – – – – –
OF THE WEST
Portage Bay
Queen Anne
QUEEN CITY – – – – – –
Rainier Valley – – – – – CITY OF FLOWERS – – – – –
RAT CITY – – – – – – – –
Ravenna
Roosevelt
Sand Point
Seward Park
Sodo
South Beach
South Lake Union
South Park
THE 206 – – – – – – – – – – – – – –
THE RATTLE – – – – – – – –
TIMBER TOWN – – – – – –
University District
View Ridge
Wallingford
Wedgwood
West Seattle
White Center
Windermere

Alki – – – – – –
Ballard – – – – – –
Beacon Hill
Belltown – – – – – –
Bitter Lake
Broadview
Capitol Hill – – – – –
Central District
Columbia
Crown Hill
Delridge – – – – –
Denny Triangle
Downtown
DUWAMPS
East lake – – – – –
EMERALD CITY – – – – –
First Hill
Fremont
Fauntleroy
Georgetown
Green Lake – – – – –
Greenwood – – – – –
Haller Lake
Harbor Island
Highland Park
Hillman City
Holly Park
Interbay – – – – –
International District
JET CITY – – – – –
Lake City
Laurelhurst
Leschi
LESSER SEATTLE – – – –
Licton Springs
Lower Queen Anne
Madison Park – – – – –
Madrona
Magnolia
Magnuson
METRONATURAL – – – –
Maple Leaf
Montlake
Mount Baker
North Beach – – – – –
Northgate

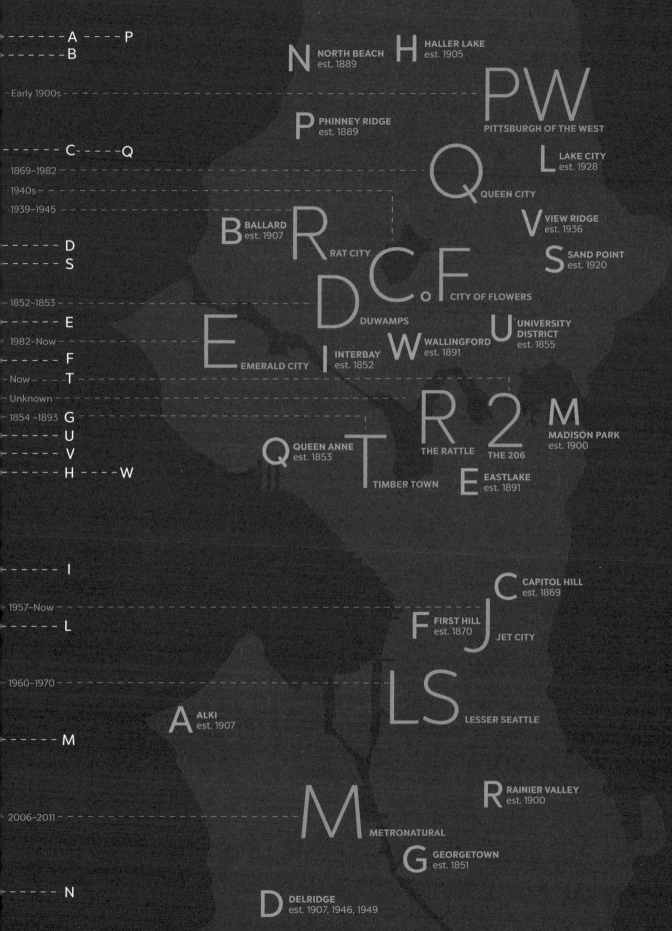

A —— P

B

Early 1900s

C ---- Q

1869–1982

1940s

1939–1945

D

S

1852–1853

E

1982–Now

F

Now --- T

Unknown

1854 –1893 G

U

G V

H ---- W

I

1957–Now

L

1960–1970

M

2006–2011

N

N NORTH BEACH
est. 1889

H HALLER LAKE
est. 1905

PW PITTSBURGH OF THE WEST

P PHINNEY RIDGE
est. 1889

Q QUEEN CITY

L LAKE CITY
est. 1928

B BALLARD
est. 1907

R RAT CITY

V VIEW RIDGE
est. 1936

S SAND POINT
est. 1920

D.C.F CITY OF FLOWERS

DUWAMPS

U UNIVERSITY
DISTRICT
est. 1855

E EMERALD CITY

I INTERBAY
est. 1852

W WALLINGFORD
est. 1891

R THE RATTLE

2 THE 206

M MADISON PARK
est. 1900

Q QUEEN ANNE
est. 1853

T TIMBER TOWN

E EASTLAKE
est. 1891

C CAPITOL HILL
est. 1869

F FIRST HILL
est. 1870

J JET CITY

LS LESSER SEATTLE

A ALKI
est. 1907

R RAINIER VALLEY
est. 1900

M METRONATURAL

G GEORGETOWN
est. 1851

D DELRIDGE
est. 1907, 1946, 1949

151

ACKNOWLEDGMENTS

For guidance, research, assistance, and advice, we are indebted to the Bigfoot Field Researchers Organization, Paul DeBarro, Andy Donovan, Paul Dorpat's *Seattle Now and Then*, Ross Eckert, Sarah Elwood, Historylink.com, Thomas Horton, Jake and Cathy Jaramillo, National USF Reporting Center, Pacific Northwest Seismic Network, Roxanne Robles, Seattle Municipal Archives, Seattle Public Library, and University of Washington Herbarium. Despite the help of so many persons, any errors, omissions, and mistakes are ours.

BIBLIOGRAPHY

AGAINST THE GRID

Berger, Knute. "The Case for Keeping Seattle's Streets Messy." *CityLab*, September 18, 2012. www.citylab.com/transportation/2012/09 /case-keeping-seattles-streets-messy/3308.

———. "The Grid vs. the Curve." *Crosscut*, August 27, 2012. http://crosscut .com/2012/08/seattle-needs-grid-olmsted-parks-boulevards.

———. "Seattle's Last Unnamed Places." *Crosscut*, March 16, 2010. http://crosscut .com/2010/03/seattles-last-unnamed-places.

Crowley, Walt. *National Trust Guide Seattle: America's Guide for Architecture and History Travelers*. New York: Wiley, 1998.

Google Maps. "Seattle." Accessed August 29, 2017. www.google.com/maps/place /Seattle,+WA.

"King County Parcels/Parcel Area." October 31, 2016. Data provided by permission of King County. Distributed by King County GIS Open Data. https://gis-kingcounty .opendata.arcgis.com/datasets/king-county-parcels—parcel-area.

Rochester, Junius. "King County, Founding of." HistoryLink.org, May 10, 1998. www.historylink.org/File/314.

Williams, David B. "Olmsted Parks in Seattle." HistoryLink.org, May 10, 1999. www.historylink.org/File/1124.

GRAY ANATOMY

Erdman, Jon. "America's Dreariest Cities." Weather.com, March 28, 2015. https://weather.com/news/news/americas-dreariest-cities.

Space Needle PanoCam. Accessed August 30, 2017. www.spaceneedle.com/webcam.

JET CITY

AirportIQ 5010. "Kenmore Air Harbor: Based Aircraft and Operations." Posted June 22, 2017. Accessed July 3, 2017. www.gcr1.com/5010web/airport .cfm?Site=W55&AptSecNum=2.

Alaska Yukon Pacific Exposition Photographs. From the University of Washington Libraries Digital Collections. Accessed August 30, 2017. http://digitalcollections.lib .washington.edu/cdm/search/collection/ayp/searchterm/balloon/field/all/mode /all/conn/and/order/title/ad/asc.

Boeing Company. "Historical Snapshot: X-15 Research Aircraft." Accessed August 30, 2017. www.boeing.com/history/products/x-15-research-aircraft.page.

Coen, Ross. "Ballooning and Aerial Photography at the Alaska-Yukon-Pacific Exposition of 1909." *Pacific Northwest Quarterly* 106, no. 1 (2014–2015): 16–24.

Davies, Ed, and Steve Ellis. *Seattle's Commercial Aviation 1908–1941*. Charleston, SC: Arcadia Publishing, 2009.

Federal Aviation Administration. "IFR Enroute Aeronautical Charts and Planning." Accessed July 3, 2017. www.faa.gov/air_traffic/flight_info/aeronav /digital_products/ifr.

——. "FAA Aeronautical Chart User's Guide." Accessed July 3, 2017. www.faa.gov /air_traffic/flight_info/aeronav/digital_products/aero_guide.

——. "VFR Raster Charts." Accessed July 3, 2017. www.faa.gov/air_traffic /flight_info/aeronav/digital_products/vfr.

Port of Seattle. "Sea-Tac Airport Yearly Activity Reports." Last modified February 8, 2017. www.portseattle.org/About/Publications/Statistics/Airport-Statistics/Pages /default.aspx.

"Rise of Boeing Industries a Romance of Aviation." *Seattle Municipal News*, June 8, 1929. From the Seattle Public Library Special Collections. Identifier: spl_ mn_198039_19_23. http://cdm16118.contentdm.oclc.org/cdm/compoundobject /collection/p16118coll7/id/10309/rec/4.

Stein, Alan J. "Silas Christofferson Shows Off Aeroplane, Bombs Seattle, on July 18, 1914." HistoryLink.org, August 2, 2001. www.historylink.org/File/3478.

VFRMap.com. "VFR Map of Sea-Tac Airport." Accessed July 3, 2017. http://vfrmap. com/?type=vfrc&lat=47.45&lon=-122.31&zoom=10.

Wikipedia. "Boeing 314 Clipper" entry. Accessed August 30, 2017. https ://en.wikipedia.org/wiki/Boeing_314_Clipper.

MOUNTAIN MORPHOLOGY

United States Geological Survey. "One Million-Scale Contours of the United States." Last modified February 6, 2017. https://nationalmap.gov/small_scale/mld/1contou .html.

Wikipedia. "List of Highest Mountain Peaks in Washington" entry. Accessed August 30, 2017. https://en.wikipedia.org/wiki /List_of_highest_mountain_peaks_in_Washington.

MOVERS + SHAPERS

Knute, Berger. "A Look at the Mountains and Rivers Moved to Build Seattle." *Crosscut*, October 9, 2015. http://crosscut.com/2015/10 /the-mountains-weve-moved-rivers-weve-created-to-build-seattle.

Wilma, David. "Harbor Island, at the Time the World's Largest Artificial Island, Is Completed in 1909." HistoryLink.org, November 6, 2001. historylink.org /File/3631.

RAISING SEATTLE

Baist, G. W. *Surveys of Seattle*. Map. Accessed August 25, 2017. http://www.edge -archive.com/maps/baist/Plates/02.pdf.

Balk, Gene. "Seattle's Population Boom Approaching Gold Rush Numbers." *Seattle Times*. Last modified September 14, 2015. www.seattletimes.com/seattle-news /data/seattles-population-boom-approaching-gold-rush-numbers.

Car in Rain, 1980s. Color photograph, ca. 1985. Seattle Municipal Archives Photograph Collection, Water Department Slides, Record Series 8200-14, Item Number 149279.

Accessed August 31, 2017. Retrieved from Flickr. www.flickr.com/photos
/seattlemunicipalarchives/11735301054. Creative Commons License (CC BY 2.0),
https://creativecommons.org/licenses/by/2.0.

Eldeby, Stefan. *DSC_228*. Color and cut-out photograph, taken May 6, 2010. Accessed
September 2, 2017. Retrieved from Wikimedia Commons. www.flickr.com
/photos/eldeby/4964322353/. Creative Commons License (CC BY 2.0), https
://creativecommons.org/licenses/by/2.0.

Emporis.com. "Fourth and Madison Building." Accessed August 25, 2017. https
://www.emporis.com/buildings/100522fourth-and-madison-building-seattle
-wa-usa.

Emporis.com. "Seattle." Accessed August 31, 2017. www.emporis.com/city/101046/
seattle-wa-usa.

Hamilton, Dennis. *West Seattle: Bicycling*. Color photograph, taken July 26, 2009.
Accessed August 31, 2017. Retrieved from Flickr. www.flickr.com
/photos/orcmid/3793215833. Creative Commons License (CC BY 2.0), https
://creativecommons.org/licenses/by/2.0.

Kemezis, Kathleen. "1411 4th Avenue Building (Seattle)." HistoryLink.org, May 4,
2009. www.historylink.org/File/9000.

King County Department of Assessments. "eReal Property: Parcel 094200-
0365." Accessed August 25, 2017. http://blue.kingcounty.com/Assessor
/eRealProperty/Detail.aspx?ParcelNbr=0942000365.

King County GIS Center. King County Parcel Viewer. Accessed August 31, 2017.
http://gismaps.kingcounty.gov/parcelviewer2.

Minnick, Benjamin. "With 58 Tower Cranes at Work, Seattle Leads the Nation—
Again." *Seattle Daily Journal of Commerce*, August 1, 2017. www.djc.com/news
/search.html?action=get&id=12102764.

Rosenberg, Mike, and Ángel González. "Thanks to Amazon, Seattle
Is Now America's Biggest Company Town." *Seattle Times*. Last
modified August 30, 2017. www.seattletimes.com/business/amazon/
thanks-to-amazon-seattle-is-now-americas-biggest-company-town.

Seafair Parade at 4th & Pike, 1954. Black-and-white photograph, taken July
31, 1954. Seattle Municipal Archives Photograph Collection, City Light
Photographic Negatives, Record Series 1204-01, Item Number 78631.
Accessed August 31, 2017. Retrieved from Flickr. www.flickr.com/photos/
seattlemunicipalarchives/35371534630/. Creative Commons License (CC BY 2.0),
https://creativecommons.org/licenses/by/2.0/deed.en.

Sherrard, Jean. "Seattle Now & Then: The Rainier Club & The Burnett
Home." *DorpatSherrardLomont* (blog). December 29, 2012. https://pauldorpat
.com/2012/12/29/seattle-now-then-the-rainier-club-the-burnett-home.

———. "Seattle Now & Then: Seattle General Hospital." *DorpatSherrardLomont*
(blog). February 28, 2014. https://pauldorpat.com/2014/02/28/
seattle-now-then-seattle-general-hospital.

Street Flusher, 1926. Black-and-white photograph, taken July 14, 1926. Seattle
Municipal Archives Photograph Collection, Department of Streets and
Sewers Photographs, Record Series 2625-10, Item Number 38183. Accessed

August 31, 2017. Retrieved from Flickr. www.flickr.com/photos
/seattlemunicipalarchives/11824321856. Creative Commons License (CC BY 2.0),
https://creativecommons.org/licenses/by/2.0.

Wikipedia. "Daniels Recital Hall" entry. Accessed August 20, 2017. https
://en.wikipedia.org/wiki/Daniels_Recital_Hall.

———. "F5 Tower" entry. Accessed August 21, 2017. https://en.wikipedia.org/wiki
/F5_Tower.

———. "Fourth and Madison Building" entry. Accessed August 21, 2017. https
://en.wikipedia.org/wiki/Fourth_and_Madison_Building.

———. "Rainier Club" entry. Accessed August 21, 2017. https://en.wikipedia.org/wiki
/Rainier_Club.

FLOATING FORTS

Abegg, Steph. "Fire Lookout Structures in Washington's Mountain Ranges."
Accessed August 30, 2017. www.stephabegg.com/home/projects/firelookouts.

Forest Fire Lookout Association, with Bill Starr, Rex Kamstra, and Ray Kresek. "Fire
Lookout Types." Accessed August 30, 2017. www.firelookout.org/fire-lookout
-types.html.

Forest History Society. "1910 Fires." Last modified December 18, 2014. www
.foresthistory.org/ASPNET/Policy/Fire/FamousFires/1910Fires.aspx.

———. "Fire Lookouts." Last modified October 25, 2013. https://foresthistory.org/
research-explore/us-forest-service-history/policy-and-law/fire-u-s-forest-service/
famous-fires/the-1910-fires.

Kamstra, Rex. "Northwest Washington Forest Fire Lookout Tower Sites." Accessed
August 30, 2017. www.firelookout.com/wanw.html.

Kresek, Ray. "Lookout Show n' Tell #2—Standard Lookout Designs." Accessed July 17,
2017. www.firelookouts.com/loshowntell.html.

"Maxine Meyers' Memories of Her Year as a Fire-Watcher, 1956." *Skagit River
Journal.* Last modified December 15, 2008. www.skagitriverjournal.com/Logging/
Firetowers/Towers02-Meyers.html.

National Historic Lookout Register. "Definitions." Last modified January 24, 2017.
http://nhlr.org/definitions.

———. "Miners Ridge Lookout US 75, WA 6." Last modified November 18, 2016. www
.nhlr.org/lookouts/us/wa/miners-ridge-lookout.

Suiter, John. *Poets on the Peaks: Gary Snyder, Philip Whalen & Jack Kerouac in the
Cascades.* Washington, DC: Counterpoint, 2002.

SummitPost. "North Mountain: Climbing, Hiking, and Mountaineering." Accessed
August 30, 2017. www.summitpost.org/north-mountain/615926.

United States Forest Service. Accessed August 30, 2017. www.fs.fed.us.

Washington Trails Association. Accessed August 30, 2017. www.wta.org.

Wilma, David. "Author Jack Kerouac Spends 63 Days as a Fire Lookout on Desolation
Peak in the Summer of 1956." HistoryLink.org. Last modified December 18, 2006.
www.historylink.org/File/8034.

SAUCERS IN THE SKY

Keeley, Sean. "Mapping the Many UFO Sightings around Puget Sound." *Curbed*, August 4, 2015. https://seattle.curbed.com/2015/8/4/9933836 /ufo-sightings-seattle-renton-bremerton-aliens-fireworks.

National UFO Reporting Center. Accessed August 30, 2017. nuforc.org.

AW, SHUCKS!

Echtle, Ed. "The Cultural History of the Olympia Oyster." City of Olympia. Last modified July 23, 2013. http://olympiawa.gov/community/parks/percival-landing /olympia-oyster.

"Kumamoto Oysters." Chefs-resources.com. Accessed August 1, 2017. www.chefs -resources.com/seafood/oysters/pacific-northwest-oysters/kumamoto-oysters.

Larson, Samantha. "The Raw Truth about Washington's Oysters." *Crosscut*, June 6, 2016. http://crosscut.com/2016/06/the-raw-truth-about-washingtons-oysters.

National Oceanic and Atmospheric Administration. Map of Puget Sound, Chart 18440. Accessed July 9, 2017. www.charts.noaa.gov/PDFs/18440.pdf.

"Oysters by Region." Oysterater.com. Accessed July 2, 2017. www.oysterater.com /oyster-map.

Oyster Guide. "Hood Canal and Southern Puget Sound." Accessed July 9, 2017. www .oysterguide.com/maps/hood-canal-and-southern-puget-sound.

——. "Northern Puget Sound." Accessed July 9, 2017. www.oysterguide.com/maps /northern-puget-sound.

Penn Cove Shellfish. "Oyster Types." Accessed July 9, 2017. www.penncoveshellfish .com/oyster-types.

"Puget Sound." Oysterater.com. Accessed August 1, 2017. https://www.oysterater .com/region/puget-sound.

Vermillion, Allecia. "The Five Oysters You Meet in Washington." *Seattle Met*. March 1, 2016, https://www.seattlemet.com/articles/2016/3/1 /the-five-oysters-you-meet-in-washington.

GUM WALL DISSECTION

Chen, Stephanie. "Kissing, Chewing—the 'Germiest' Tourist Attractions." CNN, July 20, 2009. Accessed August 20, 2017. http://edition.cnn.com/2009/TRAVEL/07/20 /germy.tourist.spots.

Crawford, Emily. "Pike Place Market's Famous Gum Wall Receives Complete Cleaning." Pike Place Market Preservation & Development Authority, November 3, 2015. www.pikeplacemarket.org/sites/default/files/Gum%20Wall%20 Announcement_11_3_15.pdf.

Donovan, Matt. Untitled color photograph of Gum Wall in Seattle, taken February 24, 2017. Reproduced with photographer's permission.

Eskenazi, Stuart. "Market Lost & Found." *Seattle Times*, August 6, 2007. www .seattletimes.com/seattle-news/market-lost-found.

Wikipedia. "Gum Wall" entry. Accessed August 1, 2017. https://en.wikipedia.org/wiki /Gum_Wall.

FERRY ROUTES

Shapely, Haley. "Scenic Washington Ferry Routes." Accessed August 22, 2017. www
.experiencewa.com/articles/scenic-washington-ferry-routes.

PIONEER SQUARE UNDERFOOT

Alliance for Pioneer Square. "Pioneer Square History." Accessed August 20, 2017.
www.pioneersquare.org/about/history.

Alliance for Pioneer Square. "Pioneer Square Street Concept Plans: Research and
Inventory." Accessed August 2, 2017. www.allianceforpioneersquare.org/what-
we-do/public-realm/streetscape-concept-plan.

Bill Speidel's Underground Tour. "A Little History." Accessed August 20, 2017. www
.undergroundtour.com/about/history.html.

Crowley, Walt. "Seattle Neighborhoods: Pioneer Square—Thumbnail History."
HistoryLink.org. Last modified May 2004. www.historylink.org/File/3392.

National Park Service. "Iron Pergola and Totem Pole." Accessed August 20, 2017.
www.nps.gov/nr/travel/seattle/s26.htm.

Pioneer Square, 1973. Black-and-white drawing, March 1973. Seattle Municipal
Archives via Flickr. Accessed August 20, 2017. www.flickr.com/photos
/seattlemunicipalarchives/2478146733. Creative Commons License (CC BY 2.0),
https://creativecommons.org/licenses/by/2.0.

Pioneer Square Pergola. Black-and-white photograph, taken October 4, 2013. From
Wikimedia Commons. Accessed August 20, 2017. https://commons.wikimedia.org
/wiki/File:Pioneer_Square_Pergola.jpg. Creative Commons License (CC BY-ND
2.0), https://creativecommons.org/licenses/by-nd/2.0.

Seattle Waterfront Streetcar, 1982. Color photograph, taken May 29, 1982. Seattle
Municipal Archives via Wikimedia Commons. Accessed August 20, 2017. https
://commons.wikimedia.org/wiki/File:Seattle_waterfront_streetcar,_1982.jpg.
Creative Commons License (CC BY 2.0), https://creativecommons.org/licenses
/by/2.0/deed.en.

Wikipedia. "Waterfront Streetcar" entry. Accessed August 20, 2017. https
://en.wikipedia.org/wiki/Waterfront_Streetcar.

———. "Smith Tower." Accessed August 20, 2017. https://en.wikipedia.org/wiki
/Smith_Tower.

TERRA-COTTA TIME CAPSULES

Archives West. University of Washington Miller Hall Façade Sculptures Photograph
Collection, ca. 1952. Accessed August 20, 2017.

Bauer, Harry C. "A Dominant Architectural Role: The Henry Suzzallo Library, A
Fitting Symbol for the University of a Thousand Years." *The Washington Alumnus,*
Winter 1951.

"Gargoyles" Subject File. University of Washington Libraries Special Collections.

Kraft, Martin. *The Suzzallo Library of the University of Washington.* Color photograph,
taken September 24, 2013. Accessed August 31, 2017. Retrieved from Wikimedia
Commons. https://en.wikipedia.org/wiki/File:MK03214_University_of
_Washington_Suzzallo_Library.jpg. Creative Commons License (CC BY-SA 3.0),
https://creativecommons.org/licenses/by-sa/3.0.

Murtagh, Bridget. "Gargoyles About on Campus." *Diversions*, Date Unknown.

Parker, Wally Lee. "The Suzzallo Statues." Clayton & Deer Park Historical Society, 2007. Accessed August 30, 2017. cdphs.org/suzzallo-statures.html.

Tiller, Pete. "UW Grotesques Revealed." *UW Daily*, Date Unknown.

UW 360: Gargoyles & Grotesques. YouTube video, 4:07, posted by UWTV, University of Washington, December 12, 2013. www.youtube.com/watch?v=HLm-3DKEQk8.

A DAMN FINE CUP OF COFFEE

Hobbes, Laural, Grace Geiger, and Rachel Hart. "Coffee Land." *Seattle*, October 2010. Accessed March 29, 2017. https://lamarzoccousa.files.wordpress.com/2010/10 /seattle-mag-timeline.jpg.

Yelp. "Seattle." Accessed March 29, 2017. www.yelp.com/seattle.

TWIN PEAKS: REAL + STRANGE

Google. "Twin Peaks Locations." www.google.com/maps/d/viewer?mid=1_ VAU78819-9BV1QmLuKvlNHLulc&hl=en_US&ll=47.734878286810954%2C- 122.1838315&z=10.

Dom, Pieter. "Twin Peaks Maps." August 10, 2011. welcometotwinpeaks.com /locations/twin-peaks-maps.

SASQUATCH SIGHTINGS

Bigfoot, Johnny. "Bigfoot Declared to Exist By US Army." *Bigfoot Research News*, July 12, 2013. www.bigfootresearchnews.com/2013/07/bigfoot-declared-to-exist-by-us -army.html.

Bigfoot Field Researchers Organization. Accessed August 30, 2017. www.bfro.net /GDB/state_listing.asp?state=wa.

ISLANDS OF THE SALISH SEA

Anderson, Ross. "One Man Is an Island." *Seattle Times*, October 19, 2006. community .seattletimes.nwsource.com/archive/?date=20061019&slug=protection19m.

Boney, Nigel. "The Forgotten San Juan Islands: Spieden and Lummi." *Snowshoe Magazine*, June 17, 2012. www.snowshoemag.com/2012/06/17 /the-forgotten-san-juan-islands-spieden-and-lummi.

Egan, Timothy. *The Good Rain: Across Time and Terrain in the Pacific Northwest*. New York: Knopf Doubleday, 2011.

Google Maps. "Puget Sound." Accessed May 7, 2017. www.google.com/maps/place /Puget+Sound.

Haupt, Jennifer. "A Whale of a Time on Spieden Island in the San Juans." *Seattle Times*, June 19, 1994. community.seattletimes.nwsource.com /archive/?date=19940619&slug=1916258.

Hillinger, Charles. "Caretakers Helping to Preserve the Peace on Protection Island: Birds Return to Where Developers Once Held Sway." *Los Angeles Times*, January 10, 1988. articles.latimes.com/1988-01-10/news/vw-34823_1_protection-island.

National Park Service. "San Juan Island Glacial Features." Accessed August 12, 2017. www.nps.gov/sajh/learn/nature/glaciers.htm.

Neumann-Rea, Kirby. "Caretaker of Wildlife Island Refuge Finds He Enjoys Solitude: Puget Sound: Volunteer and His Cat Are the Only Residents Other Than Birds, Deer and Harbor Seals." *Los Angeles Times*, February 26, 1995. articles.latimes.com/1995-02-26/local/me-36283_1_wildlife-island-refuge.

Shapiro, Talia. "Puget Sound's Hidden Island Adventures." *Seattle Weekly*, June 1, 2016. www.seattleweekly.com/news/puget-sounds-hidden-island-adventures.

United States Environmental Protection Agency. "Superfund Site: Harbor Island (Lead) Seattle, WA." Accessed May 7, 2017. https://cumulis.epa.gov/supercpad/cursites/csitinfo.cfm?id=1000949.

Weiser, Kathy. "Harbor Island—Largest Artificial Island in the U.S." December 2015. www.legendsofamerica.com/wa-harborisland.

Wilma, David. "Harbor Island, at the Time the World's Largest Artificial Island, Is Completed in 1909." HistoryLink.org. Last modified December 12, 2013. historylink.org/File/3631.

THE CITY BEAUTIFUL

10 Parks that Changed America: Episode 3. Streaming video, 56:10. PBS. Originally aired April 11, 2016. www.pbs.org/video/10-changed-america-10-parks-changed-america.

Diltz, Colin. "These 7 Photos Reveal How I-5 Construction Tore Through Old Seattle." *Seattle Times*, January 2, 2016. Last modified January 27, 2016. www.seattletimes.com/seattle-news/transportation/these-7-photos-reveal-how-i-5-construction-tore-through-old-seattle.

Friends of Mount Baker Town Center. "Olmsted System: Parks, Boulevards and Playgrounds of the City of Seattle." Color map, created December 1908. Accessed August 30, 2017. https://towncenterfriends.files.wordpress.com/2015/03/plan-for-seattle-park-system-1908.jpg.

Griffin, Tom. "Blooms in Doom." *Columns*, March 1999. www.washington.edu/alumni/columns/march99/blooms1.html.

Seattle Parks and Recreation. "Freeway Park." Accessed August 30, 2017. www.seattle.gov/parks/find/parks/freeway-park.

Wikipedia. "Gas Works Park" entry. Accessed August 30, 2017. https://en.wikipedia.org/wiki/Gas_Works_Park.

Wilma, David. "Kubota Garden (Seattle)." HistoryLink.org. Last modified November 4, 2011. www.historylink.org/File/3077.

LEGENDARY LADIES

Andrews, Mildred. "Bullitt, Dorothy Stimson (1892–1989)." HistoryLink.org, March 13, 1999. www.historylink.org/File/677.

———. "Landes, Bertha Knight (1868–1943)." HistoryLink.org, March 2, 2003. www.historylink.org/File/5343.

Becker, Paula. "Dusanne, Zoe (1884–1972), Modern-Art Dealer." HistoryLink.org, February 16, 2003. www.historylink.org/File/5222.

———. "Nishitani, Martha (1920–2014)." HistoryLink.org, October 8, 2013. www.historylink.org/File/10638.

Blecha, Peter. "Guitar, Bonnie (b. 1923): The Northwest's Trail-Blazing Pop Pioneer."
    HistoryLink.org, June 19, 2008. www.historylink.org/File/8656.

Chesley, Frank. "Chow, Ruby (1920–2008)." HistoryLink.org. Last modified June 4,
    2008. www.historylink.org/File/8063.

Denny, Brewster C. *Talk by Brewster Denny, Given to the Pioneer Association of the State
    of Washington, November 2, 1996*. Retrieved from HistoryLink.org, "Central Themes
    of Washington History: Land, Cities, Women—a Talk by Brewster Denny." Posted
    May 7, 2001. www.historylink.org/File/3262.

Eng, Lily. "Educator Roberta Byrd Barr Dies At 74—TV Host, Principal Had Key
    Community Role." *Seattle Times*, June 25, 1993. community.seattletimes.nwsource
    .com/archive/?date=19930625&slug=1708145.

Henry, Mary T. "Barr, Roberta Byrd (1919–1993)." HistoryLink.org, November 9, 1998.
    www.historylink.org/File/306.

———. "Shu, Dr. Ruby Inouye (1920–2012)." HistoryLink.org, April 11, 2012. www
    .historylink.org/File/10053.

MacIntosh, Heather M. "Ayer, Elizabeth (1897–1987), Architect." HistoryLink.org,
    October 4, 1998. www.historylink.org/File/1721.

Morgan, Murray. *Skid Road. An Informal Portrait of Seattle*. Seattle: University of
    Washington Press, 1982.

Shelton, Don. "Happy 100th Birthday to Seattle's Greatest Female Athlete." *Seattle
    Times*, June 19, 2013. http://blogs.seattletimes.com/take2/2013/06/1
    9/happy-100th-birthday-to-seattles-greatest-female-athlete.

Stein, Alan. "Madison, Helene (1913–1970)." HistoryLink.org, June 19, 2014. www
    .historylink.org/File/293.

Wong, Brad. "Ruby Chow, 1920–2008: City Loses Political, Cultural Trailblazer."
    Seattle Post-Intelligencer, June 4, 2008. www.seattlepi.com/local/article/Ruby-Chow
    -1920-2008-City-loses-political-1275470.php.

PUTTING DOWN ROOTS

American Forests. "Big Trees." Accessed August 30, 2017. www.americanforests.org
    /big-trees.

Blecha, Peter. "Ravenna Park (Seattle)." HistoryLink.org, January 23, 2011. www
    .historylink.org/File/9559.

Caldbick, John. "Henry Yesler's Steam-Powered Seattle Sawmill Cuts Its First
    Lumber in Late March 1853." HistoryLink.org, August 1, 2014. www.historylink
    .org/File/760.

City of Seattle. "Heritage Trees." Last modified June 7, 2013. Statistical table provided
    by City of Seattle My Neighborhood Map program. https://data.seattle
    .gov/Community/Heritage-Trees/5979-eagq.

Elman, Ella, and Nelson Salisbury. *The State of Seattle's Conifer Forests*. Seattle Urban
    Nature, 2009. www.seattle.gov/trees/docs/2009_State_of_Conifers.pdf.

Green Seattle Partnership. "Reference Ecosystems." Accessed August 30, 2017. www
    .greenseattle.org/information-for/forest-steward-resources/restoration-resources
    /reference-ecosystems.

Jacobson, Arthur Lee. "Tall Tales from the Northwest: Big Trees of Seattle."
    Accessed August 30, 2017. www.arthurleej.com/a-talltales.html.

Jacobson, Arthur Lee, and Jerry Clark. "Pioneering Seattle's Historical Trees." Accessed August 30, 2017. www.arthurleej.com/a-pioneering.html.

Morris, Ryan, Meg Roosevelt, Xaquín G. V., and Matthew Twombly. "Nine Cities That Love Their Trees." *National Geographic*. Accessed August 30, 2017. www .nationalgeographic.com/news-features/urban-tree-canopy.

O'Neil-Dunne, Jarlath. *2016 Seattle Tree Canopy Assessment*. University of Vermont Spatial Analysis Laboratory. Accessed August 30, 2017. www.seattle.gov/trees /docs/Seattle2016CCAFinalReportFINAL.pdf.

Seattle Department of Transportation. "Seattle Tree Inventory [Introduction and Summary]." Accessed August 30, 2017. www.seattle.gov/transportation /treeinventory.htm.

——. *Seattle Street Trees* map. Accessed August 30, 2017. web6.seattle.gov/sdot/streettrees.

Seattle Tree Map. Accessed August 30, 2017. www.seattletreemap.org/map.

Williams, David B. *Seattle Walks: Discovering History and Nature in the City*. Seattle: University of Washington Press, 2017.

HUMBLE BEGINNINGS OF SEATTLE'S PUBLIC LIBRARY

Becker, Paula. "Central Library, 1906–1957, The Seattle Public Library." HistoryLink .org, July 1, 2011. www.historylink.org/File/9869.

Long, Priscilla. "Seattle Public Library Housed in Yesler Mansion Burns Down on January 1, 1901." HistoryLink.org, January 1, 2000. www.historylink.org/File/1923.

Seattle Department of Neighborhoods. "Seattle Historical Sites: Summary for 311-1/2 Occidental Way/Parcel ID 5247800355/Inv #." Accessed August 31, 2017. web6 .seattle.gov/DPD/HistoricalSite/QueryResult.aspx?ID=-824966132.

Seattle Public Library. "History of the Central Library." Accessed August 31, 2017. www.spl.org/locations/central-library/cen-about-the-central-library/cen-history.

Wikipedia. "Seattle Central Library" entry. Accessed August 31, 2017. https ://en.wikipedia.org/wiki/Seattle_Central_Library.

SEATTLE'S LITTLE LAKE

Caldbick, John. "Builders of Classic Boats, Lake Union (Seattle)." HistoryLink.org, June 12, 2017. www.historylink.org/File/20366.

DCS Films. "Lake Union Relics." Accessed August 31, 2017. www.dcsfilms.com /Site_4/Lake_Union_Wrecks.html.

Gauvin, Brian. "For Seattle's Fremont Tugboat, Small Has Been Beautiful for 100 Years." *Professional Mariner*, April 29, 2015. www.professionalmariner.com /May-2015/For-Seattles-Fremont-Tugboat-small-has-been-beautiful-for-100-years.

Herrera Environmental Consultants. *Puget Sound No Discharge Zone for Vessel Sewage Puget Sound Vessel Population and Pumpout Facilities*. Prepared for Washington State Department of Ecology, April 27, 2012. Publication No. 12-10-031, part 3. https ://fortress.wa.gov/ecy/publications/parts/1210031part3.pdf.

MarineTraffic. "Port of Seattle (US SEA) Details." Accessed August 31, 2017. www .marinetraffic.com/en/ais/details/ports/194.

McDowell Group. *Economic Impacts of the Hiram M. Chittenden Locks*. Prepared for Lake Washington Ship Canal Users Group, June 2017. www.portseattle.org/Commercial -Marine/Documents/Final%20locks%20study%206-19-17.pdf.

National Oceanic and Atmospheric Administration. "Nautical Chart." Lake Union
Laboratory. Accessed August 31, 2017. lulab.be.washington.edu/omeka/items
/show/237.

Periscopic Map Co. "Historic Map, Seattle, WA, 1903: Main business district
periscopic Seattle." Accessed April 22, 2017. www.worldmapsonline.com/
kr-1903-se.htm.

PINBALL WIZARDS

"Data Dump!" Pincast episode 46. Skill Shot. Accessed August 31, 2017. www.skill
-shot.com/content/pincast-episode-46-data-dump,11305.

Morris-Lent, Chris. "A Journey into Seattle's Flipping Rad Pinball Scene." *Seattle
Weekly*, February 2, 2016. archive.seattleweekly.com
/home/962879-129/a-journey-into-seattles-welcoming-sprawling.

"Seattle Pinball Map." Accessed August 31, 2017. https://pinballmap.com/seattle.

Saez, Rosin. "A Pinball Rebirth Is Happening in Seattle." *Seattle Met*, July 14, 2017.
www.seattlemet.com/articles/2017/7/14/a-pinball-rebirth-is-happening-in-seattle.

Skill Shot. "Feature Audits [Seattle Pinball Scene]." Accessed August 31, 2017. www
.skill-shot.com/content/feature-audits,7435.

I ♥ THE '90s

Azzerad, Michael. "Grunge City: The Seattle Scene." *Rolling Stone*, April 16, 1992.
www.rollingstone.com/music/news/grunge-city-the-seattle-scene-19920416.

Bush, Evan. "How Chris Cornell and Soundgarden Shaped Seattle's Music
Scene—and 'Destroyed the '80s Music.'" *Seattle Times*. Last modified May 18, 2017.
www.seattletimes.com/seattle-news/how-chris-cornell-and-soundgarden
-shaped-seattles-music-scene-and-destroyed-the-80s-music.

Google Maps. "Seattle Thrift Stores." Accessed August 31, 2017. www.google.com
/maps/d/viewer?mid=1kHjWBiXsJyfQkoErrKztee733dI.

Grunge Forum. "Mother Love Bone Walls" [Discussion Board]. Accessed August 31,
2017. www.grungeforum.com/viewtopic.php?t=22974.

Hype! Directed by Doug Pray. Online format. USA: Lions Gate, 1996.

Keeley, Sean. "Mapping Seattle Thrift Stores In Macklemore's 'Thrift Shop' Video."
Curbed Seattle, January 3, 2013. https://seattle.curbed.com/maps
/mapping-seattle-thrift-stores-in-macklemores-thrift-shop-video.

Kreps, Daniel. "Grunge Era Musical in Development at Seattle Theater."
Rolling Stone, July 7, 2017. rollingstone.com/music/news/
grunge-era-musical-in-development-at-seattle-theater-w491442.

McMahon, Meredith. "Second-Hand Seattle." *Crosscut*, October 2, 2008. crosscut
.com/2008/10/secondhand-seattle.

"Mother Love Bone Mural Outside Easy Street Records." PearlJam.com discussion
board. Accessed August 31, 2017. http://community.pearljam.com
/discussion/255555/mother-love-bone-mural-outside-easy-street-records-update.

Trask, Ara. "My Great Northwestern Adventure." *South of Sanity*. Accessed August 31,
2017. https://aratrask.wordpress.com/tag/washington.

Wikipedia. "Grunge" entry. Accessed August 11, 2017. https://en.wikipedia.org/wiki/
Grunge.

Wikipedia. "Hype!" entry. Accessed August 31, 2017. https://en.wikipedia.org/wiki/Hype!.

SEATTLE STRATA

Billen, Rae Ellen. "Bertha Rescue Plan on Hold While Archaeologists Check Soil for
Sites." KNKX. http://knkx.org/post/bertha-rescue-plan-hold-while-archaeologists
-check-soil-sites, March 14, 2014.

Boswell, Sharon, and Lorraine McConaghy. "City Reshaped: Up and Down." *Seattle
Times*, March 17, 1996. old.seattletimes.com/special/centennial/march/reshaped.html.

Chiang, Connie, and Michael Reese. "Section II: Seeing the Forest for the Trees," in
Evergreen State: Exploring the History of Washington's Forests. Center for the Study of
the Pacific Northwest, University of Washington Department of History. Accessed
August 31, 2017. www.washington.edu/uwired/outreach/cspn
/Website/Classroom%20Materials/Curriculum%20Packets/Evergreen%20State
/Section%20II.html.

DeCoster, Dotty. "Colman Building (Seattle)." HistoryLink.org, July 27, 2008. www
.historylink.org/File/8708.

DeMay, Daniel. "Photos: A Tale of the Northwest's Logging Past." *Seattle Post-
Intelligencer*. Last modified September 2, 2016. www.seattlepi.com/local/seattle
-history/article/Photos-A-tale-of-the-Northwest-s-logging-past-6775332.php.

"The Exile to Ballast Island." Duwamish Tribe. http://duwamishtribe.org
/ballastisland.html.

"The Great Seattle Fire." University of Washington Libraries Digital Collections.
Accessed August 31, 2017. https://content.lib.washington.edu/extras/seattle-fire
.html.

Robinson, Robert A., Edward Cox, and Martin Dirks. "Tunneling in Seattle—A
History of Innovation." North American Tunneling Conference, Seattle, 2002.
Distributed by www.discovery.org/scripts/viewDB/filesDB-download
.php?command=download&id=3901.

THE PLACES BETWEEN

Alliance for Pioneer Square. *Pioneer Square Alleys Design Manual*. October 2015.
Retrieved from http://allianceforpioneersquare.org/what-we-do/public-realm
/alley-activation/alley-designs.

Fialko, Mary, and Jennifer Hampton. *Seattle Integrated Alley Handbook: Activating Alleys
for a Lively City*. University of Washington Green Futures Lab, October 8, 2014.
http://greenfutures.washington.edu/images/publications/Activating_Alleys
_for_a_Lively_City.pdf.

Framework. "World Cup Alley." Accessed August 31, 2017. http://weareframework
.com/portfolio/world-cup-alley.

Otárola, Miguel. "Seattle's Alleys Getting a Face-Lift." *Seattle Times*. Last modified
July 10, 2017. www.seattletimes.com/seattle-news
/fear-inducing-places-getting-fresh-look-and-lively-character-2.

Toole, Daniel. *Alleys of Seattle*. Accessed August 31, 2017. https://alleysofseattle.com.

Alaska-Yukon-Pacific Exposition Digital Collection. Identifier: mohai_
ayp_2006.3.46.5. Accessed Jan. 15, 2017. http://cdm16118.contentdm.oclc.org/cdm
/ref/collection/p200301coll1/id/274.

Becker, Paula, and Alan J. Stein. *The Future Remembered: The 1962 Seattle World's Fair
and Its Legacy*. Seattle: Seattle Center Foundation, 2011.

Century 21 Exposition. *Official Guide Book, Seattle World's Fair 1962*. Seattle: Acme
Publications, 1962. From the Seattle Public Library Century 21 Digital Collection.
Identifier: spl_c21_717441. Accessed January 15, 2017. http://cdm15015.contentdm
.oclc.org/cdm/compoundobject/collection/p15015coll3/id/2588/rec/4.

*Century 21/Seattle World's Fair. Aerial Close-Up of Top of Space Needle. Vita-
Vue Slide*. Seattle Municipal Archives Photograph Collection, World's
Fair Slides, Record Series 9955-01, Item Number 73110. Created 1962.
Accessed August 31, 2017. Retrieved from Flickr. www.flickr.com/photos/
seattlemunicipalarchives/35199816835/. Creative Commons License (CC BY 2.0),
https://creativecommons.org/licenses/by/2.0.

*Official Guide to the Alaska-Yukon-Pacific Exposition: Seattle, Washington, June 1 to
October 16, 1909*. Seattle: A.Y.P.E. Publishing Co., 1909. From the Seattle Public
Library Alaska-Yukon-Pacific Exposition Digital Collection. Identifier: mohai_
ayp_2006.3.28. Accessed January 15, 2017. http://cdm16118.contentdm.oclc.org
/cdm/ref/collection/p200301coll1/id/3629.

"Part IV. The Buildings," in *No Finer Site: The University of Washington's Early Years on
Union Bay*, web exhibition. University of Washington Libraries Special Collections.
Accessed January 16, 2017. www.lib.washington.edu/specialcollections
/collections/exhibits/site/bldgs.

Reid, Robert A. *Official Ground Plan: Alaska-Yukon-Pacific Exposition, Seattle, June 1, to Oct.
16, 1909* map. Accessed January 16, 2017. www.expomuseum.com/1909/1909-map.jpg.

Rognon, Orville J. *Dirigible Balloon "Alaska Yukon Pacific Exposition" on the Ground,
Alaska Yukon Pacific Exposition, Seattle, June 1909*. Black-and-white photograph. From
the Seattle Public Library Alaska-Yukon-Pacific Exposition Digital Collection.
Negative number: UW18372. Accessed Jan. 15, 2017. http://digitalcollections.lib
.washington.edu/cdm/singleitem/collection/ayp/id/146/rec/9.

Sanborn Map Company. *Insurance Survey of Alaska-Yukon-Pacific Exposition, March 1909*
map. From Wikimedia Commons. Accessed January 16, 2017. https://commons.
wikimedia.org/wiki/File:Sanborn_A-Y-P_map.jpg. Public Domain (PD-US).

*Secretary's Report of the Alaska-Yukon-Pacific Exposition: Held at Seattle, June 1st to October
16th, 1909*. Seattle: Gateway Print Co., 1909. From the Seattle Public Library Alaska-
Yukon-Pacific Exposition Digital Collection. Identifier: spl_ayp_324355. Accessed
January 15, 2017. http://cdm16118.contentdm.oclc.org/cdm/ref/collection
/p200301coll1/id/2835.

Space Needle Under Construction, 1961. Vita-Vue Slide. Seattle Municipal Archives
Photograph Collection, World's Fair Slides, Record Series 1204-01, Item Number
165653. Created 1961. Accessed Sept. 5, 2017. Retrieved from Flickr. www.flickr
.com/photos/seattlemunicipalarchives/6175308389. Creative Commons License
(CC BY 2.0), https://creativecommons.org/licenses/by/2.0.

World's Fair Attendance Data, October 29, 1962. Folder 11, Box 196, Wesley C. Uhlman Subject Files, 5287-02. Seattle Municipal Archives. Accessed January 15, 2017. www.seattle.gov/Documents/Departments/CityArchive/DDL/WorldsFair /Oct291962.pdf.

STEEP STREETS

"The 20 Steepest Hills in Seattle." *Seattle Post-Intelligencer*, October 13, 2011. www .seattlepi.com/local/slideshow/The-20-steepest-hills-in-Seattle-31436.php.

Fucoloro, Tom. "(Some of) The Steepest Streets in Seattle." January 17, 2013. www .seattlebikeblog.com/2013/01/17/the-steepest-streets-in-seattle.

Langston, Jennifer. "New Route-Finding Map Lets Seattle Pedestrians Avoid Hills, Construction, Accessibility Barriers." *UW News*, February 1, 2017. www .washington.edu/news/2017/02/01/new-route-finding-map-lets-seattle -pedestrians-avoid-hills-construction-accessibility-barriers.

Seattle Department of Transportation. "Steep Streets in Seattle, Based on Survey Data, 1969." Accessed August 31, 2017. www.seattle.gov/transportation/steepest.htm.

JAZZ ON JACKSON

Blecha, Peter. "AFM Seattle Local 493 (1918–1958), 'Negro Musicians' Union." HistoryLink.org, February 19, 2013. Accessed June 18, 2017. www.historylink.org /File/10329.

De Barros, Paul. *Jackson Street After Hours: The Roots of Jazz in Seattle.* Seattle: Sasquatch Books, 2006.

Faltys-Burr, Kaegan. *Jazz on Jackson Street: The Birth of a Multiracial Musical Community in Seattle*, from the Great Depression in Washington State Project. Accessed June 18, 2017. https://depts.washington.edu/depress/jazz_jackson_street_seattle.shtml.

Henry, Mary T. "Cayton, Horace (1859–1940)." HistoryLink.org, November 9, 1998. Accessed June 18, 2017. www.historylink.org/File/309.

TLINGIT TOTEM

National Park Service. "Iron Pergola and Totem Pole." Accessed August 31, 2017. www.nps.gov/nr/travel/seattle/s26.htm.

Thrush, Coll. *Native Seattle: Histories from the Crossing-Over Place*, 2nd ed. Seattle: University of Washington Press, 2017.

Wilma, David. "Stolen Totem Pole Unveiled in Seattle's Pioneer Square on October 18, 1899." HistoryLink.org, January 1, 2000. www.historylink.org/File/2076.

Wright, Robin K. "Totem Poles: Heraldic Columns of the Northwest Coast." University of Washington Libraries Digital Collections. Accessed August 29, 2017. https://content.lib.washington.edu/aipnw/wright.html.

LITERARY SEATTLE

Alexie, Sherman. *Indian Killer*. New York: Grove Atlantic, 1996.

Beck, K. K. *We Interrupt This Broadcast*. New York: Mysterious Press, 1997.

"The Best Books about Seattle." *Seattle Anne: The Ultimate Guide to Seattle*. Last modified August 4, 2017. https://seattleanne.com/seattle-books.

Boudinot, Ryan. "20 Books Every Seattleite Should
    Read." *Seattle Met*, April 1, 2015. www.seattlemet.com/
    articles/2015/4/1/20-books-every-seattleite-should-read-april-2015.
Campbell, Cate. *Benedict Hall*. New York: Kensington, 2013.
Cassella, Carol. *Oxygen*. New York: Simon and Schuster, 2008.
Ferber, Edna. *Great Son*. Garden City, NY: Doubleday, Duran, 1945.
LibraryThing. All fiction with subject "Seattle, WA". Accessed August 31, 2017. www
    .librarything.com/subject/Seattle+%28Wash.%29%09Fiction.
———. [All fiction with tag "Seattle"]. Accessed August 31, 2017. www.librarything.
    com/tag/Seattle,+fiction.
Lynch, Jim. *Truth Like the Sun*. New York: Vintage Books, 2012.
Miller, John W. *America's Most Literate Cities, 2016*. Central Connecticut State
    University Center for Public Policy & Social Research. Accessed August 20, 2017.
    http://web.ccsu.edu/americasmostliteratecities/2016/default.asp.
Priest, Cherie. *Boneshaker*. New York: Tor Books, 2009.
Raban, Jonathan. *Waxwings*. New York: Pantheon Books, 2003.
"Required Reading: 40 Books Set in the Pacific Northwest." *Powell's City of Books Blog*,
    March 10, 2014. www.powells.com/post/required-reading
    /required-reading-40-books-set-in-the-pacific-northwest.
Robbins, Tom. *Still Life With Woodpecker*. New York: Bantam Books, 1980.
"Seattle Picks: Seattle Fiction." Seattle Librarians of the Seattle Public Library. Last
    modified March 2016. https://seattle.bibliocommons.com/list
    /show/72450558__seattle_librarians/74189047_seattle_picks_seattle_fiction.
Semple, Maria. *Where'd You Go, Bernadette*. New York: Little, Brown, 2012.
Stein, Garth. *A Sudden Light*. New York: Simon and Schuster, 2014.

FLOOD LINES

Washington State Department of Natural Resources Lidar Portal [lidar]. (2011).
    Thurston County, WA: Thurston County. Available: Puget Sound Lidar
    Consortium, Seattle, WA. Accessed October 13, 2017.
Washington State Department of Natural Resources Lidar Portal [lidar]. (2000–2005).
    Thurston County, WA: Puget Sound Lowlands. Available: Puget Sound Lidar
    Consortium, Seattle, WA. Accessed October 13, 2017.

FERRIED AWAY

Egan, Timothy. "Vashon Island Journal; Islanders Envision a Bridge Too Near." *New
    York Times*, March 9, 1992. www.nytimes.com/1992/03/11/us/vashon-island-journal
    -islanders-envision-a-bridge-too-near.html.
Evergreen Fleet. "The Flying Bird of Puget Sound: The Art-Deco Kalakala." Accessed
    July 22, 2017. www.evergreenfleet.com/kalakalasplashpage.html.
Jackson, Lester T. "2015 Comparison of Operational Performance: Washington State
    Ferries to Ferry Operators Worldwide." Washington State Transportation Center
    (TRAC), March 17, 2015. Last modified October 12, 2016. Publication Number
    WA-RD 750.2. www.wsdot.wa.gov/Research/Reports/700/750.2.htm.

Kalakala.org. "Kalakala Timeline: 1926 to Present." Accessed July 22, 2017. www
.kalakala.org/history/history_timeline.html.

Washington State Department of Transportation. "WSDOT Ferries Division: Nation's
Largest Ferry System." January 2017. www.wsdot.wa.gov/NR/rdonlyres/6C78A08B
-19A1-4919-B6E6-E9EF83E6376D/116404/WSFFactSheet2017_FINAL1.pdf.

———. "Ferry Vessel Watch." Accessed July 21, 2017. www.wsdot.com/ferries
/vesselwatch/Default.aspx.

———. "Vessels by Class." Accessed July 21, 2017. www.wsdot.com/ferries
/vesselwatch/Vessels.aspx.

Waugh, Kathleen. "Guide to the Records of Washington State Ferries." Washington
State Division of Archives and Records Management, April 2004. www.sos
.wa.gov/_assets/archives/Washington-State-Ferries-findingaid.pdf.

Wikipedia. "Washington State Ferries" entry. Accessed July 21, 2017. https
://en.wikipedia.org/wiki/Washington_State_Ferries.

BRIDGING THE GAP

Caldbick, John. "Chittenden, Hiram Martin (1858–1917)." HistoryLink.org, May 1, 2017.
www.historylink.org/File/20329.

———. "Montlake Bridge (Seattle)." HistoryLink.org, February 11, 2013. www
.historylink.org/File/10216.

Historic American Engineering Record. *Montlake Bridge, State Route 513 spanning
the Lake Washington Ship Canal, Seattle, King County, WA.* Written Historical and
Descriptive Data, August 1993. PDF document. Identifiers: HAER No. WA-108;
HAER WASH 17-SEAT, 14. Retrieved from the Library of Congress. Accessed
August 31, 2017. https://cdn.loc.gov/master/pnp/habshaer/wa/wa0400/wa0441
/data/wa0441data.pdf.

Logsdon, Mike. "Seattle Bridge Openings." *Stats on the Street*, October 4, 2015. https
://statsonthestreet.org/2015/10/04/seattle-bridge-openings.

Long, Priscilla. "Ballard Bridge (Seattle)." HistoryLink.org, April 4, 2017. www
.historylink.org/File/11260.

———. "Seattle's Fremont Bridge Opens to Traffic on June 15, 1917." HistoryLink.org,
June 15, 2005. www.historylink.org/File/3129.

Pacific Northwest Analytics. "Lake Washington Ship Canal Bridges." Accessed
August 31, 2017. www.pnw-analytics.com/bridge.html.

Seattle Department of Transportation. "Bridges and Roadway Structures: Bridge
Openings." Accessed August 31, 2017. www.seattle.gov/transportation
/bridgeopenings.htm.

Wikipedia. "Montlake Bridge" entry. Accessed August 31, 2017. https://en.wikipedia
.org/wiki/Montlake_Bridge.

CITY MICROCLIMATES

ClimaTemps.com. "Seattle, Washington Climate & Temperature." Accessed August
31, 2017. www.seattle.climatemps.com.

Lacitis, Erik. "Rain, and More Rain, Is in Our DNA: Your Seattle Survival Stories."
Seattle Times. Last modified March 18, 2017. www.seattletimes.com/seattle-news
/weather/rain-and-mwore-rain-is-in-our-dna-your-seattle-survival-stories.

Lam, Linda. "Seattle's Rainy Reputation Is Well-Deserved." The Weather Channel.
October 14, 2016. https://weather.com/science/weather-explainers/news
/seattle-rainy-reputation.

Metcalfe, John. "The Wet and Slightly Less Wet Microclimates of Seattle." *CityLab*,
October 14, 2015. www.citylab.com/environment/2015/10
/the-wet-and-slightly-less-wet-microclimates-of-seattle/410428.

"Rain Stats." *Seattle Weather Blog*. Accessed August 31, 2017. www
.seattleweatherblog.com/rain-stats.

United States Department of Agriculture, Natural Resources Conservation Service.
RUSLE2 Precipitation King County graphical map, August 2006. https://efotg.sc.egov
.usda.gov/references/public/WA/King_RUSLE2.pdf.

Wikipedia. "Seattle" entry. Accessed August 31, 2017. https://en.wikipedia.org/wiki
/Seattle.

SEATTLE FLOWS

NOAA/NOS/CO-OPS Preliminary Currents Data Observed
Currents at PUG1505, Entrance to Ballard Locks, 2016. Accessed
October 9, 2017. https://tidesandcurrents.noaa.gov/cdata/
DataPlot?id=PUG1504&bin=1&bdate=20150731&edate=20150731&unit
=1&timeZone=UTC.

NOAA/NOS/CO-OPS Preliminary Currents Data Observed Currents
at PUG1642, Strait of Juan de Fuca Entrance, 2016. Accessed
October 10, 2017. https://tidesandcurrents.noaa.gov/cdata/
DataPlot?id=PUG1642&bin=50&bdate=20160731&edate=20160731&unit
=1&timeZone=UTC.

SHADOW OF SEATTLE

Catalyst Game Labs. "Shadowrun Timeline." From *Shadowrun*, 3rd ed. Accessed
August 31, 2017. www.shadowruntabletop.com/game-resources
/shadowrun-timeline.

Kenson, Steve. *Shadowrun Seattle 2072: The Definitive Seattle Sourcebook*. Catalyst Game
Labs, licensed by WizKids, Inc., 2009. https://ttop.rem.uz/Shadowrun
/Sourcebooks/26102%20-%20Seattle%202072.pdf.

Map of Shadowrun Establishments and Zones. Retrieved from *1W6-Shadownet*.
Accessed August 31, 2017. www.1w6.de/rpg/sr/map/?borders=on.

United States Geological Survey. "Lahars and Debris Flows at Mount Rainier." USGS
Volcano Hazards Program. Last modified September 3, 2015. https://volcanoes
.usgs.gov/volcanoes/mount_rainier/hazard_lahars.html.

Wikipedia. "Shadowrun (1993 Video Game)" entry. Accessed August 31, 2017. https
://en.wikipedia.org/wiki/Shadowrun_(1993_video_game).

SPLIFFS + SCHEMAS

Donovan, Andy. "A Transemantic Journey into Cannabis Strain Names." Metadata schema and poster, July 17, 2017. Seattle, WA. Used with author's permission.

Leafly. "Cannabis Strain Explorer, Results Near Seattle, WA." Accessed July 25, 2017. www.leafly.com/explore/sort-alpha#/explore/location-seattle-wa(47.6145,-122.348)/sort-alpha.

"Marijuana in Seattle." Accessed July 21, 2017. City of Seattle. www.seattle.gov/council/issues/marijuana-in-seattle.

THC Finder. "Strains Near Seattle, WA." Accessed July 25, 2017. www.thcfinder.com/strains.

Washington State Liquor and Cannabis Board. "Know the Law." Accessed July 21, 2017. http://lcb.wa.gov/mj-education/know-the-law.

Weedmaps. "Strains Near Seattle, WA." Accessed July 25, 2017. https://weedmaps.com/strains.

Young, Bob. "Better Than Bingo? Seniors Take Field Trip to Seattle Pot Store." *Seattle Times*. Last modified March 16, 2017. www.seattletimes.com/seattle-news/marijuana/better-than-bingo-seniors-take-field-trip-to-seattle-pot-store.

SEISMIC SEATTLE

Pacific Northwest Seismic Network. "2014 Green Bay at Seattle" [QuickShake]. Accessed August 31, 2017. https://pnsn.org/seahawks/quickshake/2014-green-bay-at-seattle.

———. "2014 Green Bay at Seattle" [Seismograms]." Accessed August 31, 2017. https://pnsn.org/seahawks/seismograms/2014-green-bay-at-seattle.

———. "ShakeMap." Accessed August 31, 2017. https://pnsn.org/shakemap?year=2015.

Scott, Douglas. "2,000+ Small Earthquakes Have Hit The Pacific Northwest Since New Years Day." *The Outdoor Society*. Last modified January 7, 2016. http://outdoor-society.com/2000-small-earthquakes-have-hit-the-pacific-northwest-since-new-years-day.

Seattle Seahawks. "12 Things 12s Need to Know about the Seahawks' Super Bowl Send-Off." January 23, 2015. www.seahawks.com/news/2015/01/23/12-things-12s-need-know-about-seahawks-super-bowl-send.

———. "CenturyLink Field Parade Viewing and Celebration at Capacity; Overflow Viewing Open at Safeco Field." February 4, 2014. www.seahawks.com/news/2014/02/04/centurylink-field-parade-viewing-celebration-capacity-overflow-viewing-open-safeco.

United States Geological Survey. *Latest Earthquakes* map. Accessed August 31, 2017. https://earthquake.usgs.gov/earthquakes/map.

Weisberger, Mindy. "Seahawks Score Touchdown, and Fans Shake Earthquake Monitors." *Live Science*, January 10, 2017. www.livescience.com/57441-seattle-seahawks-stadium-seismology.html.

Wikipedia. "Earthquake Game" entry. Accessed August 31, 2017. https://en.wikipedia.org/wiki/Earthquake_Game.

UPHILL BATTLE

Beyerlein, Doug. "Seattle Stairs." CommunityWalk. Accessed August 31, 2017. www
.communitywalk.com/seattle/wa/seattle_stairs/map/388644#0004p4@c.

Crowley, Walt. "Seattle's Seven Hills." HistoryLink.org. Last modified December 13,
2004. www.historylink.org/File/4131.

Dorpat, Paul. "Now & Then—Queen Anne Counterbalance (Seattle)." HistoryLink.
org, February 27, 2001. www.historylink.org/File/3027.

Jaramillo, Jake, and Cathy Jaramillo. *Seattle Stairway Walks: An Up-and-Down Guide to
City Neighborhoods*. Seattle: Mountaineers Books, 2013.

Murakami, Kery. "Piece of History Concealed within Queen Anne Hill." *Seattle Post-
Intelligencer*, March 10, 2006. www.seattlepi.com/local/article/Piece-of-history
-concealed-within-Queen-Anne-Hill-1198180.php.

Ralph, Susan Ott. "Seattle All Stairs." Accessed August 31, 2017. https://faculty
.washington.edu/smott/SeattleStairs.html.

Seattle Department of Transportation. *Seattle Municipal Street Railway Track Map, April
1933*. Accessed August 31, 2017. Retrieved from www.seattle.gov/transportation
/images/Seattle1933.jpg.

———. "Seattle Transit History." Accessed August 31, 2017. www.seattle.gov
/transportation/transit_history.htm.

Veka, Clay H. "Seattle's Street Railway System and the Urban Form: Lessons from the
Madison Street Cable Car." Research report for University of Washington class,
URBDP 565: American Urban History, taught by Professor Manish Chalana. March
14, 2007. Retrieved from https://faculty.washington.edu/chalana/urbdp565
/ClayVeka_Final.pdf.

Williams, David B. "Seven Hills of Seattle." October 21, 2014. http://geologywriter
.com/blog/seven-hills-of-seattle.

———. *Too High and Too Steep: Reshaping Seattle's Topography*. Seattle: University of
Washington Press, 2015.

CURRENT POWER

"Mount Rainer: An Icon on the Horizon." Accessed August 15, 2017. https://www.nps
.gov/mora/index.htm.

National Hydropower Association. "Western U.S. Hydro Generation Profile, 2013."
Accessed August 31, 2017. www.hydro.org/why-hydro/available
/hydro-in-the-states/west.

Seattle City Light. "Fuel Mix: How Seattle City Light Electricity Is Generated."
Accessed August 31, 2017. www.seattle.gov/light/FuelMix.

United States Army Corps of Engineers. *Pacific Northwest River System* map, January
11, 2010. Sourced from Portland District Visual Information, US Army Corps of
Engineers. Retrieved from Wikimedia Commons. Accessed August 31, 2017.
https://commons.wikimedia.org/wiki/File:Pacific_Northwest_River_System.png.
Public Domain (PD-US).

United States Energy Information Administration. "Washington: State Profile and
Energy Estimates." Last modified November 17, 2016. www.eia.gov/state/?sid=WA.

Wikipedia. "Dams in Washington State" entry. Accessed August 15, 2017. https
://en.wikipedia.org/wiki/Category:Dams_in_Washington_(state).

———. "List of Dams and Reservoirs in Washington" entry. Accessed August 15, 2017. https://en.wikipedia.org/wiki/List_of_dams_and_reservoirs_in_Washington.

———. "List of Dams in the Columbia River Watershed" entry. Accessed August 15, 2017. https://en.wikipedia.org/wiki/List_of_dams_in_the_Columbia_River_watershed.

———. "Seattle City Light" entry. Accessed August 31, 2017. https://en.wikipedia.org/wiki/Seattle_City_Light.

ACTOR LINES

Booth, Stacy. "Our Guide to Famous Movie Landmarks in Seattle." Last modified August 23, 2017. www.wheretraveler.com/seattle/play/our-guide-famous-movie-landmarks-seattle.

Kendle, Kristin. "Movies Filmed in Seattle and Tacoma." Last modified March 14, 2016. www.tripsavvy.com/movies-filmed-in-seattle-and-tacoma-2965291.

MovieMaps. "Movies Filmed in Seattle, WA." Accessed August 31, 2017. https://moviemaps.org/cities/3.

Permenter, Cody. "The Most Famous Film Landmarks in Seattle." Accessed August 16, 2017. https://www.thrillist.com/entertainment/seattle/famous-film-locations-landmarks-seattle-washington.

Rabatin, George. "Movies Filmed in Seattle." IMDb. Last modified January 23, 2014. www.imdb.com/list/ls003551803.

Seattle Office of Film and Music. "Seattle Film History Timeline." Accessed August 31, 2017. www4.seattle.gov/filmoffice/film_history.htm.

———. "Reel Life in Seattle: An Insider's Guide to Seattle Film Locations." Accessed August 31, 2017. www4.seattle.gov/filmoffice/docs/map.pdf.

Wikipedia. "List of Films Shot in Seattle" entry. Accessed August 31, 2017. https://en.wikipedia.org/wiki/List_of_films_shot_in_Seattle.

WELCOME TO SEATTLE

Balk, Gene. "Seattle's Population Boom Approaching Gold Rush Numbers." *Seattle Times*. Last modified September 14, 2015. www.seattletimes.com/seattle-news/data/seattles-population-boom-approaching-gold-rush-numbers.

"HistoryLink.org: A Look at Washington's Historical Census Data." *Seattle Times*. Last modified March 1, 2011. www.seattletimes.com/seattle-news/historylinkorg-a-look-at-washingtons-historical-census-data/.

"Milestones for Washington State History—Part 4: 1951 to Present." Last modified January 12, 2015. www.historylink.org/File/5382.

Ruggles, Steven, Katie Genadek, Ronald Goeken, Josiah Grover, and Matthew Sobek. *Integrated Public Use Microdata Series: Version 6.0* [data set]. Minneapolis: University of Minnesota, 2015. http://doi.org/10.18128/D010.V6.0.

"'Seattle Is a Wonder'—2nd and Yesler," ca. 1905. Accessed Sept. 3, 2017. Retrieved from Wikimedia Commons. www.flickr.com/photos/tigerzombie/8308568968. Creative Commons License (CC BY 2.0), https://creativecommons.org/licenses/by/2.0.

Seattle Strategic Planning Office. *Decennial Population: City of Seattle: 1900–2000*. Statistical table (PDF), April 21, 2001. Retrieved from www.seattle.gov/dpd/cs/groups/pan/@pan/documents/web_informational/dpdd017686.pdf.

Wikipedia. "Timeline of Seattle" entry. Accessed August 31, 2017. https://en.wikipedia.org/wiki/Timeline_of_Seattle.

United States Census Bureau/American FactFinder. "ACS Demographic and Housing Estimates." *2011–2015 American Community Survey 5-Year Estimates*. US Census Bureau's American Community Survey Office, 2015. Accessed August 31, 2017. https://factfinder.census.gov/bkmk/table/1.0/en/ACS/15_5YR/DP05.

——. "Selected Economic Characteristics." *2011–2015 American Community Survey 5-Year Estimates*. US Census Bureau's American Community Survey Office, 2015. Accessed August 31, 2017. https://factfinder.census.gov/bkmk/table/1.0/en/ACS/15_5YR/DP03.

——. "Selected Housing Characteristics in the United States." *2011–2015 American Community Survey 5-Year Estimates*. US Census Bureau's American Community Survey Office, 2015. Accessed August 31, 2017. https://factfinder.census.gov/bkmk/table/1.0/en/ACS/15_5YR/DP04.

——. "Selected Social Characteristics in the United States." *2011–2015 American Community Survey 5-Year Estimates*. U.S. Census Bureau's American Community Survey Office, 2015. Accessed August 31, 2017. https://factfinder.census.gov/bkmk/table/1.0/en/ACS/15_5YR/DP02.

SEATTLE BY ANY OTHER NAME

Berger, Knute. "Seattle Needs a New Nickname." *Crosscut*, February 18, 2014. http://crosscut.com/2014/02/seattle-needs-new-nickname-knute-berker.

Friedman, Spike. "How Seattle's Neighborhoods Got Their Names." *Mental Floss*, August 1, 2016. http://mentalfloss.com/article/55738/how-seattles-neighborhoods-got-their-names.

Godden, Jean. "Seattle Nickname: A Few Modest Proposals." *Crosscut*, March 21, 2014. http://crosscut.com/2014/03/jean-godden-seattle-nicknames-contests.

Muldoon, Katy. "Readers Weigh In with Ideas for a New Seattle Nickname." *Oregonian*. Last modified March 24, 2014. www.oregonlive.com/pacific-northwest-news/index.ssf/2014/03/readers_weigh_in_with_ideas_fo.html.

Nickum, Ryan. "10 Possible New Nicknames for Seattle, Not That We're Saying It Needs One or Anything." *Estately Blog*. Last modified February 18, 2014. www.estately.com/blog/2014/02/10-possible-new-nicknames-for-seattle-not-that-were-saying-it-needs-one-or-anything.

Wikipedia. "List of City Nicknames in Washington" entry. Accessed August 31, 2017. https://en.wikipedia.org/wiki/List_of_city_nicknames_in_Washington.

CREDITS

Page 6: Photo by Staffan Kjellvestad.

Page 8: Image of "Seattle, Washington. Boeing aircraft plant. Production of B-17F (Flying Fortress) bombing planes. Sections of framework" by Andreas Feininger. December 1942. Library of Congress (2017865467).

Page 21: Information from SeattleInProgress.com.

Page 26: Photo by Seattle architect and photographer Ross Eckert.

Page 32–33: Data from nuforc.org.

Page 38–39: Photo by Matt Donovan.

Page 48–49: Data derived from Yelp API and online sources.

Page 52–3: Data from bfro.net.

Page 55–57: Plant specimens from the University of Washington Herbarium collection. Horticulture and tincture expertise provided by Matteo Madero.

Page 59: Photo by Jeremy Gallman.

Page 64: Rendering by Dale Jorgensen. Collections of Richard Haag.

Page 72: Image of "Woman next to large tree in Ravenna Park" by Webster & Stevens. University of Washington Libraries, Special Collections (UW29720z).

Page 74: Map information from the Green Seattle Partnership.

Page 75: Data from SDOT Urban Forestry Tree Inventory.

Page 84: Mother Love Bone mural by Jeff Ament. Photo by Andy Donovan.

Page 90: Photo by Sergee Bee.

Page 94–95: Information from the fair's official guidebook.

Page 96: Image of "Readying the dirigible balloon, A.Y.P.E., 1909" by Orville J. Rognon. University of Washington Libraries, Special Collections (AYP302).

Page 101: Information from Paul de Barros's book *Jackson Street After Hours*.

Page 116: Data from Seattle Public Utilities.

Page 120: Timeline information from ShadowRunTabletop.com.

Page 121: Illustrations by Donny Donoghue.

Page 130–131: Data by Pacific Northwest Seismic Network Hawk-o-Gram (HWK1).

Page 136: Photo by Dale Henriksen.

Page 143: Photo by Natalie Ross.

Page 144–145: Data from IPUMS-USA, University of Minnesota, ipums.org.

ABOUT THE CONTRIBUTORS

CHRIS ADAMS is a Portland, Oregon–based tinkerer, developer, algorist, maker, and dabbler affectionately known as the55 around the internet. He also contributes to Ruins or Books, an online showcase of art books and art . . . not-books. He collaborated and coded the "Gray Anatomy" graphic illustration.

DONNY DONOGHUE is an urban designer, an aspiring cartoonist, and a rambling amateur folk musician, currently located in Los Angeles. Professionally trained in landscape architecture and urban planning, his passion for drawing developed from sketching conceptual designs for public-space projects. In art, music, and design, his driving philosophy is to boil down the emotion of a story into its simplest form. He specializes in drawing cartoon bears, faces without bodies, and people he sees on the Metro. Prior to moving to LA, he spent three years living in Seattle and loving it. Donny provided portrait illustrations for "Legendary Ladies" and "Shadow of Seattle."

ANDY DONOVAN is a librarian by profession and an artist and dabbler by hobby. He gets his news from Bill Radke and his kicks from Kid Hops, and thinks Seattle an endlessly fascinating place to call home. Andy contributed research and writing for several topics in this book: "Jet City," "Raising Seattle," "A Damn Fine Cup of Coffee," "The City Beautiful," "Legendary Ladies," "Our Fair City," "Literary Seattle," "Ferried Away," "Spliffs & Schemas," and "Aw, Shucks!"

MELISSA HAMPTON is a Saint Louis, Missouri–based artist who also loves to read, write, and edit. She holds a BA in English and an MFA in Metals and Jewelry Design. Currently she works a daytime gig as a data analyst for a nonprofit organization. Melissa lives in a cozy, STL-style bungalow with her husband and their parrot, Drummie. She contributed research and writing for: "Gum Wall Dissection," "The Places Between," "Pioneer Square Underfoot," "Steep Streets," "Actor Lines," "I ♥ the '90s," "Current Power," "Mountain Morphology," "Seismic Seattle," "City Microclimates," "Seattle by Any Other Name," and "Aw, Shucks!"

MATTEO MADERO is an amateur naturalist, herbalist, and horticulturist. He is a partner at Site Workshop, a landscape architecture firm in Seattle, Washington. He contributed copious botanical knowledge to "Bitter Seattle."

MEGAN McKISSACK is a Southerner turned Pacific Northwesterner interested in the intersection of art and technology. She spends her time exploring live cinema, video installation, creative coding, and data visualization. Lately she's been geeking out on learning to make map visualizations for the web and exploring the possibilities of virtual reality. She currently works for a non-profit open-source organization showcasing civic and public data by creating web applications, APIs, and data visualizations with volunteer groups. Megan contributed code for "Flood Lines."

ANDREW PRINDLE recently received a master's degree in landscape architecture from the University of Washington, where he focused on landscape history and political ecology. He is one of the original team members of Urban@UW and the Livable City Year program, and his current fascination with floodplains helped form the "Flood Lines" map in this book. Andrew has collaborated on other book projects centered on design for democracy, and his current research looks at how infrastructure shapes the history of a place.

ABOUT THE AUTHORS

JENNY KEMPSON is a designer, geographer, and public artist who has lived along both coasts and the middle of America. Her background spans all phases of the creative process, from research to strategy to implementation, working within nonprofit, civic, community, and private sectors. She brings experience in community-centered design and research with a foundation in psychology, skills in physical and digital design, and an entrepreneurial spirit. Jenny's work focuses on uncovering and illustrating research insights and continuously exploring ways to connect people to places and to each other through design. Her favorite way to soak in a city's personality is walking every nook and cranny while drinking coffee. Jenny lived and loved Seattle for ten years prior to moving to New York, then San Francisco. Her work on this book has kept the long-distance love affair with Seattle going strong.

TERA HATFIELD is an experience design director and writer living in Portland, Oregon. She has a background in visual design and architecture. A PNW native, she grew up on Puget Sound in Bremerton, Washington, home to monolithic battleships and forever-roving cranes. Along the way, she amassed strange credentials from Vassar College and the College of Built Environments at the University of Washington. Her curiosity and creative superpowers lie at the intersection of human-centered digital and physical design. Her work is diverse, spanning the design and fabrication of products, VR, environments, and, yes, even robots. She's won national architecture awards and, in general, is fond of prototypes, A-frames, Bucky Fuller, and f-bombs.

NATALIE ROSS is a landscape architect and geographer living in Seattle. She has a background in fine arts and tries to "make stuff" as part of her design process, whether that be full-size furniture mock-ups, funky models, or sketchy sketches. Her work with the landscape architecture firm Site Workshop focuses on parks, public open spaces, and healing spaces around Seattle. Natalie loves seeing the city at a walker's pace, exploring ideas through collage, and losing track of time in the garden.

TO ALL OUR MENTORS, FAMILY, AND
FRIENDS, NEAR AND FAR.

AND FOR JOE AND KAREN HATFIELD.

———————————————————

Printed in China

Published by Sasquatch Books
22 21 20 19 18   9 8 7 6 5 4 3 2 1

Editor: Gary Luke | Production editor: Em Gale
Design: Anna Goldstein | Copyeditor: Elizabeth Johnson
Author photo © 2018 by Derek Reeves

Library of Congress Cataloging-in-Publication Data
Names: Hatfield, Tera, author. | Kempson, Jenny, author. | Ross, Natalie,
   author.
Title: Seattleness : a cultural atlas / Tera Hatfield, Jenny Kempson, Natalie
   Ross.
Description: Seattle, WA : Sasquatch Books, 2018.
Identifiers: LCCN 2018000130 | ISBN 9781632171276 (hardback)
Subjects: LCSH: Seattle (Wash.)--Social life and customs. | Seattle
   (Wash.)--Maps. | BISAC: TRAVEL / United States / West / Pacific (AK, CA,
   HI, NV, OR, WA). | REFERENCE / Atlases. | HISTORY / United States / State
   & Local / Pacific Northwest (OR, WA).
Classification: LCC F899.S45 H37 2018 | DDC 979.7/772--dc23
LC record available at https://lccn.loc.gov/2018000130

ISBN: 978-1-63217-127-6

SASQUATCH BOOKS
1904 Third Avenue, Suite 710 | Seattle, WA 98101
(206) 467-4300 | SasquatchBooks.com